SEEING CASTANEDA

SEEING
CASTANEDA

Reactions to the "Don Juan" Writings of Carlos Castaneda

EDITED, SELECTED,
AND WITH INTRODUCTIONS

BY DANIEL C. NOEL

Capricorn Books

G. P. PUTNAM'S SONS, *New York*

Library of Congress Cataloging in Publication Data

Seeing Castaneda.

  Bibliography: p.
    1.   Castaneda, Carlos.   2.   Juan, Don, 1891–
3.   Yaqui Indians—Addresses, essays, lectures.
4.   Hallucinogenic drugs and religious experience—
Addresses, essays, lectures.   I.   Noel, Daniel C.
E99. Y3C337   1975   299′.7   75-23146

SBN: 399–11603–6

Second Impression

PRINTED IN THE UNITED STATES OF AMERICA

Grateful acknowledgement is made to the following publishers and individuals for permission to reprint material which is in copyright or of which they are the authorized publishers:

Edward H. Spicer: *Early Praise from an Authority on Yaqui Culture*, reproduced by permission of the American Anthropological Association from the American Anthropologist, Vol. 71, no. 2, copyright 1969.

Edmund Leach: *High School*, reprinted with permission from *The New York Review of Books*. Copyright © 1969 Nyrev, Inc.

Weston La Barre: *Stinging Criticism from the Author of* The Peyote Cult, © 1972 by The New York Times Company. Reprinted by permission.

Robert Buckhout: *On Being Chained to Reason,* Copyright © 1972 by the American Psychological Association. Reprinted by permission.

Paul Riesman: *A Comprehensive Anthropological Assessment,* © 1972 by The New York Times Company. Reprinted by permission.

Don Strachan: *The Word from* Rolling Stone, © 1973 by Straight Arrow Publishers Inc. All Rights Reserved. Reprinted by permission.

Elsa First: *Don Juan Is to Carlos as Carlos Is to Us,* © 1974 by The New York Times Company. Reprinted by permission.

Joyce Carol Oates: Letter to the *New York Times Book Review*; Letter to Daniel C. Noel; Don Juan's Last Laugh, © 1974 by the author, originally printed in *Psychology Today*, September, 1974. Reprinted by permission of the author.

Sam Keen: *Sorcerer's Apprentice,* reprinted from *Psychology Today* Magazine, December, 1972. Copyright © 1972 Ziff-Davis Publishing Company. All rights reserved.

Time Magazine: *Don Juan and the Sorcerer's Apprentice,* reprinted by permission from *Time*, The Weekly Newsmagazine; Copyright Time Inc.

Ronald Sukenick: *Upward and Juanward: The Possible Dream,* reprinted by permission of *The Village Voice.* Copyrighted by The Village Voice, Inc., 1973.

Jerome Klinkowitz: *The Persuasive Account: Working It Out with Ronald Sukenick and Carlos Castaneda,* © North American Review, reprinted by permission.

Theodore Roszak: *Uncaging Skylarks: The Meaning of Transcendent Symbols,* from *Where the Wasteland Ends* by Theodore Roszak. Copyright © 1972 by Theodore Roszak. Reprinted by permission of Doubleday & Company, Inc.

Carl Oglesby *et al: A Juanist Way of Knowledge,* permission granted by the author.

Joseph Chilton Pearce. Copyright © 1971, reprinted by permission of The Julian Press, Inc.

James W. Boyd: *The Teachings of Don Juan from a Buddhist Perspective,* reprinted by permission of *The Christian Century.* Copyright © 1973.

Joseph Margolis: *Don Juan as Philosopher,* reprinted by permission of the author.

Because permission to use quoted material has not been forthcoming from the copyright holders of the four Castaneda books, some Castaneda quotations which appeared in the anthology selections as originally published have had to be paraphrased, reduced, or excised here. These changes are indicated by brackets in the text.

Acknowledgments

I should like to express my indebtedness to the following persons and institutions for the stimulation, information, and/or support they have provided me in connection with this book: Salvatore Alfano, Octavio Alvarez, Harvey Bialy, Sylvia D'Arcangelo, Michael Devine, Richard Grossinger, Sam Keen, Tamarra Knapp, Otto Andrew Koehler, Linda Lewis-Williams, Terence Malley, Ross Mayberry, Pete Miller, John Mood, Christopher, Rebecca, Jennifer, and Susanna Noel, Joyce Carol Oates, Carl Oglesby, Elaine Reisler, Richard Sears, Charles Stein, Stanley Wilk, the Calais (Vermont) Recreation Association, and the astounding Adult Degree Program of Goddard College.

Special thanks are due to Mr. Richard Balkin, to Mr. Walter Betkowski of Putnam's, and to Joanna, who seeks her path with me and knows, all too well, what this apprenticeship has been.

Contents

For don B—

*and for the two persons who shared
his guilty pleasures with me*

TAKING CASTANEDA SERIOUSLY
Paths of Explanation

THE late Alan Watts used to disarm those academic critics who claimed he was not to be taken seriously by calling himself "a philosophical entertainer"—someone who does not *intend* to be taken seriously. At the same time, Watts' facility for Zen sleight-of-hand seemed geared to stressing the philosophical importance of his kind of levity. The situation with regard to Carlos Castaneda and his "don Juan" writings involves some of the same factors of intention and reaction. Castaneda's tetralogy means to be seen as most serious, even though clowning and trickery pervade it and despite the confusing public persona of its author. Aside from the successive presence of the four books on the best-seller lists, most reviewers and essayists have concluded that *The Teachings of Don Juan, A Separate Reality, Journey to Ixtlan,* and *Tales of Power* do indeed *deserve* to be taken as works of profound and lasting significance. Clearly Castaneda's writing has weathered the satirical deflation attempted by the parodies which began to appear in the periodicals after the success of the first book. By now the tetralogy itself comes to seem a kind of satire on the culture which could produce the parodies.

Castaneda has his detractors, to be sure. Sharp criticism is aimed especially at his gradual abandonment of value-free detachment in favor of what looks like sheer subjective self-expression. Counterbalancing such negative responses, however, is the extreme praise of a Joseph Chilton Pearce. He finds Carlos "the principal psychological, spiri-

tual, and literary genius of recent generations" and don
Juan "the most important paradigm since Jesus."

While most affirmations have been less lavish, some of
the parodies and condemnations can also be read as indirect acknowledgments of the volumes' importance. So
the reactions finally add up to an agreement with don
Juan's remark about don Genaro, a fellow sorcerer in
Tales of Power. There don Juan advises Carlos to be "very
careful and serious-minded about the recommendations
made by don Genaro because, although they were funny,
they were not a joke."

As far as published commentary goes, then, the question
is not really *whether* to be serious-minded about Castaneda's recommendations, but *how*: How do we best see
what his work means? We need to explore alternative
paths of explanation.

And this necessity holds notwithstanding the real danger that our pondering may become ponderous, inappro-
priately solemn rather than properly thoughtful. It is true
that in searching out something so lofty-sounding as "interpretive options" we run the risk of forgetting to laugh
at what remains a very funny series of literary escapades.
Moreover, we may ourselves become fit targets for the
caustic wit of don Juan if our choice of interpretations
turns out to be heavy-handed. Still, this fate must be
tempted; the danger of mishandling Castaneda's meanings with an anti-intellectual nervous giggle is even greater. For better or worse, most of us are *already* interpreting
Castaneda in ways which unwittingly prefer one cognitive
path to the exclusion of others, so a deliberate mindlessness simply will not do for us. It would be, and is, inauthentic to refuse all careful reflection on the tetralogy's
words when our laughter is filled with ideological presumption.

In other words, although a truly Buddhist "no-minded-
ness" might qualify us to titter in lieu of proposing explanations, few of us can actually claim such a clean mental
slate. Therefore, we are forced back to the intellectual im-

perative of taking Castaneda seriously and to the difficult questions that entails. Do we even know how to *begin* exploring alternative paths of explanation? Where are these paths? How do we find them?

Perhaps a path, or a clue to finding one, is already laid out for us by what Carlos—as a "character" *in* Castaneda's books—does to explain the bizarre phenomena he experiences, the nonordinary reality he encounters with and without chemical assistance. We note that in the tetralogy, as his apprenticeship to the aged Yaqui proceeds, Carlos sometimes calls upon particular conceptual resources to help him make sense of what happens to him. Georg Simmel, structuralism, Juan Ramon Jimenez, *The Tibetan Book of the Dead*, phenomenology, Cesar Vallejo—these are the specific social theorists, methodologies, poets, and spiritual visions Carlos appeals to in the four books.

On the other hand, such tools are never used in a systematic way, except conceivably in the "Structural Analysis" section of the first book (where the total absence of footnotes and the notable *failure* of the analysis suggest a system within a surrealistic dream or schizophrenic episode). The fact is, the anthropological training and philosophical perspectives Carlos employs to cope interpretively are scarcely spelled out. Furthermore, it appears that all explanatory resources, implicit and general or specific and obvious, to which Carlos has recourse in the books become the *butt* of don Juan's teachings as much as the keys to understanding those teachings.

Where does this leave us? If Carlos' attempts to explain his experience are unavailing, how can we learn from *him* how to find the most promising angles of vision on Castaneda's books? The clue Carlos' own efforts appear to offer is further complicated by the sense the writings themselves foster that the reader is superior to Carlos. His reasoning can seem inadequate to rationalist and irrationalist alike. Indeed, we are hard pressed, at times, to see any virtue whatsoever in following Carlos' uncertain lead.

But we should challenge our feelings of superiority

here. Not only are they uncomfortably similar to Carlos'
smug attitude in approaching don Juan; they may also
prevent us from appropriating the lesson of Carlos' failures. The clue is complex, admittedly. Nevertheless, the
kinds of adventures Carlos has in Castaneda's pages provide our best beginnings for seeing how to be serious-
minded about these books. That is, what goes on in Castaneda's text is our initial access to understanding what
they recount.

If we look, then, to the major motifs of Carlos' apprenticeship in the tetralogy, four paths of explanation or interpretive options open up. Others, less clearly marked,
present themselves as a result of exploring the first four.

Psychedelic Experience

First of all, we need to examine the overwhelming influence, early in Carlos' apprenticeship, of the psychotropic
power plants. It is undeniable that the initial sales appeal
of the books can largely be attributed to this emphasis.
Many a drug-oriented reader was "hooked" by it, only to
find with Carlos that don Juan's knowledge is in no way
dependent upon the ingestion of Jimson weed, mushrooms, or peyote. The retrospective revelations of *Journey
to Ixtlan* would seem to have hit the reading public just as
the psychedelic absolutisms of the 1960's were fading. But
despite reading there that the long hallucinogenic tutelage
detailed in the first two books was only undertaken grudg-
ingly by don Juan after realizing Carlos' insensitivity,
many Castaneda aficionados stubbornly see psychotropic
plants as the only path to a knowledge of what the tetralogy has to teach.

Do such readers fail to register anything in Castaneda's
chronicle which conflicts with their ideology? Or are they
confessing that *their* insensitivity to transchemical lessons is
even greater than Carlos'? It is unclear. In any case, it will
probably remain true that in outright contradiction of the

narrative, the four books will often be read as riddles whose solution is straightforward: Turn on, get off, and *be* (here, now) the man of knowledge Carlos could not become in almost a decade and a half of note-taking.

Don Juan's intermittent critique of intellectuality, it should be added, is too tempting a weapon to pass up in this acidheaded arsenal of rationalizations. As implied above, an inauthentic mindlessness, a *false* sense of *insecurity*, is a powerful lure today. Perhaps drug-tripping, once a promising avenue to honest confrontation with the powers and mysteries, has now become a part of the very cultural reality we are advised by Castaneda's writing to relativize. Such world-stopping advice, as a don Juan represents it, is never welcomed. It is much easier to presume, settled comfortably within a culture (or counterculture), that one is an impeccable warrior than to acknowledge one's apprenticeship to an apprentice.

Anthropology

But if what we are dealing with are texts, not plants, it is nonetheless the case that the texts do refer to the use of natural hallucinogens in an alien cultural context. And here we have a body of anthropological scholarship to supply us with edifying parallels. Carlos is far from the first researcher to do field work among peyote-using native Americans. In fact, he mentions at the outset of the third book that he read reports on such research during his initial year of hunting for don Juan's supposed information on medicinal plants.

Unfortunately, in light of his patent lack of success in understanding what he viewed as don Juan's "system," Carlos' anthropological acumen poses more questions for us than it answers. Does his *mis*understanding teach us that by gathering the *right* data on, say, hallucinogens and shamanism, we can avoid the naïveté so obvious to us as we look back at Carlos' early apprenticeship? Or can we take it that no amount of mere *information,* however sophisticated, will make us warriors—or even help us see what becoming one might mean?

It seems that for Carlos, "the facts" about power substances were no more an open sesame to Juanist knowledge than was his actual ingestion of the plants themselves. Moreover, don Juan's isolation from almost everything that is identifiably Yaqui in culture hardly argues for cultural anthropology as an especially privileged vantage point for seeing the tetralogy. Certainly Carlos considers himself an ethnographer in all his endeavors, but what he encounters just as clearly pushes us all beyond an *exclusive* reliance upon anthropological patterns and precedents.

Psychology

Castaneda's books give us "participant-observation" with a vengeance, the hyphenation of the term as readily reflecting the scholar's deepening schizophrenia as his careful field methodology. Such a cleavage, induced by don Juan in Carlos' sober mindset, may suggest to the reader that a reconciling comprehension is best sought in the forces of contemporary *psychological* thought. Surely the recent insights of social psychology and psychopharmacology into the nature of human consciousness are pertinent to seeing Castaneda's point. Once again, however, the path may not lead to the understanding we need.

The problem is that the results of biofeedback experiments or research on "psi phenomena" can turn out to be cultural baggage, too—the Altered States of America: a rhetoric and a reality in which one can be trapped at least as insidiously as in the world of sorcery. Like the data of anthropology, the concepts of psychology are called into play by a reading of Castaneda only to be called into question. They are *necessary* to explain the tetralogy, but insufficient to do so alone.

In short, neither psychedelic experience nor the two

academic disciplines with which we usually conceptualize it, despite their evidently close connection to the apprenticeship narrated in the four books, provides a broad enough perspective to encompass the issues which confront anyone who reflects seriously upon Castaneda's writing. These issues—they involve cultural relativity, the sociology of knowledge, the philosophy of interpretation itself—require to be dealt with in an interdisciplinary approach.

Body Awareness

The fourth path implied by Castaneda's text would appear to contradict the impressions gained by exploring the first three. For the sensitivities of the body seem primal enough to outstrip any and all purely intellectual disciplines in taking the measure of don Juan's knowledge. Carlos' experience urges upon him a "body-knowledge" which Western culture has generally repressed as part of its psychological denial of death. The tetralogy shows that, knowing its own ever-imminent end in a way the mind finds very hard to reason out, the body can also interact with its physical surroundings more variously than we can conceive.

In actuality, this body awareness is not a matter of learning unusual styles of breathing, standing, running, or even focusing one's eyes *per se*. Don Juan's teaching, as Castaneda describes it, puts such experiential techniques together with an attitude toward the processes of perception to form a thoroughly convincing picture of the metaphorical way we create our worlds. That is, the minutely coached environmental interactions of Carlos' apprenticeship add up to a physiological parable. The need to use terms like "metaphorical" and "parable" here is owing to our pervasively intellectualized vantage point.

Aside from the fact of our dependence on language in writing and reading about the body, we have to acknowl-

edge that for most of us our own bodies are a very intellectual affair. Like the prereflective and preverbal possibilities of psychedelic experience, body awareness is fitted out
with abstract ideologies—"bioenergetics," "structural integration," "martial arts" are some of the labels—even when
we try to get at it most directly. These ideological garments
no doubt feature zippers and buttons which allow, even
encourage, easier access to our essential nakedness. But
while we still wear them we must admit that Carlos' body
comes to be aware of playful dogs, drooling gnats, burned
clumps of desert bush, or fluttering moths in a manner *we*
could not now sustain.

To sum up: As long as we seek explanations to Castaneda's work with minds that need to do all their own
knowing, body awareness (or what it presents us) cannot
be taken literally. Such is our culturally trained incapacity
that, for instance, "poetry" and "imagination"—the etymo-
logy here involves image-making—are the most accurate
words we have for conveying to one another the *power* of
Carlos' eyes actually to transform ordinary natural objects,
to breathe life into them. It certainly will not do, by the
way, to call what Carlos sees illusions, hallucinations, or
tricks of the eye. The physical ability don Juan teaches him
is meant to be exercised even *after* he realizes that Mescalito is "only" a dog, the guardian is "only" a gnat, the
beaked mammal is "only" a burned bush, and knowledge
is "only" a moth.

The fourth path thus proves to be no alternative to an
interdisciplinary effort at interpretation, but an additional
challenge to participant-observers of Castaneda's writings.
Or rather, the stress on body awareness finally suggests
that whether we draw upon a combination of intellectual
methodologies or try to avoid them all, there is an irreducible elusiveness to don Juan's knowledge. In a simile
offered by the first book, what we are seeking is like "dust
particles in the eyelashes, or the blood vessels in the cornea
of the eye, a wormlike shape that can be seen as long as

one is not looking at it directly." Because the simile is itself based on a concrete physical experience it ought to have pointed up for us how bodily as well as mental paths of explanation must be indirect. But in case we read on through the tetralogy with the growing hope that the body is the bedrock goal of our seeking, the grounded and graspable center of Castaneda's seriousness, don Juan undeceives us in *Tales of Power* by telling Carlos that he cannot understand the teachings if he thinks he is "a solid body."

And so it seems that both the abstract vastness of emerging interdisciplinary concerns and the concrete minutiae of Carlos' "physical education" take us away from the middling literal meaning we should like to have for Castaneda's work. Indeed, they both propose as central the sort of evanescently "symbolic" possibilities we have been trained to overlook.

By the same token, the power of the tetralogy is that *in reading it* we are dramatically involved in these very possibilities to such an extent that we are freed, however fleetingly, from the cultural pressure to find the plain truth, the unambiguous doctrines, of don Juan's way. What this in turn implies is that the interpretive resources which can most effectively *maintain* this sense of possibility and pluralistic openness *after we stop* reading can probably be of great help in our quest for an explanation of the books.

Fact, Fiction, Literary Reality

This raises a related point about the controversy over whether Castaneda's writing is straight documentary reportage, as he claims, or a purely fictional narrative, as certainly cannot be *dis*proven with the hard evidence at hand.

The debate should be considered salutary. It contributes to understanding the writings because it tends to replicate in the way we look back at the books from the *outside* some of the same ambiguity Carlos confronts *within* them, the wonder and terror we, too, experience as we are caught up uncritically in the act of reading. The surprising interpretive relevance of this dispute—its tendency to undermine our confident categorization of the writings as *either* fact or fiction—also means that any specifically literary expertise will give us important guidance when we come to reflect upon our reading of Castaneda.

It has already been mentioned that the books are texts, not plants, but literary-critical tools that help us explore more deeply the implications of *this* elusive actuality. Words are the only psychotropic agents Castaneda gives us, and the black marks on his pages are our eyes' only path through his desert. What kind of writing does this anthropologist apprentice us to? Is Carlos' multistaged confessional narrative the next step in the history of ethnography, or do we find that his social-scientific research notes are "in fact," "in reality," a further development in the novel, an ultimate innovative fiction which suspends unto mis-shelving even the disbelief of library cataloguers?

"Illusion," says the literary theorist Northrop Frye, "is whatever is fixed and definable," and one of Wallace Stevens' poetic adages states the obverse: "Reality is not what it is. It consists of the many realities which it can be made into." These literary insights come close to specifying the relativity and open-endedness embodied in Castaneda's texts. Faced with that which refuses to be fixed and defined as either fact or fiction, we readers are edged toward the situation of the warrior as described in *Tales of Power.* The warrior does not merely believe; he "*has* to believe"—deliberately choosing to accept as true what he just as consciously knows might *not* be true at all. This again recalls one of Stevens' central insights into the relation of imagination and reality in a time bereft of naïve relgous faith: We are obliged to "believe without belief, beyond belief." If Castaneda has written a sacred text, a new generation of biblical scholars may be required to unravel the appeal of its *challenge* to our credulity.

Language and the Metaphysical

In addition to the controversy about the *veracity* of Castaneda's words, there is the question don Juan repeatedly raises about the *value* of words in general. It not only recurs in regard to the intricate intimacies of body-knowledge but also becomes, as we approach the end of the tetralogy, a profound matter of mystical theology.

Don Juan does not, it must be stressed, endorse any cut-rate denunciation of language or champion a conventionally unitive mysticism. The entire apprenticeship, after all, is built upon conversations, and in the final book don Juan's explanations are invariably prefaced by phrases which suggest the necessary, even if insufficient, place of language in the way of a warrior. Likewise, there is no "true reality" behind or above the ordinary one in don Juan's teachings, no "proper abode" for man's "immortal soul" beyond the *maya* of gross matter. The intricate "sorcerers' explanation" about the *tonal* and the *nagual* is a fit topic for a metaphysician's skills, to be sure, but it issues in paradox rather than in a positive assertion of otherworldly absolutism.

"Let's say that God is the tablecloth," don Juan tells Carlos, completing a list of the components of the *tonal* which admits no language Carlos can conceive, however cosmic, as applicable to the *nagual*, "the area beyond the boundaries of the table." The late Protestant theologian Paul Tillich was forced to speak similarly of "the God beyond the God of theism" and once declared that the only nonsymbolic statement one could make about this transtheistic God is that all statements about "Him" are symbolic. This complicates, but does not deny, the positive role of religious language, and St. Augustine's remark that "God should not be said to be ineffable, for when this is said something is said" also bears repeating—especially when Lao-tse's classic *dictum* downgrading "the Tao which can be spoken" is quoted too confidently.

The silent power for which don Juan's pedagogy pre-

pares his apprentice is never far from the narrations the
two men exchange, or from the internal dialogue to which
Carlos always returns in reflecting upon what has befallen
him during its interruption. Clearly what happens to the
reader is radically dependent on language. But once having
emphasized the indispensable linguistic scaffolding, must
we not acknowledge that the structure erected by Castaneda's words transcends those words in a manner we can
call "mystical"?

Perhaps. (Which is a way of saying we cannot presume
to jump off the final mountain with Carlos without having
reached his precipice of learning.)

Negative Mysticism and the Postmodern

In any case, the *negative* mysticism epitomized by a Buddhism focused on "nothingness" or "openness" *(sunyata)*
seems the only pertinent variety to apply, and it gives us no
firmer foothold, no surer path, than don Juan's teachings
themselves. At this point we perhaps recall don Juan's
forthright testimony in the first book, where the old sorcerer reminisces that none of the many paths he has taken
has led him anywhere.

Do the paths of explanation we are exploring get us anywhere? By attending to Castaneda's texts we have determined that the appropriate manner of taking him seriously is to seek an interpretation which is interdisciplinary,
sensitive to the poetry of our carnal experience in the eco-
sphere, indirect in approaching its object, faithful to the
indeterminacy we encounter as we read. But does this not
lead us *away* from all explanation, into the paradoxical, the
ineffable, the unknown?

Not quite; and besides, what alternative do we have?
The serious reader eventually realizes that no nonordinary occurrence anywhere in the four books is left without
its *possible* ordinary, naturalistic explanation in terms of
"misperception," "suggestibility," "the manipulation of

cues," "hypnosis," "conditioning," "wishful thinking," "drug-induced states," and so on. Like a compressed reliving of Western modernity, every "transcendent" vision *can* be debunked, if we wish, and reduced to what are really quite prosaic secular categories. The problem—and part of what makes Castaneda's texts *post*modern—comes with the striking discovery that these perfectly accessible interpretations simply will not suffice for us. The option of a clear and distinct rational explanation of all that Carlos undergoes fails us precisely in its success. Just as Carlos had to pursue the entire apprenticeship in order to understand why his success as a social scientist in *The Teachings of Don Juan* was humanly empty, without "heart," we may need to traverse the paths of explanation long enough to learn, with Nietzsche, that a "will to *conscious* illusion" can validly follow the skeptical destruction of unconsciously held superstitions and pieties.

If Castaneda's books lead us to be disillusioned with our modern disillusionments, we may be ready to accept something akin to the sorcerers' explanation in *Tales of Power*: a mode of interpretation matching what we found to be the upshot of our explorations into explaining the tetralogy, a mode of interpretation deliberately bordering on the paradoxical, the ineffable, the unknown.

The Sorcerers' Last Trick: Self-Knowledge

Throughout the four books Carlos's assumptions about knowledge, about what comprises adequate interpretation, are under the attack of don Juan's sorcery. However, when we see in our reading that it is not exactly an *irrational* explanation which is being proposed as the "correct" alternative, we begin actually to feel the sense of don Juan's own solitary perspective. "Rational explanation," "fact," "ordinary reality" whisper in one ear; "irrational explanation," "fiction," "nonordinary reality" whisper in the other. Our minds go out of their familiar focus, the clear distinctions disappear. We now see that surrounding these distinctions are determinants other than correctness for our relationships with everything from a gnat to the *nagual.* "Intent, "purpose," "predilection," "will"—these are some of the Juanist terms indicating a revised orientation on the path. In this process, as Carlos learned, the seeker of explanations finds himself tricked into self-knowledge.

And what of the various disciplines the tetralogy suggests as applicable to itself? What of the anthropology, the psychology, the literary theory, the metaphysics, not to mention the psychedelic speculations and body awareness?

They are not to be discarded. In fact, such an absolutist reaction would reflect one of the attitudes we are to be tricked *out* of along the way. It is rather a matter of these disciplines clarifying their own foundations and contexts in the attempt to answer the puzzle posed by don Juan and his cohorts. This, too, is a kind of self-knowledge, and no doubt a part of the reflexive and personalizing direction Western fields of thought are taking in order to move beyond the characteristic dilemmas of modernity. But this is to state the situation too abstractly, as if *we* were not the ones doing the thinking, the students, in one way or the other, of these disciplines.

Don Juan says it is constantly necessary to remember that any total orientation, even sorcery, is "only a path," and that the prerequisite for keeping *this* clearly in mind is a "disciplined life." The meaning of discipline in one's life—including the life of the mind—may finally be what is at stake here. For with this discipline, the old sorcerer suggests, one may find among the million paths—including the paths of explanation—one's own path with a heart, the path which goes nowhere and yet makes for "a joyful journey." Even a glimpse of such a path would be a far from meager reward for a careful and serious-minded look at the writings of Carlos Castaneda. And, following the glimpse, laughter might be our next step.

Part One
REVIEWS

1

THE TEACHINGS OF DON JUAN

A Yaqui Way of Knowledge

TWO OF THE earliest reviews of Carlos Castaneda's writings were by prominent scholars in the field in which he was still a graduate student: anthropology. In April, 1969, the year after *The Teachings of Don Juan* was published by the University of California Press—and the same month Ballantine Books first printed its psychedelically packaged paperback edition—Edward H. Spicer discussed the book for *American Anthropologist*. Two months later the acidly intellectual *New York Review of Books* published a titled review by the Cambridge University cultural anthropologist Edmund Leach. Both reviews contributed to the largely affirmative reception Castaneda's work was to receive over the next six years. More importantly, each reviewer raised points which quickly placed it in the tantalizing cultural category it has occupied ever since.

Spicer, a distinguished professor of anthropology at the University of Arizona and the foremost academic authority on Yaqui Indian culture, had written *Pascua: A Yaqui Village in Arizona* about thirty years earlier. He does not hesitate to say in his review that Castaneda fails to establish any strong connection between don Juan and what we know of Yaqui culture. In fact, Spicer indicates that the author describes a figure with several characteristics quite *opposed* to Yaqui custom. Spicer therefore erases from the subtitle of the first book an adjective which had promised to narrow the possible meanings of don Juan's alien philosophy. At the same time, while praising Castaneda's ac-

29

counts of hallucinogenic episodes and his picture of the "field behavior" of a student anthropologist, and even giving good marks to the "structural analysis" which glazes the eyes of most readers of *The Teachings of Don Juan*, Spicer emphasizes something which was to become the focus of controversy. "Castaneda's literary skill," he testifies, "led me to complete absorption in what seemed almost the direct experience itself."

Not only is Professor Leach's reaction more critical than Professor Spicer's, it is couched in caustic phrases which occasionally verge upon ridicule. Agreeing that don Juan's relation to the Yaquis is too tenuously set forth to tell us anything about his ethnic setting, Leach considers Castaneda's book "a diary of unusual personal experience." Although he is especially unsympathetic to the philosophizing of don Juan, he feels that as "a work of art rather than of scholarship" *The Teachings of Don Juan* is "very good indeed." So Leach comes out in favor of Castaneda, on balance, but transfers the discussion from the realm of ethnography to that of "literary aesthetics," and goes even further than Spicer in highlighting the author's literary skill. His arch appraisal of Castaneda's writing is aptly summed up in the judgment that it is "certainly not a complete spoof . . . but if it had been spoof, it might not have been very different."

It is important to note that whereas Spicer sees Castaneda's novelistic flair as serving proper anthropological purposes, Leach feels this skill was exercised to the detriment of ethnographic effectiveness (structural analyses notwithstanding).

EDWARD H. SPICER
Early Praise from an Authority on Yaqui Culture

This small book achieves three things: (1) it presents a description of personal experience with peyote, datura, and hallucinogenic mushrooms; (2) it describes the relationship between a student anthropologist and an elderly North Mexican Indian; and (3) it offers an analysis of a set of concepts and a pattern of thought concerning a realm of knowledge important in the Indian's world view. The first two goals (if indeed they may be spoken of as goals of the author) are achieved with great success, and the book should attain a solid place in the literature of both the hallucinogenic drugs and the field behavior of anthropologists. The third goal (which I would guess is the major objective of the author) is achieved with only somewhat less success.

The description of the young anthropologist's hallucinogenic experiences, under the tutelage of the Indian, is remarkably vivid and compelling. Certainly what Castaneda has put on paper, recording the highlights of his several experiences with each of the three drugs, ranks with the best accounts by experimental psychologists, such as those by Havelock Ellis and Weir Mitchell with peyote and the Wassons with hallucinogenic mushrooms. They seem to me superior to the various literary accounts, such as those of Aldous Huxley. While the evocative descriptions are at least on a par with Huxley's, Castaneda's accounts seem based on more systematic use of notes and less after-the-experience reworking Castaneda's literary skill led me to complete absorption in what seemed almost the direct experience itself I think that this comes about in part through the skillful delineation of the immediate setting, namely, the personal relationship between the author and his teacher, which provided the motivation and the meaning of the activities.

It is in the presentation of this relationship that Castaneda is at his very best. With the skill of an accomplished novelist, utilizing suspense in character unfoldment and compelling suggestion rather than full exposition of place and situation, the intense relationship developed between the young and groping anthropologist and the richly experienced old teacher engrosses the reader. To me this is the chief value of the book and represents a remarkable achievement. It seems to me, further, that anthropologists concerned with preparing students for significant field relationships will find Castaneda's presentation of his experience immensely useful. The many facets of participant observation are available here for illuminating analysis and discussion of what this kind of fieldwork involves.

Castaneda was unable to understand immediately the nature of the viewpoint regarding the realm of knowledge to which Don Juan introduced him. Only some six years after the time of his first introduction did he attain what he felt was adequate understanding. The processes of relating the unfamiliar set of concepts and their interrelations to Castaneda's own world view is presented in what is called a "structural analysis." This consists in a concise exposition of the basic concepts held by Don Juan and a sort of operational analysis of Don Juan's application of the concepts to the process of teaching a neophyte to become aware of, accept, and handle the sort of knowledge which the hallucinogenic drugs help a person to acquire. Of particular interest in this analysis is Castaneda's concept of "special consensus."

It seems wholly gratuitous to emphasize, as the subtitle does, any connection between the subject matter of the book and the cultural traditions of the Yaquis. One suspects that the publisher went beyond Castaneda's intention, for the text itself provides no data for such a connection. It is true that Don Juan is at one point called a Yaqui. Moreover, the brief outline of his life describes a pattern that is common among persons of Yaqui descent, namely, early residence in Sonora, "exile" to central Mexico, and later residence in Arizona and somewhere in northern Mexico. However, the use of the three drugs is not consistent with our ethnographic knowledge of the Yaquis, and Don Juan is not described as having any role in any Yaqui community life. No Yaqui words are mentioned, not even in connection with the most distinctive concepts in Don Juan's "way of knowledge." In fact, all the internal evidence suggests that the two men talked with each other wholly in Spanish. I am forced to the conclusion that Don Juan is one of those many persons to be encountered in Mexico and Arizona who, although Yaqui in family origin perhaps, have never participated in Yaqui group life or at best have done so only sporadically. Persons of this sort have come to participate in an interesting mélange of custom and belief that derives from a number of Indian sources but is largely dominated by one or another of the mestizo variants of Spanish-derived culture. It is therefore misleading to describe the content of this study as a Yaqui "way of knowledge," even though, when pushed to do so, Don Juan may have identified himself with the (under certain circumstances) prestigious label of Yaqui.

Insofar as the reader is informed by this book, the teachings of Don Juan exist in a cultural limbo. Within the bounds of this serious limitation, it is nevertheless an excellent piece of work. One hopes that Castaneda will cultivate his exceptional gift for writing expressive prose and continue to employ it in his further contributions to anthropology.

EDMUND LEACH
High School

Mysticism is in fashion. Just at the moment nothing brings in the bread more easily than a careful description of the horrors and delights of hippydom, pot, LSD, St. Teresa, or what have you. So any book of this sort invites caution. The general tone is Coleridge-de Quincey by Rousseau out of eighteenth-century Gothik:

> I saw his eyes looking through half-closed eyelids. I jumped up; I knew then that whoever or whatever was in front of me was not don Juan. . . . I felt a strange vigor filling me, in a matter of seconds. Then I yelled and hurled the rock at him. I thought it was a magnificent outcry. At that moment I did not care whether I lived or

died. I felt the cry was awesome in its potency. It was
piercing and prolonged and it actually directed my aim.
The figure in front wobbled and shrieked. . . .

Clearly the atmosphere is that of *The Ancient Mariner*—

> I closed my lids, and kept them
>   close and the balls like pulses
>   beat. . . .
> The body of my brother's son stood
>   by me, knee to knee
> The body and I pulled at one rope
>   but he said nought to me

But even if the images are familiar it needs a *guru* to get
you through "the caverns measureless to man down to the
sunless sea" and if Maharishis from the Himalayas are in
short supply, an Indian from Arizona may do just as well.
The outcome need not be contemptible, but it is more likely to emerge as poetry rather than science. In other words,
the reader of this often entrancing slice of autobiography
can ignore the fact that at all relevant times the author was
a graduate student in the Department of Anthropology at
the University of California, Los Angeles. Despite the last
fifty pages of jargon-loaded "structural analysis," this is a
work of art rather than of scholarship, and it is as a diary
of unusual personal experience that the book deserves attention. Assessed on this basis the book is not of superla-
tive quality perhaps, but very good indeed.
   The don Juan of the title is an old man, a Yaqui Indian
from Sonora in Mexico, who now lives at an unspecified lo-
cality in Arizona. This is all we are told about him. The
book contains no bibliography and no further clues about
the Yaqui and their way of life. Indeed if don Juan had
been described as a man from Mars it would have made little difference. The text is narrowly confined to the personal interactions between don Juan and the author between
the summer of 1960 and the autumn of 1965. It is a rela-

tionship which is at once intimate yet tense, as between Moby Dick and Ahab, God and Job, or any psychoanalyst and his patient.

The start of the matter was that Castaneda, in his role as anthropologist, was interested in collecting information about the Indian use of hallucinogenic plants such as peyote. He was introduced to don Juan because the latter had the reputation of being a *brujo* (witch, medicine man, sorcerer). The book is a step by step record of how, in seeking to learn about don Juan's secrets, Castaneda gradually became his apprentice. Don Juan taught his craft by initiation. The pupil was first induced to take a drug; then, while under its influence or subsequently, he was persuaded, by means of hypnotic commands or less direct modes of suggestion, to accept the teacher's interpretation of the drug-induced experience. From the teacher's point of view, this was a road to true knowledge. Just how far Castaneda himself came to believe in don Juan's fantasies is left carefully obscure. And the undoubted fascination of the book lies precisely in this: the uncertainty of the author's own attitude. It is don Juan, not Castaneda, who has the dominant voice.

So this is not just another account of the joys and terrors of mescalin-induced visions, for it has the novelty that we are led to apprehend the contours of the other world according to don Juan's categories rather than as figments of a bemused American's imagination. Cut down to the barest skeleton, what actually happens in the story is that the apprentice Castaneda is trained to experience three different kinds of hallucination consequent upon partaking of concoctions made of (1) the *Datura* plant ("Jimson's Weed"), (2) a variety of the mushroom species *Pscilocybe,* and (3) the cactus peyote (*Lophophora williamsii*). Don Juan interprets these states as resulting from the influence of supernatural personal powers (familiars). The Datura is woman-like, violent, unpredictable; the mushroom is male-like, gentle, predictable; the peyote cactus, which don Juan knows as Mescalito, is a higher order of being, more independent and more subtle in the way it leads the addict into an understanding of philosophic mysteries. The novice apprentice starts off by interpreting his visions as glimpses of another world of "non-ordinary reality," but as the book progresses he comes to accept more and more completely the non-rational logic which underlies don Juan's magical premises. At this critical point, when he is approaching a position in which the hallucinatory state seems real and normal experience an illusion, Castaneda, perhaps wisely, but without explanation, suddenly decides that he has had enough and breaks off the analysis.

In between descriptions of the techniques of drug preparation and vivid accounts of Castaneda's personal hallucinations, don Juan is presented as a mystic spouting the universal jargon of the apocalypse—

> The particular thing to learn is how to get to the crack between the worlds and how to enter the other world. There is a crack between the two worlds, the world of the diableros and the world of living men.

But just how much of this "philosophy" is really that of don Juan and how much is Castaneda (or even don Juan himself) regurgitating the Book of Revelations is hard to say. The Yaqui Indians incidentally have been Catholic Christians of a sort for several hundred years. What I find worrying is that although the reader is likely to end up with a strong impression of what don Juan must be like, we are, in fact, told practically nothing about him. All that we know concerns his attitudes toward the sources of his magic, and although these seem coherent enough in the setting of this book, they have no obvious connection with Yaqui culture as it has been described for us by other authors.

The dustjacket draws our attention to the parallels between don Juan's teachings and "Taoism, Yoga, Vedanta, and Zen"—the ancient "ways of liberation." But that is just the trouble: it is too much alike to be true. Some years ago T. Lobsang Rampa's *The Third Eye* (1956) created quite a

sensation. The book purported to be an autobiographical
account by an emigré Tibetan Lama of metaphysical go-
ings on in pre-communist Lhasa. It seemed convincing because it fitted with the reader's expectations. "Rampa" is
actually an Englishman, and I doubt if he has ever been
within a 1000 miles of the Himalayas. Castaneda's book is
certainly not a complete spoof in this sense, but if it had
been spoof, it might not have been very different. The pa-
tients of psychoanalysts are unreliable witnesses of either
the personality or the doctrine of their mentors, and Castaneda is no exception. It seems to me that he has just
fitted don Juan into a mold that is ready-made.

Potentially his theme is very big. He is trying to describe
a non-logical cosmos in terms which we can accept as con-
stituting a "reality." But somehow, despite the author's
sensitivity to the poetic symbolism which is implicit in his
often terrifying experiences, the whole business gets reduced to triviality. Perhaps it is simply that the size of the
canvas is too small for what it is meant to portray. Or perhaps the sadistic reader feels frustrated because, when it
comes to the point, Castaneda does not commit himself to
final destruction. We know from Melville what to ex
pect:—

"Oh! Ahab," cried Starbuck, "not too late is it, even now,
the third day to desist. See! Moby Dick seeks thee not. It is
thou, thou, that madly seekest him!"

So we feel let down by Castaneda's modesty and discre-
tion:

I remained in a state of profound distress for several
hours. Afterwards don Juan explained my disproportion-
ate reaction as a common occurrence. I said I could not
figure out logically what had caused my panic, and he replied that it was not fear of dying, but rather the fear of
losing my soul, a fear common among men who do not
have unbending intent. That experience was the last of

don Juan's teachings. Ever since that time I have re-
frained from seeking his lessons.

In this area of literary aesthetics the competition is pretty
tough.

2

A SEPARATE REALITY
Further Conversations with Don Juan

LOOKING BACK to the beginning of his apprenticeship, Carlos says that during the second half of 1960, following his initial encounter with don Juan, he had diligently studied books on Amerind peyotism. For Weston La Barre, author of a compendious study, *The Peyote Cult*—one of the works to which Carlos refers—this reading must not have "taken." Reviewing *A Separate Reality*, which appeared in 1971 and got us used to the idea of a *series* of works on don Juan, La Barre thoroughly condemns Castaneda. La Barre is a Duke University professor who, like Edward Spicer and Edmund Leach, is an internationally prominent anthropologist. He goes far beyond even Leach's misgivings in his review (commissioned and paid for by the *New York Times Book Review* but never published), denigrating the success of the books, their ethnographic competence, even their literary quality. From his resolutely Freudian perspective, La Barre sees Castaneda's work as an ego trip only, and "longs for sheer information" on hallucinogens and peyotism.

Contrasting sharply with La Barre's negative reaction is the review by Robert Buckhout, a psychologist at City University of New York. A comparison of the two pieces clearly reveals a basic difference of criteria in the reviewers. "Castaneda," Buckhout allows, "violates the rules of the game of science." La Barre would hardly differ here, but where he had found "sophomoric and deeply vulgar" consequences to this violation, Buckhout is able to praise it. He sees Castaneda as "getting 'too close' to his subject in a very successful effort to enlighten his audience." Considering the first two books as "crucial, transitional volumes" on altered states of consciousness, Buckhout is impressed with the *challenge* to positivist notions of reason and reality Castaneda poses. In a sense this is precisely opposite to La Barre's feeling that Castaneda leads his audience into authoritarianism and *away* from "fresh inquiries of That Which Is, reality." Although Buckhout's assessment has carried the day, it is helpful to ponder the deeply divergent standards at work in these two brief reviews by respected social scientists.

WESTON LA BARRE
Stinging Criticism from the Author of The Peyote Cult

All men seek some touchstone for the validity of their beliefs, whether that authority be of persons (tribal, or historic tradition, or individual visionary experience, immediate or borrowed), or of things (the scientific reference to validation by impersonal nature). For those inexperienced in the use of this last technique, and for those alienated from their own society and culture, it is all too easy to think they find that authority for belief or world-view in still another tribe. Thus, scientifically uneducated youngsters move easily, in a matter of mere years, from Zen Buddhism to Hindu Vedantism, in their quest for some impressive cultural authority, and even turn on soon again as "Jesus freaks."

One can be sympathetic with other world-views and yet ask the question: Is not the endless quest for a *guru* in fact diagnostic of the authoritarian personality, a sign of eternal adolescence in the seeker? That is, such persons dependently seek in the mere authority of other persons what can only be found in fresh inquiries of That Which Is, reality. The purpose of comparative culture studies is

properly to discover the nature of culture itself, not to indulge in individual daisy-picking over the problem of
"what can a man believe." As for finding cosmic truth by
searching "inner space"—often deplorably unfurnished—
with the aid of drugs, this epistemology is too noodlehead-
ed and naïve to merit comment.

Having made out with a good thing in "The Teachings
of Don Juan: A Yaqui Way of Knowledge," Carlos Castaneda now writes a kind of "Don Juan Revisited." There
is a certain poignancy in the picture of a raw young anthropologist in his encounter with a wise old man of another culture, and in both books Castaneda has played this for
all it is worth, even to his own indignity. But no professional anthropologist who read the first book was ever able to
suppose it made any contribution to Yaqui ethnography,
and it is even unclear to what degree Don Juan was Yaqui
in culture. The Appendix purporting to be "A Structural
Analysis" shows an abrupt change of style and was evidently tacked on at the behest of a thesis committee, in order to
retrieve otherwise woefully inadequate ethnography. But
this tedious attempt to play dutiful Lévi-Straussian games
can have satisfied neither committee nor the general
reader.

The long disquisition of Don Juan and the detailing of
each confused emotional reaction of the author, in the
present volume, imply either total recall, novelistic talent,
or a tape recorder. No banality goes unrecorded, nothing
is summarized, nothing is spared us, and yet the nourishment of it all hardly matches that in Jello. The total effect
is self-dramatizing and vague, and Castaneda curiously
manages to be at once disingenuous and naïve. Even as
belles lettres the book is wanting, for the writing is preten-
tious (twice we read of "insidious hair," as though the writer were enamoured of his concoction). The *smoking* of the
"psilocybe" (mushroom) raises some wonder too.

There seems to exist a sizeable public with a taste for the
plastic flowers of science-writing in Ardrey, Heyerdahl,
and Desmond Morris, and that public will no doubt be

pleased with this new production. One longs for sheer information on datura and narcotic mushrooms beyond the oblique words of Don Juan and the empty feelings of the acolyte, and both books together advance our knowledge of peyotism not a whit. But perhaps it is unfair to expect this of an ego trip. Everything is smarmy with self-important and really quite trivial feelings and narcissistic self-preoccupation.

One's impatience is aroused by the most obvious questions being left unasked. For example, is "a separate reality" the same for every society, or even for two individuals? And is a toxic state of the brain any earnest for the existence of another "reality"? The book is pseudo-profound, sophomoric and deeply vulgar. To one reader at least, for decades interested in Amerindian hallucinogens, the book is frustratingly and tiresomely dull, posturing pseudo-ethnography and, intellectually, kitsch.

ROBERT BUCKHOUT
On Being Chained to Reason

The psychologist who has overlearned logical positivism will be both frustrated and enlightened by taking this voyage into the personalized ethnography of a sorcerer. The voyage involves the conscious suspension of a social scientist's well-developed standards for credibility of evidence and a period of participative education that is usually only theorized upon. Through the medium of peyote or psilocybin, Carlos Castaneda experiences, as an apprentice, the separate reality of the 'man of knowledge,' Don Juan, a Yaqui Indian *brujo,* or sorcerer.

Castaneda's account of his experiences impresses on the reader, often in a chilling fashion, a world of experience which is paradoxical, violent, transcending, and challenging to a modern western man's comfortable sense of what is real. Like R. D. Laing's exploration of the world of the 'mad,' Castaneda violates the rules of the game of science; getting 'too close' to his subject in a very successful effort to enlighten his audience.

The popularity of these two books in head shops around the US might be written off, because they present a sympathetic portrayal of the benefits derived from the disciplined use of psychedelic drugs. But, regardless of the motivations of 'Don Juan' readers, Castaneda is a trained social scientist, whose own analytical frame of reference is constantly getting in the way of learning from Don Juan, who comes across as a very eloquent philosopher of science. In one case, in which Castaneda is directed to perceive as a crow, the vividness of the experience prompts the author to ask if his body really flew. The exasperated Don Juan replies [that such a question is pointless, since he flew not like a bird—which is the corroboration Castaneda wants—but like someone who has used the devil's weed (as Castaneda did)!].

The first book, which has the earmarks of a far out doctoral dissertation, is more analytical, containing an explanatory Appendix on the alleged process of using "nonordinary reality" in the drug-taking rituals of the Yaqui Indian. But as Castaneda experiences more, his preconceived notions disappear—the observer becomes the learner and the observed. The conversations—presented as solid reportage—are the fascinating data which could only come from mutual trust and the willingness of the author to discover rather than to explain.

These books will disturb the psychologist, the philosopher of science, and any 'rational man.' They must be read and experienced; I cannot convey their impact in a review. In the emerging literature on altered states of consciousness, Castaneda has contributed two crucial, transitional volumes. The reader shares the anguish of a professional social scientist whose sense of reason and borders of 'reality' are shaken to their very foundations. To the teachers of psychology courses, I can only urge that you catch up with some of your students and ponder, if you will, the words of Don Juan, Sorcerer: "A phony sorcerer tries to explain everything in the world with explanations he is not sure about . . . and so everything is witchcraft. But then you're no better [. . .] you're not sure of your explanations either."

3

JOURNEY TO IXTLAN
The Lessons of Don Juan

ONE INDICATION that Robert Buckhout's affirmation has prevailed over Weston La Barre's condemnation is the omnibus review of the first three Castaneda books which the *New York Times Book Review* published after the appearance of *Journey to Ixtlan* in 1972. Paul Riesman, a Carleton College anthropologist, remarks that he does not have the space to put down his own reading of just what don Juan's teachings mean, but he goes a long way toward explaining the challenge of those teachings pointed to by Buckhout. In dramatizing some of the shibboleths and shortcomings of the conventional anthropological understanding of alien cultures, Castaneda's work is for Riesman "among the best that the science of anthropology has produced."

A major point in this review is the subtlety with which even the most sensitive students of other worldviews can cling to their own sense of superiority, their assumption of having a privileged access to a single reality which primitive conceptions try quaintly but poorly to approximate. Riesman stresses how radically Castaneda's writing undermines this pervasive Western presumption, and how unsettling it actually is to be cut adrift from an anchorage of hidden absolutism when we had already thought ourselves free of all dogmatic beliefs. "Castaneda makes it clear that the teachings of don Juan do tell us something of how the world really is," Riesman concludes, and while he commends the author's "great artistry" he treats the books as totally factual.

In the more playful style of the principal literary organ of the rock music-youth-drug culture, Don Strachan's discussion of *Journey to Ixtlan* for *Rolling Stone* pushes the experiential response to Castaneda. In his view, the don Juan writings are primarily books of practical exercises for the reader. This "go thou and do likewise" literalism, relieved by Strachan's self-deprecating humor, is prevalent among those—in or out of the *Rolling Stone* audience—who have grown tired of merely intellectual responses to revelatory texts.

But Strachan also rehearses what he calls the "axioms," the paradoxical concepts of don Juan's teachings, and he raises again in the context of *Journey to Ixtlan* the intellectual riddle which crept into Spicer's and Leach's reviews: "Is Don Juan a real live Peter Pan who grew up or just a literary flight in the Never-Never Land of Castaneda's imagination?" Strachan goes on to imply that he doubts the existence of don Juan, and perhaps the true reason it doesn't *matter* to him whether don Juan is real or illusory is that as long as the effectiveness of recipes is the main issue, the correct identity of the chef counts for little.

PAUL RIESMAN
A Comprehensive Anthropological Assessment

Anthropology is, for many of its American practitioners and amateurs, a way of trying to get out of our particular culture, or at least a way of finding out whether "other ways of life" are possible and, if so, perhaps better than our own. Yet despite the impetus of such curiosity, the bulk of the writing actually published in this field only tends to confirm what we think we already know about the nature of man, society, the human condition. For when we study "other cultures" this way, we assume in advance that "understanding" means "explanation" in terms with which we are already familiar from our own experience and knowledge of what the world is like. To put it another way, anthropological understanding is a way of making the world feel safer, a way of extending the edge of order so that we can comfortably say that people are fundamentally the same everywhere and that "cultural differences" are merely something like different mental images of the same basic reality.

I used to think, in fact, that one of anthropology's great humanistic contributions to our civilization was the notion of a basic humanity common to all mankind—a humanity that was only differently emphasized or differently expressed in different cultures. This idea has been repeatedly used to argue that no race is superior or inferior to any other, and that different cultural accomplishments are not the result of different genetic endowments. Although I have used this argument myself, I believe now that it has been an ineffective and perhaps even irrelevant one for the fight against racism, and that it has actually held back the progress of anthropology because it has almost invariably led us, as Dorothy Lee has shown, in her book "Freedom and Culture" (Prentice Hall, 1959), to confuse equality with sameness and inequality with difference.

Paradoxically, then, the belief that all people are human leads to a *disrespect* for other people as they are, for in the back of our minds we are saying: They could be just as good as we if they tried, or if they adopted different cultural patterns, or if they learned how to read, etc. The belief that all people are human has not saved Western anthropologists from feeling superior to the people they study and write about, and it has not prevented serious distortions in our picture of non-Western peoples (and of ourselves) from arising and influencing our actions.

In light of this we are incredibly fortunate to have Carlos Castaneda's books. Taken together—and they should be read in the order they were written—they form a work which is among the best that the science of anthropology has produced. Three aspects of the work have profoundly influenced my response to it: first, the interest and value of the teachings of Don Juan are extraordinary in themselves; second, Carlos Castaneda has conveyed these teachings with great artistry so that they affect us at many levels; third, he shows us the conditions under which the teachings were transmitted to him, and not only makes us feel the relation he had with his teacher, but also reveals something of his personal struggle with standard Western reality whose thrall kept preventing him from accepting Don Juan's lessons on their own terms.

Though these three aspects are obviously interconnected, I will try to deal with them separately here. I needn't dwell on the artistic value of these books. The story they tell is so good, and the descriptions so vivid, that I was utterly fascinated as I read. What makes these books great is that Castaneda has not been afraid to commit things to paper that he himself does not understand. This is true of all the volumes, but it is most obvious in the first, "The Teachings of Don Juan," where Castaneda largely separates his description of what happened from his attempt to make sense of it. The "structural analysis," the second part of that book, is awful but useful all the same because of what it reveals about our approach to the world: rather than deal with what the teachings of Don Juan are, the structural analysis pays attention to the fact that they seem to be systematic and consistent with themselves. The structural analysis, then, is a pathetic denial of the reality of the experiences presented in the first part of the book and thus exemplifies the arrogance and fright of most of us Western anthropologists, who carry on as if we know reality while "other cultures" merely have approximate "versions" of that reality. Luckily, something in Castaneda's guts told him that there was more to his experiences than what he could understand, so rather than give us the pabulum of analyzed data, he has done a wonderful job of conveying his experiences while under the tutelage of Don Juan.

Carlos Castaneda was a graduate student in anthropology at the University of California at Los Angeles when he began to work with Don Juan. He had undertaken a study of the medicinal plants used by the Indians of the Southwest; presumably this study, if it had ever been done, would have added something to the body of our knowledge. Somebody, if not Castaneda himself, might have written a paper on it, called "Cross-Cultural Transformations in the Lexical Structure of the Plant Lore of the Indians of the Southwestern United States." This did not happen, however, because Castaneda met Don Juan, a Yaqui "sorcerer," and Don Juan, after feeling Castaneda out, decided to try to teach him what he knew.

Actually, that is not what happened; writing that sentence was an easy out for me; writer and reader could both go on to the next sentence feeling they had understood: what really happened is that Mescalito, the "spirit" of the Peyote plant, indicated to Don Juan that Carlos was the "chosen" one, the person to whom Don Juan should pass on his knowledge.

The result of this has been for us, a very happy collaboration, and it is because of the collaborative nature of the work that it is appropriate, I think, to call it science. Castaneda modestly says that he is letting Don Juan's words speak for themselves, but this is true only in that Castaneda does not burden them with qualifications or alter them while trying to explain them. The fact is that the words would not be there at all if Castaneda had not been there "with unbending intent," and if he had not put his very being on the line so that Don Juan would also give him his utmost. It is not the object we are trying to know that makes knowledge scientific, nor is it the kind of knowledge we have about it (e.g. intuitive, quantifiable, dream, etc.) but rather the fact that the person knowing has done the best he could to show others exactly how he came by that knowledge.

Although I feel he should do even more of this, Castaneda does reveal enough of himself for us to see some of the ways in which we are like him (or unlike him, as the case may be). In fact, his courage lies not only in the fact

that he persists in his effort to become a "man of knowledge"—a path that involves continuing openness to the
unknown—but also in the fact that he is willing to speak of
things concerning himself that most people would prefer
to hide from themselves as well as others. Yet it is these
things, the truths that hit you in the pit of the stomach,
that enable us to see that our image of man is just that—an
image—and that suggest entirely other ways of perceiving
man and the world. I am not thinking here of Castaneda's
strange, beautiful and disconcerting experiences in what
he calls "non-ordinary reality," but rather of some simpler,
more every-day ones which I am sure nearly every reader
of these books can recognize as his own. Let me illustrate
with two examples.

Near the beginning of "A Separate Reality," Carlos tells
Don Juan of his experience watching a group of street urchins who lived by shining shoes around a hotel in a Mexican city and eating the scraps left on the plates in the
hotel's restaurant. He told Don Juan that [he had been
saddened to consider the hopelessness of these children's
situation, their imprisonment in lives which were, so early,
determined by pathetic scavenging.

Don Juan then startles Carlos by taking issue with his
pity for the urchins. He forces Carlos to defend his seemingly unassailable position, which the latter does by pointing to the contrast between his own life, open as it is to a
variety of courses of action and cultural possibilities, and
the children's confining world.

Don Juan's rejoinder to this is that the only men he is
familiar with as having successfully traversed the path of
knowledge began as just such pathetic street children.
Since Carlos' feeling sorry for the scavengers is based not
on their economic but on their intellectual prospects, and
since progress on the way of knowledge is, by then, Carlos'
own highest *intellectual* goal, he confronts the disturbing
realization that, as he confesses], "My reason for pitying
them was incongruous. Don Juan had nailed me neatly."

While "A Separate Reality" is a sequel to "The Teachings of Don Juan," "Journey to Ixtlan" is not a sequel except fot the last three of its 20 chapters. Rather, because of a new sense of his relationship to the world which arose in him through experiences described in those chapters, Carlos saw the significance of a whole series of other "lessons" which Don Juan had given him during the period described in "The Teachings of Don Juan" and he recounts those "lessons" in "Journey to Ixtlan." Carlos had omitted them from his first book because, at the time, he hadn't been able to see how they fitted in with his psychedelic experiences: in fact, none of the experiences described in "Journey to Ixtlan" take place under the influence of psychotropic plants, but simply in relation to hills, valleys, animals and plants and, of course, Don Juan himself. The following passage describes a portion of one of Don Juan's lessons. After Don Juan had told Castaneda about the time when he changed his way of living, Castaneda replied [that he was content with his life as it was, and saw no reason for altering it.

At that point Don Juan had challenged Carlos to say whether he thought they were "equals." Growing nervous at such probing, Carlos had at last attested to their equality, but he secretly held to a deep-rooted sense of superiority and condescension. When Don Juan had then disagreed with his affirmation, Carlos hastened to reassure the old Indian, but was silenced and enraged by the latter's quiet reply: " 'We are not equal. I am a hunter and a warrior, and you are a pimp.' "

Don Juan had explained this startling diagnosis by accusing Carlos of seeking the knowledge of sorcery not for himself but merely so as to gather data for others, and by adding that, compared to his own carefully controlled life, Carlos' is one of "blinding idiocy"].

This lesson took place very near the beginning of Castaneda's apprenticeship as described in "The Teachings of Don Juan"; in fact, it was the day after he had found his "spot." The lesson given here exemplifies in a highly dramatic way some of the points I was making at the beginning of this article. Castaneda, like nearly every member of Western civilization, feels himself to be superior to members of other cultures and in fact to all other entities in the world. But since such feelings conflict with our democratic ideology, he claims that Don Juan is his equal. Don Juan not only sees through this, but also sees that Castaneda is pimping in the sense that Castaneda's reason for being there in the first place is not to learn something but to collect information for someone else: to add to the corpus of anthropological knowledge, for instance, by writing a Ph.D. thesis that will add to what is already known so that others can then add even more and it will appear that our knowledge is actually increasing.

But knowledge of what? This is the crux of the matter. Our social sciences generally treat the culture and knowledge of other peoples as forms and structures necessary for human life that those people have developed and imposed upon a reality which we know—or at least our scientists know—better than they do. We can therefore study those forms in relation to "reality" and measure how well or ill they are adapted to it. In their studies of the cultures of other people, even those anthropologists who sincerely love the people they study almost never think that they are learning something about the way the world really is. Rather, they conceive of themselves as finding out what other people's *conceptions* of the world are. For the longest time Castaneda, too, thought this way about what Don Juan was telling him.

It is stupid and wasteful, however, to think of Don Juan's knowledge—and that of other non-Western peoples—as no more than conceptions of some fixed reality. Castaneda makes it clear that the teachings of Don Juan do tell us something of how the world really is, and I feel that this is knowledge of great value. I don't have the space to put down my own reading of what Don Juan is saying, and I can't even begin to point out all the delights to be found in these books. In any case, the excellence of Castaneda's writing ensures, I believe, that readers will discover these things for themselves. In losing, let me give Don Juan the last word by quoting an apparently simple but really unsettling remark. Earlier in the conversation from which this is taken, Don Juan described how his parents were murdered by the Mexicans. Then, after an interchange concerning Castaneda's childhood, Don Juan said:

"I promised my father that I would live to destroy his assassins. I carried that promise with me for years. Now I . . . have learned that the countless paths one traverses in one's life are all equal. Oppressors and oppressed meet at the end, and the only thing that prevails is that life was altogether too short for both. Today I feel sad not because my mother and father died the way they did; I feel sad because they were Indians. They lived like Indians and died like Indians and never knew that they were, before anything else, men."

DON STRACHAN
The Word from Rolling Stone

Peter Pan and Wendy glided gracefully across the stage and off into the mini-bubbled night. Later I went home and flapped my arms off the end of my bed until I finally flew an airy two feet. I was eight. (All right, I was 12.) Carlos Castaneda found his beneficial spot and his enemy spot on Don Juan's porch by *crossing his eyes*; that is, by shifting glances so quickly that his eyes did not rest on any object. This forced each eye to see the same image separately, allowing him to [perceive normally unnoticed alterations in his environment].

While I was reading about it, a mouse appeared at my feet. Being now a culture-bound 29, had not Mescalito's little brother been floating through my frontal lobe, and had I not heard a voice in the dark after finishing *A Separate Reality,* I might not have recognized this rodent as an ally. Forewarned by Don Juan not to look him head on, I

crossed my eyes at him. After about 15 minutes, a balloon exploded behind my eyes. I looked for the writing but it was
blank. The ally minced off toward the kitchen and my
frontal lobe ached.

If *crossing your eyes* gives you only headaches instead of
access into the world of a sorcerer, you might try *setting up
dreaming.* Begin tonight by looking at your hands in your
dreams. . . .

Such exercises prepare you for *stopping the world,* the
first step in becoming a *brujo.* Maybe a bilingual coyote will
walk up and chat with you, as one did with Carlos; maybe
you'll see a shadow slide off a rock into the ground, to be
absorbed by the soil [. . .]. *Ixtlan* is even richer than Castaneda's previous books in these eerie, supernatural events
and flickering glimpses at retina's edge.

Carlos and Juan's Flakey Foont-Mr. Natural relationship is honed to a hilarious edge. [Flakey Carlos whines,
for instance, that the "omen" announcing his power is not
forthcoming.] The more he questions his mentor, the
more exacerbatingly disdainful, enigmatic or silent the
sage becomes. Juan rocks with the laughter of superiority
from cover to cover, at one point has Carlos walk three
paces behind him, and regularly scares the shit out of his
apprentice to prepare him for his cryptic gems of resonant
wisdom.

Carlos, although he actually *stops the world* toward the
end of the book, is more the obtuse Ugly American than
ever. [When he condescends to Don Juan that they are
equals he is brought up short by the sorcerer's retort that it
is Carlos who is the inferior one.] Crazy Juan views the
world as "stupendous, awesome, mysterious, unfathomable," while Carlos' university-ordered mind can churn
out only indecision, depression and fear.

In the sense that there are no new jokes, there is no new
wisdom. Juan enhances the palatability of his advice by
tacking it onto superb dramatizations and parables, but
even out of context it holds up well. Erase personal
history, he counsels. Give up self-importance. [. . .] Use

death as an advisor. [. . .] (Assume responsibility for your acts; perform each as if it were "your last battle on earth.") Become inaccessible. [. . .]

To measure the truth in these axioms, assume their opposites: They are equally true. Juan has Carlos describe his personality exactly the opposite of the way he perceives it; shortly Carlos finds, to his surprise, that these descriptions fit him, too . . . The mood of a warrior calls at once for "control and abandon" . . . "Power commands you and obeys you." Juan is a master at yin-yang, or what Carlos calls the paradoxical unity of opposites.

Carlos has succeeded best at becoming inaccessible. As a white-collar *brujo* (he teaches at the University of California), he moves in a fog of mystery, allowing no image to form around him and limit his actions. The fog permeates even to the books: Is Don Juan a real live Peter Pan who grew up or just a literary flight in the Never-Never Land of Castaneda's imagination?

Not that it matters—the books convincingly erase the line each of us draws to separate "reality" from "illusion"— but I'll believe Don Juan is a breathing entity when I see him on *The Dick Cavett Show*. (All right, I'm over 30.)

4

TALES OF POWER

THE publication of *Tales of Power,* the fourth volume of the tetralogy, late in 1974, prompted another extremely favorable reaction in the *New York Times Book Review.* Elsa First, a New York psychoanalyst interested in the relation between Freudian and Buddhist therapies, feels that Castaneda's unique contribution is to have "placed us inside the shaman's consciousness." Through techniques of trance, controlled dreaming, and the ritual use of hallucinogens, these religious virtuosi have for countless centuries in many cultures undertaken "vision-flights" of dismemberment and transfiguration. Scholars like Eliade (and, indeed, Weston La Barre) have shown us enough of the externals of this tradition to suggest connections with don Juan's sorcery, but First stresses how the writing in *Tales of Power* draws the observing reader into participation along with Carlos.

Calling it "Castaneda's most improbable book," she gives a fuller description of its actual contents than most reviews of Castaneda's work: the roles of don Genaro and Pablito, his apprentice; the surprising appearance of a well-tailored don Juan in Mexico City; the sophisticated categories of *tonal* and *nagual;* the logic-defying leaps of the concluding section. Even more than Robert Buckhout, Elsa First appeals to the experience of "altered states" to explain what happens to Carlos. "Don Juan and Don Genaro," she claims, "were directly manipulating Carlos's consciousness," although the absence of any stage directions or terminology in the text which would highlight the manipulation allows the skeptical reader to retain his skepticism.

Her focus also suggests an additional consideration. From our psychologized standpoint, can we be as indifferent to the "location" of states of consciousness as don Juan would have Carlos be to the metaphysical whereabouts of the *tonal* and the *nagual*? According to First it makes no difference where these realities exist: "In the course of 'Tales of Power,' Carlos learns how to accept the unwonted 'at its face value.'"

Reviewers who do more than merely quote from Castaneda's tetralogy are hard pressed to accept the unwonted in it at face value. But in the five and a half years between Spicer's article and Elsa First's, they helped see to it that the don Juan writings were accepted as serious works worthy of attention by even the most sophisticated reader.

ELSA FIRST
Don Juan Is to Carlos as Carlos Is to Us

Over the last decade the scientific study of altered states of consciousness has given us a new perspective on the history of religion and in particular on shamanism—a form of religion in tribal cultures that are being rapidly extinguished just when we have begun to appreciate what they can teach us about the potentialities of the human mind operating in modes other than those we have cultivated so exclusively in modern Western civilization.

Today we are no longer in the parochial position of 19th-century ethnographers scratching their heads over the peculiar magical beliefs of tribal peoples, nor in the position of the anthropologists of a generation ago who saw shamanism largely as a socially sanctioned form of schizophrenia. We can now see that shamanism is not just magic but metaphysics: it maintains that this world—the world of

everyday appearances—is not more real than the other
world—the world of powers, energies, demons and gods—
because this world is only the "lie" which our minds construct in one particular state: ordinary waking consciousness. We have discovered the essential continuity between
shamanism and the psychological sophistication of Buddhism, which maintains that all worlds are only the product of the mind in various states of consciousness. Mircea
Eliade, the historian of religion, has in effect argued this
throughout his career by elucidating the inner meaning of
the myths of shamanism.

Eliade has not, however, placed us inside the shaman's
consciousness. Carlos Castaneda has—and this is why his
work is original and important. Castaneda is, of course,
the deliberately elusive anthropologist (his method involves the "disrupting of routines" and "erasing personal
history") who has become a best-selling writer and a nearly
legendary figure for his unique and courageous project of
trying to learn how to experience the world as a shaman
does. His reports on his intermittent apprenticeship to a
Mexican Indian shaman which has extended now over 14
years—"The Teachings of Don Juan" (1968), "A Separate
Reality" (1971), "Journey to Ixtlan" (1972)—have been
widely acclaimed for their vividness, and increasingly
widely suspected for the evident art Castenada uses to
shape his picture of shamanism seen from the inside.

In order to show us a world in which "non-ordinary"
states of reality are given an equal valence with waking
consciousness, Castaneda has devised a powerful literary
strategy. He describes "non-ordinary" experiences as they
occurred subjectively, often taking him overwhelmingly by
surprise. Only afterwards does he give his attempts to understand them rationally—and always in the form of dialogues with his teacher, so that the terms of the discussion
are those of Don Juan's world, not ours. Castaneda's narrative surface thus modulates from one state of consciousness to another without transition.

This has caused considerable bewilderment among the

group of naïve skeptics who say that such things don't occur. Castaneda deliberately leaves out the helpful sign-
posts that might read "hallucinatory state" or "trance." In
fact, many of the phenomena Castaneda reports—such as
conscious dreaming, shared trance states, uncannily rapid
trance running, the use of spirit guides or "allies," the cul-
tivation of synaesthesias—are familiar phenomena in a
wide variety of non-Western cultures.

There is a more knowledgeable form of skepticism
which holds that Castaneda's experiences are almost too
good to be true: Don Juan's teachings are strikingly similar
to those of all of the world's great esoteric traditions (such
as Sufism, the higher yogas or Tantric Buddhism) and the
figure of Don Juan himself has increasingly assumed the
outline of paradigmatic spiritual teacher or guru. Why, for
example, do Castaneda's shamans seem to possess a close
analogue to the Hindu Chakra system when this has not
been reported by others? At this point all we can say is that
Castaneda's reported experiences closely resemble much
cross-cultural data—and this could well be explained by
the fact that the "natural mind" everywhere perceives similarly.

Before the publication of "Tales of Power," an anecdote
began circulating in Berkeley, Calif., about Carlos Castaneda's recent visit to Yogi Chen, an elderly Chinese prac-
titioner of esoteric Buddhism who is something of a local
saint. Castaneda, it seems, told Yogi Chen that he was now
being taught how to produce a "double" of himself. Was
there anything similar in Chen's traditions? Of course, said
Yogi Chen, there were methods for producing up to six
emanations of oneself. "But why bother? Then you only
have six times as much trouble."

"Tales of Power," Castaneda's most improbable book, is
partly about the role of such "magical" practices in the
spiritual training of a shaman and, more largely, about the
knowable and the unknowable. It was difficult to imagine
what could possibly follow Castaneda's "Journey to Ixtlan." The stunning antic sorcery of Don Genaro and Don

Juan had finally "stopped the world" for Carlos as they made his car apparently disappear and reappear before his eyes. This salutary shock had enabled Carlos, alone the next day in the wilderness, to have a magical bilingual conversation with a talking coyote, thereby entering the sorcerer's world without the use of drugs. "Journey to Ixtlan" is the most lyrical of Castaneda's books (especially in Don Genaro's lambent fable at the end) but also the most explicit about what Don Juan has been trying to teach. Carlos had been brought to accept [a sorceric vision of reality], not to make him a sorcerer, but to make him realize that our ordinary experience of the world is also only "a description."

"Tales of Power" starts out only a few months after "Journey to Ixtlan" left off (it is based on Castaneda's experiences in 1971 and '72) but we soon see that the pace is accelerated and the scale is grander. Carlos, along with his fellow apprentice Pablito, is to be led toward his full initiation, and Don Juan, as all good gurus must, de-mystifies himself at the end (more or less) with a comprehensive explanation of the strategies used throughout Carlos's apprenticeship. Some of these explanations we would not be surprised to hear from psychologist Robert Ornstein or others in the field of consciousness research.

This is a splendid book, for all that it may seem ungainly, at times ponderous, at others overwrought. Never has Carlos shivered, puked, lost control of his bowels or fainted so often in terror. The systematic derangement of Carlos's senses goes farther than ever. "Tales of Power" could well be read as a farcical picaresque epic of altered states of consciousness. Carlos adventures through many strange modes of perceptions and suffers many enchantments as well. The farce begins early on when Carlos the dogged note-taker drops his pencil and the two sorcerers dive to retrieve it, producing instead, in a wonderfully slapstick scene, all manner of zanily banal paraphernalia [without, apparently, employing any sort of stage trickery]. (Here, as elsewhere, the reader is left to work out for himself that Don Juan and Don Genaro were directly manipulating Carlos' consciousness.)

In all the great examples of the picaresque genre we meander through tales within tales until we feel we are in danger of getting lost. The central section of "Tales of Power" takes place largely in Mexico City where Don Juan shatters Carlos's romanticism and ours by appearing in a well-tailored suit, and there we do seem to get definitely lost: Suddenly, Carlos finds himself whirled away from an acquaintance who has been tailing him in the hopes of being led to the real Don Juan. Carlos lands a mile and a half away near some familiar market stalls which, as he discovers when he tries to confirm the event later, were not in fact open that day. . . .

"Tales of Power," it is explained, are stories of magical feats that are told to an apprentice at the point when he has progressed too far to turn back but is still unable to perform [such feats] himself. The occult feat this book revolves around is an ability Don Genaro is said to possess—borne out by his opportune impromptu appearances—of sending forth a "double" of himself.

In Part One, Carlos receives further instruction in the techniques of conscious "dreaming" which is the take-off point for that curious journey known in anthropology as the shamanistic vision flight, in yogic traditions as astral travel, and in current psychology as an "out-of-the-body-experience." "Dreaming," Carlos is shown, is the first step toward the realization that the "self" is a dream. We see how "dreaming" sets up new experiences of the self and undoes the ordinary distinction between dream and reality. In Part Two, Carlos and Don Juan engage in a series of philosophical dialogues in Mexico City. In Part Three, in initiation scenes, with Don Juan whispering in one ear and Don Genaro whispering in the other, Carlos's consciousness does split in two. He finds afterward that he has been able to perceive things in two separate places at once. In a spectacular climax, Carlos recounts what a ritual test is like from the inside as his awareness shatters into [fragments and he learns he is a] "cluster."

Carlos has come a long way. Just as Castaneda's style has changed from the factual precision of the first book to the lunatic extravagance of this last, so too his *persona* Carlos's understanding of the states of "non-ordinary reality" has grown from book to book. His relationship with Don Juan has developed too, since that moment in "A Separate Reality" when Don Juan uncovered Carlos's forgotten childhood vow that he would fail—a striking example of how the shaman-guru may act as a psychotherapist as he deals with the interferences to his apprentice's "seeing." One of the finest things in "Tales of Power," however stylized or fictional it may be, is the convincing portrait of a spiritual teacher working away at his student's tendency to "indulge" in self-dramatization and self-pity. There are interesting statements also on how and how much such teaching can rearrange the elements of personality.

Now, in some simple and elusively concrete conversations with Don Juan over restaurant tables and on the park benches of Mexico City, the perspective widens further. These comic dialogues, with Don Juan clowningly piling up dishes, cutlery and a chili sauce bottle on the tablecloth to illustrate his meaning, are probably the most poetic statement we have of the epistemological position that seems to arise whenever states of consciousness are taken as primary data.

Don Juan introduces two new terms, the *tonal* and the *nagual,* which are taken from the vocabulary of shamanism. The *tonal* is everything we have words for (let us say, roughly, the world of the ego and of culture), while the *nagual* is everything else that cannot be named; the two, says Don Juan, make up [man's totality]. Then comes a quietly dazzling dialectical turn: [Carlos inquires whether these two dimensions are within us or outside of us. Don Juan replies that while his own *tonal* would lead him to say the latter and Carlos' would have *him* choose the former, neither answer would be correct]. "Inside, outside, it really doesn't matter."

Over the last six years the figures of Carlos and Don Juan have assumed a peculiar status in the imagination of an entire generation. They loom as do the great characters of fiction, Sancho Panza and Don Quixote, say, who marked Western civilization's fall into materialism as Carlos and Don Juan signify the attempt to emerge from it. But we also remain aware that somewhere there is a real Carlos who apparently has painstakingly learned how to "stop the internal dialogue" which continually reconstitutes the ego-bound world.

Can Don Genaro really emanate a double? Is Carlos Castaneda really in touch with a network of Central and South American "sorcerers" whose skills flourished in response to the Conquest and who continue to initiate apprentices? What happened when Carlos "saw" Pablito leap off a cliff and disintegrate in the air, just as, when it was Carlos's turn, he too "exploded" into [a loose collection of separate points of equally personal awareness]?

What happened? Where? Inside, outside, it really doesn't matter. In the course of "Tales of Power," Carlos learns how to accept the unwonted "at its face value." Confronted with the inexplicable, a warrior simply responds, Don Juan explains, without either pretending that nothing has happened or pretending that he understands. Eventually Carlos stops asking anxious questions, stops trying to reduce everything to rational categories. He has learned the warrior's stance of "believing without believing," a kind of metaphysical aplomb. Neurotic Carlos has been freed to use his "reason" where it is called for, but also to use those buried faculties the sorcerers call "will."

"Tales of Power" is extravagant and outrageous on purpose. Castaneda is doing to his audience exactly what Don Juan and Don Genaro do to Carlos from the moment they begin rambunctiously teasing him out of his wits with the possibility that he is seeing their "doubles." In teaching his readers to "believe without believing," Castaneda enlarges his achievement as the chronicler of ancient methods for restructuring the sense of reality. He has brought us closer to understanding the teaching behind all the magic. In Don Juan's words, "Life in itself is sufficient, self-explanatory, and complete."

Part Two
CORRESPONDENCE AND CONTROVERSY

5

ANTHROPOLOGY—OR FICTION?
Two Letters

IN LATE November, 1972, responding to Paul Riesman's review the previous month, the National Book Award-winning novelist Joyce Carol Oates wrote a letter to the *New York Times Book Review* which brought to a boil the simmering controversy over the actual nature of Castaneda's writing. Coming from a correspondent with a reputation as a brilliant writer of fiction and an astute literary critic, her bewilderment over Riesman's treatment of the first three books as nonfiction was worth contending with. Her own quickly rejected surmise that she might be trying to reason her way out of believing something too strange to accept—a surmise which is curiously consistent with Elsa First's later recommendation to accept Juanist phenomena at face value—was tempting to follow up, too.

Accordingly, in light of her desire to know if other Castaneda readers were as bewildered as she, I wrote Ms. Oates. My letter expressed the opinion that the Castaneda volumes could well be nonfiction, but that in any case their ambiguity in this regard might be an important part of their impact. I was therefore baffled by her reply to me, in which she refers confidently to a "hoax." Although I had mentioned to her the similarities I saw between Castaneda and the fiction of the Argentinian J. L. Borges (I hadn't thought of the ones between Castaneda and Laing or Suzuki), I had never heard any *conclusive* argument for the view that the books were an outright hoax, and I still haven't. I was never able to determine what Ms. Oates had in mind by her statement, but her knowledgeably dogged resistance to the supposed factuality of Castaneda's accounts left me skeptical of my own acceptance of it.

JOYCE CAROL OATES
Letter to the *New York Times Book Review*

To The Editor

Paul Riesman's review of Carlos Castaneda's three books ("The Teachings of Don Juan," "A Separate Reality," and "Journey to Ixtlan"), while a respectful and illuminating commentary, left me more bewildered than ever.

Since I am by no means familiar with anthropology, and have not yet read Castaneda's most recent book, "Journey," I should make it clear that my reaction is certainly an amateur's and no doubt very private . . . but is it possible that these books are non-fiction?

I realize that everyone accepts them as anthropological studies, yet they seem to me remarkable works of art, on the Hesse-like theme of a young man's initiation into "another way" of reality. They are beautifully constructed. The dialogue is faultless. The character of Don Juan is unforgettable. There is a novelistic momentum—rising suspenseful action, a gradual revelation of character . . . the moment when Don Juan sees in the narrator a certain secret he clung to as a child, which must be overcome if he is to become a "man of knowledge."

It is quite possible that Don Juan represents a "nonordinary reality" so strange to me that I cannot accept it, and must try to reason my way out of believing. But I don't think so. The voice of Don Juan has always been with us . . . and though his vocabulary is different, he is saying basically much the same thing that Buddhists have always said. However, because I am unfamiliar with anthropological studies and with the response these books have received from professionals, I would be very interested in knowing whether other readers share my bewilderment.

JOYCE CAROL OATES
Windsor, Ontario

JOYCE CAROL OATES
Letter to Daniel C. Noel

. . . I only read Carlos' first two books about 3 weeks ago—enjoyed them immensely. But now that it's a "hoax" I doubt that I'll read the third; for me Borges has done this sort of thing so beautifully, and I must confess a temperamental preference for the "seeing" of—let's say—a Dr. Suzuki, if one desires a guru. Or Dr. Laing. . . .

Best wishes,
JOYCE CAROL OATES

6

AN INTERVIEW, AN EXPOSÉ, A STORY ABOUT STORIES

AT about the time Joyce Carol Oates' note to me arrived, the December, 1972, *Psychology Today* carried an article by Sam Keen in which he interviewed Castaneda himself and tried to get to the bottom of the controversy. Keen, in addition to being a contributing editor for the magazine, is the theologically trained author of two books—*Apology for Wonder* and *To A Dancing God*—which set forth lyrical arguments for a "Dionysian" and autobiographical approach to religion. His questions and comments to Castaneda reflect this background, as the search for the "true facts" about the (then) trilogy becomes a serious conversation about some of the most esoteric concepts of don Juan's teaching and Carlos's learning: "glosses," "desocializing and resocializing," the deficiencies of drugs as a means of interrupting our descriptions of reality, perceiving with one's entire body, and so forth.

Meanwhile, Castaneda's comments about the artistry of don Juan's teaching methods *could* account for the fictive polish of works which he claims are straight reportage, and his discussion of how he disrupts his routines *could* account for his elusiveness without undermining his role as a reliable reporter. The fact is, after the interview we still do not know the truth in the anthropology vs. fiction dispute, but Castaneda's careful responses to all the philosophical parallels Keen proposes are instructive. Moreover, Castaneda's confession—contrary to his students' expectation—that "understanding is important" to him is an extremely suggestive piece of iconoclasm, as is his description of the practical attitude with which he seeks to live out don Juan's disciplines. "For me the way to live—the path with heart—is not introspection or mystical transcendence but presence in the world."

A few months after the Keen interview-article came out, the importance and impact of Castaneda's trilogy in American popular culture were certified by a *Time* magazine cover story. If the *Psychology Today* piece at all supported Castaneda's protestations of anthropological accuracy, *Time*'s attempt at an exposé certainly rekindled the controversy.

To readers for whom the Watergate-widened credibility gap had not also swallowed up such an Establishment periodical, the details unearthed by the *Time* investigators seemed to tip the scales back toward Joyce Carol Oates' skepticism (her bewildered letter is actually quoted at one point). In its characteristic clipped and quipping style, the straight society's *Rolling Stone* summarizes the three books and gathers testimonies from Castaneda himself and several friends, colleagues, and former professors. The magazine's final verdict is guarded: Although Castaneda may have falsified his personal history, and no don Juan can be found, the books cannot yet be *proven* fictional.

It was time for a less brittle and legalistic consideration of the controversy, and, as it turns out, one had already been published *between* the appearances of the more widely circulated *Sorcerer's Apprentice* by Sam Keen and *Don Juan and the Sorcerer's Apprentice* in *Time.* Writing in the *Village Voice* late in January, 1973, Ronald Sukenick presents the case for Castaneda's credibility in terms of the function of stories and fictions in *all* our dealings with "reality," including our confident appeals to solid factuality. He ends up amplifying a theme already sounded by Sam Keen: the social and political implications of sorcery's abandonment of ordinary consensus. But as the author of a critical study of Wallace Stevens (the Hartford businessman-poet who could say "Reality is not what it is") and several books of experimental fiction, Sukenick is especially well equipped to tell us that "the secret of the sorcerer's power . . . is to know that reality is imagined and, as if it were a work of art, to apply the full force of imagination to it." Citing deep congruities between his own writing techniques, Anaïs Nin's theories of fiction, and don Juan's teachings about controlled dreaming, he comes to a decision about the Castaneda books: "These are works of art, Ms. Oates, to answer your questions directly, but works of art don't have to be novels."

Sam Keen had mentioned that Castaneda was a good "sociologist of knowledge." A major tenet of the sociology of knowledge, in the work of an Alfred Schutz or a Peter Berger, is that our sense of reality turns upon a socially constructed "plausibility structure." This is strikingly close to Ronald Sukenick's storyteller's judgment that the crucial thing for Castaneda's account is not that it be "true" rather than "false," but that it be "persuasive." Each reader is capable of deciding privately on the persuasiveness of the tetralogy. Whether, in our fact-focused age, he or she can consciously shift sights to the artistic perspective on the real such a decision implies is a more difficult matter, one which approximates the challenge of don Juan's "seeing."

SAM KEEN
Sorcerer's Apprentice

PROLOGUE. Sorcerers are not fond of statistics, verifiable knowledge or established identities. Their tradition is ancient, their knowledge is esoteric and their way of life is surpassing strange. When Carlos Castaneda began to report on the teachings of don Juan he was more than a spectator to the world of sorcery but something less than a convert. In subsequent years he found the wisdom of don Juan to be the most certain guide on "the path with heart."

He is more elusive as a disciple than he was as an anthropologist. The more notoriety his books gain, the farther he retreats from public attention. His books, *The Teachings of Don Juan, A Separate Reality,* and *Journey to Ixtlan,* have sold half a million copies.

To compensate for his growing image and legend, Carlos Castaneda erases his personal history and deliberately withholds information that would destroy the anonymity he needs so that he can wander freely in whatever worlds there are or may be. When he is caught in the official world, where withholding autobiographical information is tantamount to treason, he may give his name, rank and serial number. Then, like the Lone Ranger, he disappears in a cloud of rumor.

COOL. Usually reliable sources report that Castaneda was born in Brazil 33 or 34 years ago. He spent most of his early life in Argentina before he came to the United States to study anthropology. In the summer of 1960 he set out to gather information on medicinal plants.

He met and became a friend of an old Indian—don Juan Matus—who was reputed to know something about peyote. After a year of slow-growing friendship don Juan explained that he was a *brujo* (sorcerer, medicine man, or healer) and had decided to pass along his secret knowledge to Carlos. Castaneda accepted, confident of his ability to rationalize and transcend the weird world of sorcery and keep his anthropological cool. For the next 12 years Castaneda commuted between the halls of the University of California at Los Angeles and the haunted hills of Mexico. While he played on the margins of madness he managed to retain his sanity and to work on a Ph.D. in anthropology.

CROW. More interesting than the putative facts about Castaneda are the transformations he has undergone and the marvels he has witnessed. Once he became a crow. With only a little help from the smoke of a magical plant, he watched crow's wings sprout from what had been his cheekbones and a tail grow from his neck. And then he flew off with three other crows on a three-day trip. (Any-one who has ever hunted crows would envy anyone who had a chance to crawl inside their uncanny heads. As ex-perts in carrion—sanitation engineers—they must be able to distinguish between the living and the dead. This makes them experts in motion. Their wisdom consists in the abili-ty to tell when things are moving too fast, too slow and just right. And that is no mean knowledge. It might serve well in our culture in which we worship a demon god called Progress who keeps us moving and changing at an insane rate.)

COYOTE. And that is only the beginning. In the course of his apprenticeship Castaneda encountered creatures sel-dom found this side of the looking glass. When he tried to enter the separate reality of the sorcerer's world he was stopped by a gnat that was close to 100 feet tall. There were other dangers. A beautiful sorceress, la Catalina, tried to steal his soul and forced him into deadly combat. Once he almost killed her with a shotgun when she made the mistake of assuming the form of a blackbird and flying too near don Juan's house. When Carlos finally sum-moned sufficient nerve to ram a wild boar's hoof into la Catalina's navel she saw that his intent was strong and she ceased to bug him. Much of Carlos' power came from his meeting with Mescalito, the strawberry-headed, green-skinned spirit of peyote. But there were times when he saw unbelievable things without even a little help from his psy-chotropic friends. One day don Juan and his friend don Genaro made Carlos' car disappear before his stone-sober eyes. And there was the time he had a conversation with a luminous, bilingual coyote.

CONSENSUS. All of these are but minor tricks, occasional far-out trips. The marvel of marvels was Castaneda's steady journey to the heart of ordinary reality. Things are seldom what they seem. In sharing the sources of his sor-cery, don Juan sought to develop in Carlos the ability to see the everyday world with wondering eyes. Don Juan is a good sociologist of knowledge. He knows that the world of common-sense reality is a product of a social consensus. To marvel we need to strip ourselves of the explanations and assumptions that shape and limit our vision. If we bracket our normal ways of perceiving the world we can see how arbitrary they are. Don Juan used sorcery and psychotropic plants to help Carlos in this process of bracketing. The most sophisticated philosophers of our century have tried to accomplish the same thing by pure thought or intellection.

CONDITION. Here fiction and fact entwine to turn event into allegory. A student of the German phenomenologist Edmund Husserl, knowing of Castaneda's interest in phenomenology, gave him a piece of ebony that once sat on Husserl's writing desk. Carlos had read and discussed passages of Husserl's *Ideas* with don Juan and passed the gift on to him. Don Juan fondled the ebony, as Husserl had done a generation before, and gave it an honored place in his treasury of power objects that are used for conjuring. And it is wholly appropriate. Husserl sought to escape from the subjectivity and solipsism that was the legacy of Descartes' definition of man as a rational being enclosed within the certainties of his own mind. Don Juan likewise taught that it is a mistake to get caught in the world of the psyche and neglect the marvels that are all around us. There is no salvation or sanity to be found within the isolated self. If we can discover ways of deconditioning consciousness, of erasing the barriers to perception that are imposed on us by common sense, there is no telling what strange things we may discover. There are certainly more things under heaven than philosophers or psychologists or stock brokers imagine.

CHANGE. In his most recent book, *Journey to Ixtlan,* Castaneda shows that it was more the realistic than the fantastic aspects of don Juan's teachings that convinced him that there was no other way to live an exuberant life. "Don Juan kept reminding me that I had to die," he says. When death became a reality for Castaneda he was able to change, to become more decisive, and to be less governed by the expectations of others and by ordinary social routines. He accepted the ideal of the life of the warrior who must discipline his body and accumulate personal power. By experiment with living impeccably Carlos discovered the paradoxical unity of opposites. Discipline and abandon, realism and fantasy, secondary- and primary-process thinking go hand in hand. There need be no enmity between sanity and ecstasy.

CHARISMA. Every age discovers or creates the heroes it needs. Ours has a strange bunch. Perhaps we feel that we are increasingly strangers in a strange land and so we populate our new world with Hobbits and gurus, charismatics and explorers of altered states of consciousness. The names of Carlos Castaneda, don Juan, Timothy Leary, John Lilly, and other psychonauts are known to many persons who think that Neil Armstrong is the all-American boy who used to be on the radio just before "Terry and the Pirates." Our occult heroes testify to the desire for a new age of enchantment. We have become disenchanted with the old dreams. We thought accumulated wealth would bring us security, and that technological power would allow us to manipulate the environment until it satisfied our every wish. We have found as much anxiety as happiness and more chaos than progress. Now it seems to be time to try another way. Neither technology nor government can change the world sufficiently to satisfy the needs of persons who understand eventually that they must die. So we revive the ancient notion of the power of personal vision. The new mysticism proclaims that enlightenment must take precedence over projects for social change. The eye of the beholder must be purified before it can see new possibilities. There is danger in enchantment. We know that the tyrannical dominion of machines, profit, and power politics will bring only increasing alienation and injustice. But it does not follow that a retreat from politics into nature mysticism or privatism will serve the cause of survival. Vision without politics is as dangerous as politics without vision. We need the disconcerting marvels of don

Juan's world no less than we need the prophetic protests of the Berrigans. And we all might borrow crows' eyes and take a hard look at our rate and direction of movement. When Castaneda returned from his flight with the crows he was shaken for many days. He lived with the anxiety common to all voyagers who enter the world on the other side of the looking glass. For a time he did not know whether he was a professor pretending to be a crow or a crow pretending to be a professor. Then he laughed and knew that literal truth and poetry can never be separated. What is important is to fly high and return to earth.

SAM KEEN: As I followed don Juan through your three books, I suspected, at times, that he was the creation of Carlos Castaneda. He is almost too good to be true—a wise old Indian whose knowledge of human nature is superior to almost everybody's.

CARLOS CASTANEDA: The idea that I concocted a person like don Juan is inconceivable. He is hardly the kind of figure my European intellectual tradition would have led me to invent. The truth is much stranger. I didn't create anything. I am only a reporter. I wasn't even prepared to make the changes in my life that my association with don Juan involved.

KEEN: How and where did you meet don Juan and become his apprentice?

CASTANEDA: I was finishing my undergraduate study at UCLA and was planning to go to graduate school in anthropology. I was interested in becoming a professor and thought I might begin in the proper way by publishing a short paper on medicinal plants. I couldn't have cared less about finding a weirdo like don Juan. I was in a bus depot in Arizona with a high-school friend of mine. He pointed out an old Indian man to me and said he knew about peyote and medicinal plants. I put on my best airs and introduced myself to don Juan and said: "I understand you know a great deal about peyote. I am one of the experts on peyote (I had read Weston La Barre's *The Peyote Cult*) and it might be worth your while to have lunch and talk with me." Well, he just looked at me and my bravado melted. I was absolutely tongue-tied and numb. I was usually very aggressive and verbal so it was a momentous affair to be silenced by a look. After that I began to visit him and about a year later he told me he had decided to pass on to me the knowledge of sorcery he had learned from his teacher.

KEEN: Then don Juan is not an isolated phenomenon. Is there a community of sorcerers that shares a secret knowledge?

CASTANEDA: Certainly. I know three sorcerers and seven apprentices and there are many more. If you read the history of the Spanish conquest of Mexico, you will find that the Catholic inquisitors tried to stamp out sorcery because they considered it the work of the devil. It has been around for many hundreds of years. Most of the techniques don Juan taught me are very old.

KEEN: Some of the techniques that sorcerers use are in wide use in other occult groups. Persons often use dreams to find lost articles, and they go on out-of-the-body journeys in their sleep. But when you told how don Juan and his friend don Genaro made your car disappear in broad daylight I could only scratch my head. I know that a hypnotist can create the illusion of the presence or absence of an object. Do you think you were hypnotized?

CASTANEDA: Perhaps, something like that. But we have to begin by realizing, as don Juan says, that there is much more to the world than we usually acknowledge. Our normal expectations about reality are created by a social consensus. We are taught how to see and understand the world. The trick of socialization is to convince us that the descriptions we agree upon define the limits of the real world. What we call reality is only one way of seeing the world, a way that is supported by a social consensus.

KEEN: Then a sorcerer, like a hypnotist, creates an alternative world by building up different expectations and manipulating cues to produce a social consensus.

CASTANEDA: Exactly. I have come to understand sorcery in terms of Talcott Parsons' idea of glosses. A gloss is a total system of perception and language. For instance, this room is a gloss. We have lumped together a series of isolated perceptions—floor, ceiling, window, lights, rugs, etc.—to make a single totality. But we had to be taught to put the world together in this way. A child reconnoiters the world with few preconceptions until he is taught to see things in a way that corresponds to the descriptions everybody agrees on. The world is an agreement. The system of glossing seems to be somewhat like walking. We have to learn to walk, but once we learn there is only one way to walk. We have to learn to see and to talk, but once we learn we are subject to the syntax of language and the mode of perception it contains.

KEEN: So sorcery, like art, teaches a new system of glossing. When, for instance, Vincent van Gogh broke with artistic tradition and painted *The Starry Night* he was in effect saying: here is a new way of looking at things. Stars are alive and they whirl around in their energy field.

CASTANEDA: Partly. But there is a difference. An artist usually just rearranges the old glosses that are proper to his membership. Membership consists of being an expert in the innuendoes of meaning that are contained within a culture. For instance, my primary membership like most educated Western men was in the European intellectual world. You can't break out of one membership without being introduced into another. You can only rearrange the glosses.

KEEN: Was don Juan resocializing you or desocializing you? Was he teaching you a new system of meanings or only a method of stripping off the old system so that you might see the world as a wondering child?

CASTANEDA: Don Juan and I disagree about this. I say he was reglossing me and he says he was deglossing me. By teaching me sorcery he gave me a new set of glosses, a new language and a new way of seeing the world. Once I read a bit of the linguistic philosophy of Ludwig Wittgenstein to don Juan and he laughed and said: "Your friend Wittgenstein tied the noose too tight around his neck so he can't go anywhere."

KEEN: Wittgenstein is one of the few philosophers who

would have understood don Juan. His notion that there are many different language games—science, politics, poetry, religion, metaphysics, each with its own syntax and rules—would have allowed him to understand sorcery as an alternative system of perception and meaning.

CASTANEDA: But don Juan thinks that what he calls seeing is apprehending the world without any interpretation; it is pure wondering perception. Sorcery is a means to this end. To break the certainty that the world is the way you have always been taught you must learn a new description of the world—sorcery—and then hold the old and the new together. Then you will see that neither description is final. At that moment you slip between the descriptions; you stop the world and see. You are left with wonder; the true wonder of seeing the world without interpretation.

KEEN: Do you think it is possible to get beyond interpretation by using psychedelic drugs?

CASTANEDA: I don't think so. That is my quarrel with people like Timothy Leary. I think he was improvising from within his European membership and merely rearranging old glosses. I have never taken LSD, but what I gather from don Juan's teachings is that psychotropics are used to stop the flow of ordinary interpretations, to enhance the contradictions within the glosses, and to shatter certainty. But the drugs alone do not allow you to stop the world. To do that you need an alternative description of the world. That is why don Juan had to teach me sorcery.

KEEN: There is an ordinary reality that we Western people are certain is *the* only world, and then there is the separate reality of the sorcerer. What are the essential differences between them?

CASTANEDA: In European membership the world is built largely from what the eyes report to the mind. In sorcery the total body is used as a perceptor. As Europeans we see a world out there and talk to ourselves about it. We are here and the world is there. Our eyes feed our reason and we have no direct knowledge of things. According to sorcery this burden on the eyes is unnecessary. We know with the total body.

KEEN: Western man begins with the assumption that subject and object are separated. We're isolated from the world and have to cross some gap to get to it. For don Juan and the tradition of sorcery, the body is already in the world. We are united with the world, not alienated from it.

CASTANEDA: That's right. Sorcery has a different theory of embodiment. The problem in sorcery is to tune and trim your body to make it a good receptor. Europeans deal with their bodies as if they were objects. We fill them with alcohol, bad food, and anxiety. When something goes wrong we think germs have invaded the body from outside and so we import some medicine to cure it. The disease is not a part of us. Don Juan doesn't believe that. For him disease is a disharmony between a man and his world. The body is an awareness and it must be treated impeccably.

KEEN: This sounds similar to Norman O. Brown's idea that children, schizophrenics, and those with the divine madness of the Dionysian consciousness are aware of things and of other persons as extensions of their bodies. Don Juan suggests something of the kind when he says the man of knowledge has fibers of light that connect his solar plexus to the world.

CASTANEDA: My conversation with the coyote is a good illustration of the different theories of embodiment. When he came up to me I said: "Hi, little coyote. How are you doing?" And he answered back: "I am doing fine. How about you?" Now, I didn't hear these words in the normal way. But my body knew the coyote was saying something and I translated it into dialogue. As an intellectual my relation to dialogue is so profound that my body automatically translated into words the feeling that the animal was communicating with me. We always see the unknown in terms of the known.

KEEN: When you are in that magical mode of consciousness in which coyotes speak and everything is fitting and luminous it seems as if the whole world is alive and that human beings are in a communion that includes animals and plants. If we dropped our arrogant assumptions that

we are the only comprehending and communicating form
of life we might find all kinds of things talking to us.

John Lilly talked to dolphins. Perhaps we would feel less
alienated if we could believe we were not the only intelli-
gent life.

CASTANEDA: We might be able to talk to any animal. For
don Juan and the other sorcerers there wasn't anything
unusual about my conversation with the coyote. As a matter of fact they said I should have gotten a more reliable
animal for a friend. Coyotes are tricksters and are not to
be trusted.

KEEN: What animals make better friends?

CASTANEDA: Snakes make stupendous friends.

KEEN: I once had a conversation with a snake. One night
I dreamt there was a snake in the attic of a house where I
lived when I was a child. I took a stick and tried to kill it. In
the morning I told the dream to a friend and she remind-
ed me that it was not good to kill snakes, even if they were
in the attic in a dream. She suggested that the next time a
snake appeared in a dream I should feed it or do something to befriend it. About an hour later I was driving my
motor scooter on a little-used road and there it was waiting
for me—a four-foot snake, stretched out sunning itself. I
drove alongside it and it didn't move. After we had looked
at each other for a while I decided I should make some
gesture to let him know I repented striking his brother in
my dream. I reached over and touched his tail. He coiled
up and indicated that I had rushed our intimacy. So I
backed off and just looked. After about five minutes he
went off into the bushes.

CASTANEDA: You didn't pick it up?

KEEN: No.

CASTANEDA: It was a very good friend. A man can learn
to call snakes. They sense everything, your activity and
your feeling. But you have to be in very good shape, calm,
collected—in a friendly mood, with no doubts or pending
affairs.

KEEN: My snake taught me that I had always had paranoid feelings about nature. I considered animals and snakes dangerous. After my meeting I could never kill another snake and it began to be more plausible to me that we might be in some kind of living nexus.

Our ecosystem might well include communication between different forms of life.

CASTANEDA: Don Juan has a very interesting theory about this. Plants, like animals, always affect you. He says that if you don't apologize to plants for picking them you are likely to get sick or have an accident.

KEEN: The American Indians had similar beliefs about animals they killed. If you don't thank an animal for giving up his life so that you may live, his spirit may cause you trouble.

CASTANEDA: We have a commonality with all life. Something is altered every time we deliberately injure plant life or animal life. We take life in order to live but we must be willing to give up our lives without resentment when it is our time. We are so important and take ourselves so seriously that we forget that the world is a great mystery that will teach us if we listen.

KEEN: Perhaps psychotropic drugs momentarily wipe out the isolated ego and allow a mystical fusion with nature. Most cultures that have retained a sense of communion between man and nature also have made ceremonial use of psychedelic drugs. Were you using peyote when you talked with the coyote?

CASTANEDA: No. Nothing at all.

KEEN: Was this experience more intense than similar experiences you had when don Juan gave you psychotropic plants?

CASTANEDA: Much more intense. Every time I took psychotropic plants I knew I had taken something and I could always question the validity of my experience. But when the coyote talked to me I had no defenses. I couldn't explain it away. I had really stopped the world and, for a short time, got completely outside my European system of glossing.

KEEN: Do you think don Juan lives in this state of awareness most of the time?

CASTANEDA: Yes. He lives in magical time and occasionally comes into ordinary time. I live in ordinary time and occasionally dip into magical time.

KEEN: Anyone who travels so far from the beaten paths of consensus must be very lonely.

CASTANEDA: I think so. Don Juan lives in an awesome world and he has left routine people far behind. Once when I was with don Juan and his friend don Genaro I saw the loneliness they shared and their sadness at leaving behind the trappings and points of reference of ordinary society. I think don Juan turns his loneliness into art. He contains and controls the power, the wonder and the loneliness, and turns them into art.

His art is the metaphorical way in which he lives. This is why his teachings have such a dramatic flavor and unity. He deliberately constructs his life and his manner of teaching.

KEEN: For instance, when don Juan took you out into the hills to hunt animals was he consciously staging an allegory?

CASTANEDA: Yes. He had no interest in hunting for sport or to get meat. In the 10 years I have known him don Juan has killed only four animals to my knowledge, and these only at times when he saw that their death was a gift to him in the same way his death would one day be a gift to something. Once we caught a rabbit in a trap we had set and don Juan thought I should kill it because its time was up. I was desperate because I had the sensation that I was the rabbit. I tried to free him but couldn't open the trap. So I stomped on the trap and accidentally broke the rabbit's neck. Don Juan had been trying to teach me that I must assume responsibility for being in this marvelous world. He leaned over and whispered in my ear: "I told you this rabbit had no more time to roam in this beautiful desert." He consciously set up the metaphor to teach me about the ways of the warrior. The warrior is a man who hunts and accumulates personal power. To do this he must develop patience and will and move deliberately through the world. Don Juan used the dramatic situation of actual hunting to teach me because he was addressing himself to my body.

KEEN: In your most recent book, *Journey to Ixtlan,* you reverse the impression given in your first books that the use of psychotropic plants was the main method don Juan intended to use in teaching you about sorcery. How do you now understand the place of psychotropics in his teachings?

CASTANEDA: Don Juan used psychotropic plants only in the middle period of my apprenticeship because I was so stupid, sophisticated and cocky. I held on to my description of the world as if it were the only truth. Psychotropics created a gap in my system of glosses. They destroyed my dogmatic certainty. But I paid a tremendous price. When the glue that held my world together was dissolved, my body was weakened and it took months to recuperate. I was anxious and functioned at a very low level.

KEEN: Does don Juan regularly use psychotropic drugs to stop the world?

CASTANEDA: No. He can now stop it at will. He told me that for me to try to see without the aid of psychotropic plants would be useless. But if I behaved like a warrior and assumed responsibility I would not need them; they would only weaken my body.

KEEN: This must come as quite a shock to many of your admirers. You are something of a patron saint to the psychedelic revolution.

CASTANEDA: I do have a following and they have some strange ideas about me. I was walking to a lecture I was giving at California State, Long Beach the other day and a guy who knew me pointed me out to a girl and said: "Hey, that is Castaneda." She didn't believe him because she had the idea that I must be very mystical. A friend has collected some of the stories that circulate about me. The consensus is that I have mystical feet.

KEEN: Mystical feet?

CASTANEDA: Yes, that I walk barefooted like Jesus and
have no callouses. I am supposed to be stoned most of the
time. I have also committed suicide and died in several
different places.

A college class of mine almost freaked out when I began
to talk about phenomenology and membership and to explore perception and socialization. They wanted to be told
to relax, turn on and blow their minds. But to me understanding is important.

KEEN: Rumors flourish in an information vacuum. We
know something about don Juan but too little about Castaneda.

CASTANEDA: That is a deliberate part of the life of a warrior. To weasel in and out of different worlds you have to
remain inconspicuous. The more you are known and identified, the more your freedom is curtailed. When people
have definite ideas about who you are and how you will
act, then you can't move. One of the earliest things don
Juan taught me was that I must erase my personal history.
If little by little you create a fog around yourself then you
will not be taken for granted and you will have more room
for change. That is the reason I avoid tape recordings
when I lecture, and photographs.

KEEN: Maybe we can be personal without being historical. You now minimize the importance of the psychedelic
experience connected with your apprenticeship. And you
don't seem to go around doing the kind of tricks you describe as the sorcerer's stock-in-trade. What are the elements of don Juan's teachings that are important for you?
How have you been changed by them?

CASTANEDA: For me the ideas of being a warrior and a
man of knowledge, with the eventual hope of being able to
stop the world and see, have been most applicable. They
have given me peace and confidence in my ability to control my life. At the time I met don Juan I had very little
personal power. My life had been very erratic. I had come
a long way from my birthplace in Brazil. Outwardly I was

aggressive and cocky, but within I was indecisive and unsure of myself. I was always making excuses for myself. Don Juan once accused me of being a professional child because I was so full of self-pity. I felt like a leaf in the wind. Like most intellectuals, my back was against the wall. I had no place to go. I couldn't see any way of life that really excited me. I thought all I could do was make a mature adjustment to a life of boredom or find ever more complex forms of entertainment such as the use of psychedelics and pot and sexual adventures. All of this was exaggerated by my habit of introspection. I was always looking within and talking to myself. The inner dialogue seldom stopped. Don Juan turned my eyes outward and taught me how to see the magnificence of the world and how to accumulate personal power.

I don't think there is any other way to live if one wants to be exuberant.

KEEN: He seems to have hooked you with the old philosopher's trick of holding death before your eyes. I was struck with how classical don Juan's approach was. I heard echoes of Plato's idea that a philosopher must study death before he can gain any access to the real world and of Martin Heidegger's definition of man as being-toward-death.

CASTANEDA: Yes, but don Juan's approach has a strange twist because it comes from the tradition in sorcery that death is a physical presence that can be felt and seen. One of the glosses in sorcery is: death stands to your left. Death is an impartial judge who will speak truth to you and give you accurate advice. After all, death is in no hurry. He will get you tomorrow or next week or in 50 years. It makes no difference to him. The moment you remember you must eventually die you are cut down to the right size.

I think I haven't made this idea vivid enough. The gloss—"death to your left"—isn't an intellectual matter in sorcery; it is a perception. When your body is properly tuned to the world and you turn your eyes to your left, you can witness an extraordinary event, the shadowlike presence of death.

KEEN: In the existential tradition, discussions of responsibility usually follow discussions of death.

CASTANEDA: Then don Juan is a good existentialist. When there is no way of knowing whether I have one more minute of life I must live as if this is my last moment. Each act is the warrior's last battle. So everything must be done impeccably. Nothing can be left pending. This idea has been very freeing for me. I don't have any more loose ends; nothing is waiting for me. I am here talking to you and I may never return to Los Angeles. But that wouldn't matter because I took care of everything before I came.

KEEN: This world of death and decisiveness is a long way from psychedelic utopias in which the vision of endless time destroys the tragic quality of choice.

CASTANEDA: When death stands to your left you must create your world by a series of decisions. There are no large or small decisions, only decisions that must be made now.

And there is no time for doubts or remorse. If I spend my time regretting what I did yesterday I avoid the decisions I need to make today.

KEEN: How did don Juan teach you to be decisive?

CASTANEDA: He spoke to my body with his acts. My old way was to leave everything pending and never to decide anything. To me decisions were ugly. It seemed unfair for a sensitive man to have to decide. One day don Juan asked me: "Do you think you and I are equals?" I was a university student and an intellectual and he was an old Indian but I condescended and said: "Of course we are equals." He said: "I don't think we are. I am a hunter and a warrior and you are a pimp. I am ready to sum up my life at any moment. Your feeble world of indecision and sadness is not equal to mine." Well, I was very insulted and would have left but we were in the middle of the wilderness. So I sat down and got trapped in my own ego involvement. I was going to wait until he decided to go home. After many hours I saw that don Juan would stay there forever if he had to. Why not? For a man with no pending business that is his power. I finally realized that this man was not like my father who would make 20 New Year's resolutions and cancel them all out. Don Juan's decisions were irrevocable as far as he was concerned. They could be canceled out only by other decisions. So I went over and touched him and he got up and we went home. The impact of that act was tremendous. It convinced me that the way of the warrior is an exuberant and powerful way to live.

KEEN: It isn't the content of decision that is important so much as the act of being decisive.

CASTANEDA: That is what don Juan means by having a gesture. A gesture is a deliberate act which is undertaken for the power that comes from making a decision. For instance, if a warrior found a snake that was numb and cold, he might struggle to invent a way to take the snake to a warm place without being bitten. The warrior would make the gesture just for the hell of it. But he would perform it perfectly.

KEEN: There seem to be many parallels between existential philosophy and don Juan's teachings. What you have said about decision and gesture suggests that don Juan, like Nietzsche or Sartre, believes that will rather than reason is the most fundamental faculty of man.

CASTANEDA: I think that's right. Let me speak for myself. What I want to do, and maybe I can accomplish it, is to take the control away from my reason. My mind has been in control all of my life and it would kill me rather than relinquish control. At one point in my apprenticeship I became profoundly depressed. I was overwhelmed with terror and gloom and thoughts about suicide. Then don Juan warned me this was one of reason's tricks to retain control. He said my reason was making my body feel that there was no meaning to life. Once my mind waged this last battle and lost, reason began to assume its proper place as a tool of the body.

KEEN: "The heart has its reasons that reason knows nothing of" and so does the rest of the body.

CASTANEDA: That is the point. The body has a will of its

own. Or rather, the will is the voice of the body. That is why don Juan consistently put his teachings in dramatic form. My intellect could easily dismiss his world of sorcery as nonsense. But my body was attracted to his world and his way of life. And once the body took over, a new and healthier reign was established.

KEEN: Don Juan's techniques for dealing with dreams engaged me because they suggest the possibility of voluntary control of dream images. It is as though he proposes to establish a permanent, stable observatory within inner space. Tell me about don Juan's dream training.

CASTANEDA: The trick in dreaming is to sustain dream images long enough to look at them carefully. To gain this kind of control you need to pick one thing in advance and learn to find it in your dreams. Don Juan suggested that I use my hands as a steady point and go back and forth between them and the images. After some months I learned to find my hands and to stop the dream. I became so fascinated with the technique that I could hardly wait to go to sleep.

KEEN: Is stopping the images in dreams anything like stopping the world?

CASTANEDA: It is similar. But there are differences. Once you are capable of finding your hands at will, you realize that it is only a technique. What you are after is control. A man of knowledge must accumulate personal power. But that is not enough to stop the world. Some abandon also is necessary. You must silence the chatter that is going on inside your mind and surrender yourself to the outside world.

KEEN: Of the many techniques that don Juan taught you for stopping the world, which do you still practice?

CASTANEDA: My major discipline now is to disrupt my routines. I was always a very routinary person. I ate and slept on schedule. In 1965 I began to change my habits. I wrote in the quiet hours of the night and slept and ate when I felt the need. Now I have dismantled so many of my habitual ways of acting that before long I may become unpredictable and surprising to myself.

KEEN: Your discipline reminds me of the Zen story of two disciples bragging about miraculous powers. One disciple claimed the founder of the sect to which he belonged could stand on one side of a river and write the name of Buddha on a piece of paper held by his assistant on the opposite shore. The second disciple replied that such a miracle was unimpressive. "My miracle," he said, "is that when I feel hungry I eat, and when I feel thirsty I drink."

CASTANEDA: It has been this element of engagement in the world that has kept me following the path which don Juan showed me. There is no need to transcend the world. Everything we need to know is right in front of us, if we pay attention. If you enter a state of nonordinary reality, as you do when you use psychotropic plants, it is only to draw from it what you need in order to see the miraculous character of ordinary reality. For me the way to live—the path with heart—is not introspection or mystical transcendence but presence in the world. This world is the warrior's hunting ground.

KEEN: The world you and don Juan have pictured is full of magical coyotes, enchanted crows and a beautiful sorceress. It's easy to see how it could engage you. But what about the world of the modern urban person? Where is the magic there? If we could all live in the mountains we might keep wonder alive. But how is it possible when we are half a zoom from the freeway?

CASTANEDA: I once asked don Juan the same question. We were sitting in a café in Yuma and I suggested that I might be able to learn to stop the world and to see, if I could come and live in the wilderness with him. He looked out the window at the passing cars and said: "That, out there, is your world. You cannot refuse it. You are a hunter of that world." I live in Los Angeles now and I find I can use that world to accommodate my needs. It is a challenge to live with no set routines in a routinary world. But it can be done.

KEEN: The noise level and the constant pressure of masses of people seem to destroy the silence and solitude that would be essential for stopping the world.

CASTANEDA: Not at all. In fact, the noise can be used. You can use the buzzing of the freeway to teach yourself to listen to the outside world. When we stop the world the world we stop is the one we usually maintain by our continual inner dialogue. Once you can stop the internal babble you stop maintaining your old world. The descriptions collapse. That is when personality change begins. When you concentrate on sounds you realize it is difficult for the brain to categorize all the sounds, and in a short while you stop trying. This is unlike visual perception which keeps us forming categories and thinking. It is so restful when you can turn off the talking, categorizing, and judging.

KEEN: The internal world changes but what about the external one? We may revolutionize individual consciousness but still not touch the social structures that create our alienation. Is there any place for social or political reform in your thinking?

CASTANEDA: I came from Latin America where intellectuals were always talking about political and social revolution and where a lot of bombs were thrown. But revolution hasn't changed much. It takes little daring to bomb a building, but in order to give up cigarettes or to stop being anxious or to stop internal chattering, you have to remake yourself. This is where real reform begins.

Don Juan and I were in Tucson not long ago when they were having Earth Week. Some man was lecturing on ecology and the evils of the war in Vietnam. All the while he was smoking. Don Juan said, "I cannot imagine that he is concerned with other people's bodies when he doesn't like his own." Our first concern should be with ourselves. I can like my fellow men only when I am at my peak of vigor and am not depressed. To be in this condition I must keep my body trimmed. Any revolution must begin here in this body. I can alter my culture but only from within a body that is impeccably tuned-in to this weird world. For me, the real accomplishment is the art of being a warrior, which, as don Juan says, is the only way to balance the terror of being a man with the wonder of being a man.

TIME MAGAZINE
Don Juan and the Sorcerer's Apprentice

> Glendower: "I can call spirits from the vasty deep."
> Hotspur: "Why, so can I, or so can any man;
> But will they come when you do call for them?"
> —*Henry IV, Part I*

The Mexican border is a great divide. Below it, the accumulated structures of Western "rationality" waver and plunge. The familiar shapes of society—landlord and peasant, priest and politician—are laid over a stranger ground, the occult Mexico, with its *brujos* and *carismaticos,* its sorcerers and diviners. Some of their practices go back 2,000 and 3,000 years to the peyote and mushroom and morning-glory cults of the ancient Aztecs and Toltecs. Four centuries of Catholic repression in the name of faith and reason have reduced the old ways to a subculture, ridiculed and persecuted. Yet in a country of 53 million, where many village marketplaces have their sellers of curative herbs, peyote buttons or dried hummingbirds, the sorcerer's world is still tenacious. Its cults have long been a matter of interest to anthropologists. But five years ago, it could hardly have been guessed that a master's thesis on this recondite subject, published under the conservative imprint of the University of California Press, would become one of the best-selling books of the early '70s.

OLD YAQUI. The book was *The Teachings of Don Juan: a Yaqui Way of Knowledge* (1968). With its sequels, *A Separate Reality* (1971) and the current *Journey to Ixtlan* (1972), it has made U.S. cult figures of its author and subject—an anthropologist named Carlos Castaneda and a mysterious old Yaqui Indian from Sonora called Juan Matus. In essence, Castaneda's books are the story of how a European rationalist was initiated into the practice of Indian sorcery. They cover a span of ten years, during which, under the weird, taxing and sometimes comic tutelage of Don Juan, a young academic labored to penetrate and grasp what he calls the "separate reality" of the sorcerer's world. The learning of enlightenment is a common theme in the favorite reading of young Americans today (example: Hermann Hesse's novel *Siddhartha*). The difference is that Castaneda does not present his Don Juan cycle as fiction but as unembellished documentary fact.

The wily, leather-bodied old *brujo* and his academic straight man first found an audience in the young of the counterculture, many of whom were intrigued by Castaneda's recorded experiences with hallucinogenic (or psychotropic) plants: Jimson weed, magic mushrooms, peyote. *The Teachings* has sold more than 300,000 copies in paperback and is currently selling at a rate of 16,000 copies a week. But Castaneda's books are not drug propaganda, and now the middle-class middlebrows have taken him up. *Ixtlan* is a hardback bestseller, and its paperback sales, according to Castaneda's agent, Ned Brown, will make its author a millionaire.

To tens of thousands of readers, young and old, the first meeting of Castaneda with Juan Matus—which took place in 1960 in a dusty Arizona bus depot near the Mexican border—is a better-known literary event than the encounter of Dante and Beatrice beside the Arno. For Don Juan's teachings have reached print at precisely the moment when more Americans than ever before are disposed to consider "non-rational" approaches to reality. This new openness of mind displays itself on many levels, from ESP experiments funded indirectly by the U.S. Government to the weeping throngs of California 13-year-olds getting blissed-out by the latest child guru off a chartered jet from Bombay. The acupuncturist now shares the limelight with Marcus Welby, M.D., and his needles are seen to work— nobody knows why. However, with Castaneda's increasing fame have come increasing doubts. Don Juan has no other verifiable witness, and Juan Matus is nearly as common a name among the Yaqui Indians as John Smith farther

north. Is Castaneda real? If so, did he invent Don Juan? Is
Castaneda just putting on the straight world?

Among these possibilities, one thing is sure. There is no
doubt that Castaneda, or a man by that name, exists: he is
alive and well in Los Angeles, a loquacious, nut-brown anthropologist, surrounded by such concrete proofs of existence as a Volkswagen minibus, a Master Charge card, an
apartment in Westwood and a beach house. His celebrity is
concrete too. It now makes it difficult for him to teach and
lecture.

At present he lives "as inaccessibly as possible" in Los
Angeles, refreshing his batteries from time to time at what
he and Don Juan refer to as a "power spot" atop a mountain north of nearby Malibu: a ring of boulders overlook-
ing the Pacific. So far he has fended off the barrage of film
offers. "I don't want to see Anthony Quinn as Don Juan,"
he says with asperity.

Anyone who tries to probe into Castaneda's life finds
himself in a maze of contradictions. But to Castaneda's admirers, that scarcely matters. "Look at it this way," says
one. "Either Carlos is telling the documentary truth about
himself and Don Juan, in which case he is a great anthropologist. Or else it is an imaginative truth, and he is a
great novelist. Heads or tails, Carlos wins."

Indeed, though the man is an enigma wrapped in mystery wrapped in a tortilla, the work is beautifully lucid.
Castaneda's story unfolds with a narrative power un-
matched in other anthropological studies. Its terrain—
studded with organ-pipe cacti, from the glittering lava
massifs of the Mexican desert to the ramshackle interior of
Don Juan's shack—becomes perfectly real. In detail, it is as
thoroughly articulated a world as, say, Faulkner's Yok-
napatawpha County. In all the books, but especially in
Journey to Ixtlan, Castaneda makes the reader experience
the pressure of mysterious winds and the shiver of leaves
at twilight, the hunter's peculiar alertness to sound and
smell, the rock-bottom scrubbiness of Indian life, the raw

fragrance of tequila and the vile, fibrous taste of peyote, the dust in the car and the loft of a crow's flight. It is a superbly concrete setting, dense with animistic meaning. This is just as well, in view of the utter weirdness of the events that happen in it.

The education of a sorcerer, as Castaneda describes it, is arduous. It entailed the destruction, by Don Juan, of the young anthropologist's interpretation of the world; of what can, and cannot, be called "real." *The Teachings* describes the first steps in this process. They involved natural drugs. One was *Lophophora williamsii,* the peyote cactus, which, Don Juan promised, revealed an entity named Mescalito, a powerful teacher who "shows you the proper way of life." Another was Jimson weed, which Don Juan spoke of as an implacable female presence. The third was *humito,* "the little smoke"—a preparation of dust from *Psilocybe* mushrooms that had been dried and aged for a year, and then mixed with five other plants, including sage. This was smoked in a ritual pipe, and used for divination.

Such drugs, Don Juan insisted, gave access to the "powers" or impersonal forces at large in the world that a "man of knowledge"—his term for sorcerer—must learn to use. Prepared and administered by Don Juan, the drugs drew Castaneda into one frightful or ecstatic confrontation after another. After chewing peyote buttons Castaneda met Mescalito successively as a black dog, a column of singing light, and a cricket-like being with a green warty head. He heard awesome and uninterpretable rumbles from the dead lava hills. After smoking *humito* and talking to a bilingual coyote, he saw the "guardian" [. . .] rise before him as a hundred-foot-high gnat with spiky tufted hair and drooling jaws. After rubbing his body with an unguent made from datura, the terrified anthropologist experienced all the sensations of flying.

Through it all, Castaneda often had little idea of what was happening. He could not be sure what it meant or whether any of it had "really" happened at all. That interpretation had to be supplied by Don Juan.

Why, then, in an age full of descriptions of good and bad trips, should Castaneda's sensations be of any more interest than anyone else's? First, because they were apparently conducted within a system—albeit one he did not understand at the time—imposed with priestly and rigorous discipline by his Indian guide. Secondly, because Castaneda kept voluminous and extraordinarily vivid notes. A sample description of the effects of peyote [refers to his experience of crawling through a long enclosure with walls which seemed to be made of "solid tinfoil"]. Perhaps most important, Castaneda remained throughout a rationalist Everyman. His one resource was questions: a persistent, often fumbling effort to keep a Socratic dialogue going with Don Juan. [A prime example of this is his frustrated attempt to get the aged sorcerer to admit that a psychotropically induced sensation of flight was not objectively birdlike.]

By his account, the first phase of Castaneda's apprenticeship lasted from 1961 to 1965, when, terrified that he was losing his sense of reality—and by now possessing thousands of pages of notes—he broke away from Don Juan. In 1968, when The Teachings appeared, he went down to Mexico again to give the old man a copy. A second cycle of instruction then began. Gradually Castaneda realized that Don Juan's use of psychotropic plants was not an end in itself, and that the sorcerer's way could be traversed without drugs.

But this entailed a perfect honing of the will. A man of knowledge, Don Juan insisted, could only develop by first becoming a "warrior"—not literally a professional soldier, but a man wholly at one with his environment, agile, unencumbered by sentiment or "personal history." The warrior knows that each act may be his last. He is alone. Death is the root of his life, and in its constant presence he always performs "impeccably." This existential stoicism is a key idea in the books. The warrior's aim in becoming a "man of knowledge" and thus gaining membership as a sorcerer, is to "see." "Seeing," in Don Juan's system, means experiencing the world directly, grasping its essence, without interpreting it. Castaneda's second book, *A Separate Reality,* describes Don Juan's efforts to induce him to "see" with the aid of mushroom smoke. *Journey to Ixtlan,* though many of the desert experiences it recounts predate Castaneda's introduction to peyote, datura and mushrooms, deals with the second stage: "seeing" without drugs.

[Castaneda points to the central imperative of developing a total bodily awareness in order to discern even the smallest fleeting occurrences in the surrounding world.] Easier said than done. Part of the training involved minutely, even piously attuning the senses to the desert, its animals and birds, its sounds and shadows, the shifts in its wind, and the places in which a shaman might confront its spirit entities: spots of power, holes of refuge. When Castaneda describes his education as a hunter and plant-gatherer, learning about the virtues of herbs, the trapping of rabbits, the narrative is absorbing. Don Juan and the desert enable him, sporadically and without drugs, to "see" or, as the Yaqui puts it, "to stop the world." But such a state of interpretation-free experience eludes description—even for those who believe in Castaneda wholeheartedly.

SAGES.   Not everybody can, does or will. But in some quarters Castaneda's works are extravagantly admired as a revival of a mode of cognition that has been largely neglected in the West, buried by materialism and Pascal's despair, since the Renaissance. Says Mike Murphy, a founder of the Esalen Institute: "The essential lessons Don Juan has to teach are the timeless ones that have been taught by the great sages of India and the spiritual masters of modern times." Author Alan Watts argues that Castaneda's books offer an alternative to both the guilt-ridden Judaeo-Christian and the blindly mechanistic views of man: "Don Juan's way regards man as something central and important. By not separating ourselves from nature, we return to a position of dignity."

But such endorsements and parallels do not in any way validate the more worldly claim to importance of Cas-

taneda's books: to wit, that they are anthropology, a specific and truthful account of an aspect of Mexican Indian
culture as shown by the speech and actions of one person,
a shaman named Juan Matus. That proof hinges on the
credibility of Don Juan as a being and Carlos Castaneda as
a witness. Yet there is no corroboration—beyond Castaneda's writings—that Don Juan did what he is said to
have done, and very little that he exists at all.

Ever since *The Teachings* appeared, would-be disciples
and counterculture tourists have been combing Mexico for
the old man. One awaits the first Don Juan Prospectors'
Convention in the Brujo Bar-B-Q of the Mescalito Motel.
Young Mexicans are excited to the point where the au-
thorities may not even allow Castaneda's books to be re-
leased there in Spanish translation. Said one Mexican student who is himself pursuing Don Juan: "If the books do
appear, the search for him could easily turn into a gold-
rush stampede."

His teacher, Castaneda asserts, was born in 1891, and
suffered in the diaspora of the Yaquis all over Mexico
from the 1890s until the 1910 revolution. His parents were
murdered by soldiers. He became a nomad. This helps explain why the elements of Don Juan's sorcery are a combination of shamanistic beliefs from several cultures. Some
of them are not at all "representative" of the Yaquis. Many
Indian tribes, such as the Huichols, use peyote ritually,
both north and south of the border—some in a syncretic
blend of Christianity and shamanism. But the Yaquis are
not peyote users.

Don Juan, then, might be hard to find because he wisely
shuns his pestering admirers. Or maybe he is a composite
Indian, a collage of others. Or he could be a purely fictional shaman concocted by Castaneda.

Opinions differ widely and hotly, even among deep admirers of Castaneda's writing. "Is it possible that these
books are nonfiction?" Novelist Joyce Carol Oates asks
mildly. "They seem to me remarkable works of art on the
Hesse-like theme of a young man's initiation into 'another

way' of reality. They are beautifully constructed. The character of Don Juan is unforgettable. There is a novel-istic momentum, rising, suspenseful action, a gradual revelation of character."

GULLIVER. True, Castaneda's books do read like a highly orchestrated *Bildungsroman*. But anthropologists worry less about literary excellence than about the sha-man's elusiveness, as well as his apparent disconnection from the Yaquis. "I believe that basically the work has a very high percentage of imagination," says Jésus Ochoa, head of the department of ethnography at Mexico's Na-tional Museum of Anthropology. Snaps Dr. Francis Hsu of Northwestern University: "Castaneda is a new fad. I en-joyed the books in the same way that I enjoy *Gulliver's Travels.*" But Castaneda's senior colleagues at U.C.L.A., who gave their student a Ph.D. for *Ixtlan,* emphatically dis-agree: Castaneda, as one professor put it, is "a native ge-nius," for whom the usual red tape and bureaucratic rig-marole were waived; his truth as a witness is not in ques-tion.

At the very least, though, it is clear that "Juan Matus" is a pseudonym used to protect his teacher's privacy. The need to be inaccessible and elusive is a central theme in the books. Time and again, Don Juan urges Castaneda to emulate him and free himself not only of daily routines, which dull perception, but of the imprisoning past itself. [In *Ixtlan* the old man explains that no one, including him-self, can be sure of his identity, past or present, and that the only way we can avoid a life of boredom and routine is to "create a fog around us" in the way he has done.]

Unhappily for anyone hot for certainties about Carlos Castaneda's life, Don Juan's apprentice has taken the les-son very much to heart. After *The Teachings* became an underground bestseller, it was widely supposed that its au-thor was El Freako the Acid Academic, all buckskin fringe and pinball eye, his brain a charred labyrinth lit by mys-terious alkaloids, tripping through the desert with a crow on his hat. But *castañeda* means chestnut grove, and the man looks a bit like a chestnut: a stocky, affable Latin American, 5 ft. 5 in., 150 lbs. and apparently bursting with vitamins. The dark curly hair is clipped short, and the eyes glisten with moist alertness. In dress, Castaneda is conservative to the point of anonymity, decking himself either in dark business suits or in Lee Trevino-type sports shirts. His plumage is words, which pour from him in a ceaseless, self-mocking and mesmeric flow. "Oh, I am a bullshitter!" he cackles, spreading his stubby, calloused hands. "Oh, how I love to throw the bull around!"

FOG.   Castaneda says he does not smoke or drink hard liquor; he does not use marijuana; even coffee jangles him. He says he does not use peyote any more, and his only drug experiences took place with Don Juan. His own encounters with the acid culture have been unproductive. Invited to a 1964 East Village party that was attended by such luminaries as Timothy Leary, he merely found the talk absurd: "They were children, indulging in incoherent revelations. A sorcerer takes hallucinogens for a different reason than heads do, and after he has gotten where he wants to go, he stops taking them."

Castaneda's presentation of himself as Mr. Straight, it should be noted, could not be better designed to foil those who seek to know his own personal history. What, in fact, is his background? The "historical" Carlos Castaneda, anthropologist and apprentice shaman, begins when he met Don Juan in 1960; the books and his well-documented career at U.C.L.A. account for his life since. Before that, a fog.

In spending many hours with Castaneda over a matter of weeks, TIME Correspondent Sandra Burton found him attractive, helpful and convincing—up to a point—but very firm about warning that in talking about his pre-Don Juan life he would change names and places and dates without, however, altering the emotional truth of his life. "I have not lied or contrived," he told her. "To contrive would be to pull back and not say anything or give the assurances that everybody seeks." As the talks continued,

Castaneda offered several versions of his life, which kept changing as Burton presented him with the fact that much of his information did not check out, emotionally or otherwise.

By his own account, Castaneda was not his original name. He was born, he said, to a "well-known" but anonymous family in São Paulo, Brazil, on Christmas Day, 1935. His father, who later became a professor of literature, was then 17, and his mother 15. Because his parents were so immature, little Carlos was packed off to be raised by his maternal grandparents on a chicken farm in the back country of Brazil.

When Carlos was six, his story runs, his parents took their only child back and lavished guilty affection on him. "It was a hellish year," he says flatly, "because I was living with two children." But a year later his mother died. The doctors' diagnosis was pneumonia, but Castaneda's is accidie, a condition of numbed inertia, which he believes is the cultural disease of the West. He offered a touching memory: "She was morose, very beautiful and dissatisfied; an ornament. My despair was that I wanted to make her something else, but how could she listen to me? I was only six."

Now Carlos was left with his father, a shadowy figure whom he mentions in the books with a mixture of fondness and pity shaded with contempt. His father's weakness of will is the obverse to the "impeccability" of his adopted father, Don Juan. Castaneda describes his father's efforts to become a writer as a farce of indecision. But, he adds, "I am my father. Before I met Don Juan I would spend years sharpening my pencils, and then getting a headache every time I sat down to write. Don Juan taught me that's stupid. If you want to do something, do it impeccably, and that's all that matters."

Carlos was put in a "very proper" Buenos Aires boarding school, Nicolas Avellaneda. He says he stayed there till he was 15, acquiring the Spanish (he already spoke Italian and Portuguese) in which he would later interview Don Juan. But he became so unmanageable that an uncle, the family patriarch, had him placed with a foster family in Los Angeles. In 1951 he moved to the U.S. and enrolled at Hollywood High. Graduating about two years later, he tried a course in sculpture at Milan's Academy of Fine Arts, but "I did not have the sensitivity or the openness to be a great artist." Depressed, in crisis, he headed back to Los Angeles and started a course in social psychology at U.C.L.A., shifting later to an anthropology course. Says he: "I really threw my life out the window. I said to myself: If it's going to work, it must be new." In 1959 he formally changed his name to Castaneda.

BIOGRAPHY. Thus Castaneda's own biography. It creates an elegant consistency—the spirited young man moving from his academic background in an exhausted, provincial European culture toward revitalization by the shaman; the gesture of abandoning the past to disentangle himself from crippling memories. Unfortunately, it is largely untrue.

For between 1955 and 1959, Carlos Castaneda was enrolled, under that name, as a pre-psychology major at Los Angeles City College. His liberal arts studies included, in his first two years, two courses in creative writing and one in journalism. Vernon King, his creative-writing professor at L.A.C.C., still has a copy of *The Teachings* inscribed "To a great teacher, Vernon King, from one of his students, Carlos Castaneda."

Moreover, immigration records show that a Carlos Cesar Arana Castaneda did indeed enter the U.S., at San Francisco, when the author says he did: in 1951. This Castaneda too was 5 ft. 5 in., weighed 140 lbs. and came from Latin America. But he was Peruvian, born on Christmas Day, 1925, in the ancient Inca town of Cajamarca, which makes him 48, not 38, this year. His father was not an academic, but a goldsmith and watchmaker named César Arana Burungaray. His mother, Susana Castaneda Novoa, died not when Carlos was six, but when he was 24. Her son spent three years in the local high school in Cajamarca and then moved with his family to Lima in 1948, where he graduated from the Colegio Nacional de Nuestra Señora de Guadalupe and then studied painting and sculpture, not in Milan, but at the National Fine Arts School of Peru. One of his fellow students there, José Bracamonte, remembers his pal Carlos as a resourceful blade who lived mainly off gambling (cards, horses, dice), and harbored "like an obsession" the wish to move to the U.S. "We all liked Carlos," recalls Bracamonte. "He was witty, imaginative, cheerful—a big liar and a real friend."

SISTER.   Castaneda apparently wrote home sporadically, at least until 1969, the year after *Don Juan* came out. His cousin Lucy Chavez, who was raised with him "like a sister," still keeps his letters. They indicate that he served in the U.S. Army, and left it after suffering a slight wound or "nervous shock"—Lucy is not sure which. (The Defense Department, however, has no record of Carlos Arana Castaneda's service.)

When TIME confronted Castaneda with such details as the time and transposition of his mother's death, Castaneda was opaque. "One's feelings about one's mother," he declared, "are not dependent on biology or on time. Kinship as a system has nothing to do with feelings." Cousin Lucy recalls that when Carlos' mother did die, he was overwhelmed. He refused to attend the funeral, locked himself in his room for three days without eating. And when he came out announced he was leaving home. Yet Carlos's basic explanation of his lying generally is both perfect and totally unresponsive. "To ask me to verify my life by giving you my statistics," he says, "is like using science to validate sorcery. It robs the world of its magic and makes milestones out of us all." In short, Castaneda lays claim to an absolute control over his identity.

Well and good. But where does a writer's license, the "artistic self-representation" Castaneda lays claim to, end? How far does it permeate his story of Don Juan? As the books' sales mount, the resistance multiplies. Three parodies of Castaneda have appeared in New York magazines and papers lately, and the critics seem to be preparing to skewer Don Juan as a kind of anthropological Ossian, the legendary third century Gaelic poet whose works James Macpherson foisted upon 18th century British readers.

Castaneda fans should not panic, however. A strong case can be made that the Don Juan books are of a different order of truthfulness from Castaneda's pre-Don Juan past. Where, for example, was the motive for an elaborate scholarly put-on? *The Teachings* was submitted to a university press, an unlikely prospect for bestsellerdom. Besides, getting an anthropology degree from U.C.L.A. is not so difficult that a candidate would employ so vast a confabulation just to avoid research. A little fudging, perhaps, but not a whole system in the manner of *The Teachings*, written by an unknown student with, at the outset, no hope of commercial success.

For that was certainly Castaneda's situation in the summer of 1960: a young Peruvian student with limited ambitions. There is no reason to doubt his account of how the work began. "I wanted to enter graduate school and do a good job of being an academic, and I knew that if I could publish a little paper beforehand, I'd have it made." One of his teachers at U.C.L.A., Professor Clement Meighan, had interested him in shamanism. Castaneda decided the easiest field would be ethnobotany, the classification of psychotropic plants used by sorcerers. Then came Don Juan.

The visits to the Southwest and the Mexican desert gradually became the spine of Castaneda's life. Impressed by his work, the U.C.L.A. staff offered him encouragement. Recalls Professor Meighan: "Carlos was the type of student a teacher waits for." Sociology Professor Harold Garfinkel, one of the fathers of ethnomethodology, gave Castaneda constant stimulus and harsh criticism. After his first peyote experience (August 1961), Castaneda presented Garfinkel with a long "analysis" of his visions. "Garfinkel said, 'Don't *explain* to me. You are a nobody. Just give it to me straight and in detail, the way it happened. The richness of detail is the whole story of membership.'" The abashed student spent several years revising his thesis, living off odd jobs as taxi driver and delivery boy, and sent it in again. Garfinkel was still unimpressed. "He didn't like my efforts to explain Don Juan's behavior psychologically. 'Do you want to be the darling of Esalen?' he asked." Castaneda rewrote the thesis a third time.

Like the various versions of Castaneda's life, the books are an invitation to consider contradictory kinds of truth. At the core of his books and Don Juan's method is, of course, the assumption that reality is not an absolute. It comes to each of us culturally determined, packaged in advance. "The world has been rendered coherent by our description of it," Castaneda argues, echoing Don Juan. "From the moment of birth, this world has been described for us. What we see is just a description."

MULTIVERSE.   In short, what men take as reality, as well as their notions of the world's rational possibilities, is determined by consensus, in effect by a social contract that varies from culture to culture. Through history, the road has been hard for any person who questions its fine print—especially if, like Castaneda, he tries to persuade others to accept his vision.

Anthropology by its nature deals with different descriptions, and hence literally with separate realities, within different cultures. As Castaneda's colleague Edmund Carpenter of Adelphi College notes, "Native people have many separate realities. They believe in a multiverse, or a biverse, but not a universe as we do." Yet even this much scholarly relativism is indigestible for many people who like to reassure themselves that there is only one world and that the "validity" of a culture's interpretations can and should be measured only against this norm. Any myth, they would say, can conveniently be seen as an embryonic form of what the West accepts as linear history; a Hopi rain dance is merely an "inefficient" way of doing what cloud-seeding does well.

Castaneda's books insist otherwise. He is eloquent and convincing on how useless it is to explain or judge another culture entirely in terms of one's own particular categories. "Suppose there was a Navajo anthropologist," he says. "It would be very interesting to ask him to study us. He would ask extraordinary questions, like 'How many in your kinship group have been bewitched?' That's a terribly important question in Navajo terms. And of course, you'd say 'I don't know,' and think 'What an idiotic question.' Meanwhile the Navajo is thinking, 'My God, what a creep! What a primitive creep!'"

Turn the situation around, Castaneda argues, and there is your typical Western anthropologist in the field. Yet a "very simple" alternative exists: the crux of anthropology is acquisition of real membership. "It's a hell of a lot of work," he says, explaining the years he spent with Don Juan. "What Don Juan did with me was simply this: he was making his sorcery membership available, handing down the necessary steps." Professor Michael Harner of The New School for Social Research, a friend of Castaneda's and an authority on shamanism, explains: "Most anthropologists only give the result. Instead of synthesizing the interviews, Castaneda takes us through the process."

It is not those years of study but the nature of the revelation he offers that has run Castaneda afoul of rationalists. To join another man's consensus of reality, one's own must go, and since nobody can easily abandon his own accustomed description it must be forcibly broken up. The historical precedents, even in the West, are abundant. Ever since the ecstatic mystery religions of Greece, our culture has been continually challenged by the wish to escape its own dominant properties: the linear, the categorical, the fixed.

Whether Carlos Castaneda is, as some leading scholars think, a major figure in an evolution of anthropology or only a brilliant novelist with unique knowledge of the desert and Indian lore, his work is to be reckoned with. And it goes on. At present, he is finishing the fourth and last volume of the Don Juan series, *Tales of Power,* scheduled for publication next year.

"POWER SPOT." It may confront, more clearly than the first three books, the final purpose of Don Juan's painful teachings: a special case of the ancient desire to know, propitiate and, if possible, use the mysterious forces of the universe. In that pursuit, the splitting of the atom, the sin of Prometheus and Castaneda's search for a "power spot" near Los Angeles can all be remotely linked. A good deal of the magic Don Juan works on Castaneda in the books (making Carlos believe his car has disappeared, for instance) sounds like the kind of fakir rope trickery that gurus think frivolous. Yet all in all, the books communicate a primal sense of power running through the world, arranging our perceptions of reality like so many iron filings in a huge magnetic field.

A sorcerer's power, Castaneda insists, is "unimaginable," but the extent to which a sorcerer's apprentice can hope to use it is determined by, among other things, the degree of his commitment. The full use of power can only be acquired with the help of an "ally," a spirit entity which attaches itself to the student as a guide—of a dangerous sort. The ally challenges the apprentice when he learns to "see," as Castaneda did in the earlier books. The apprentice may duck this battle. For if he wrestles with the ally—like Jacob with the Angel—and loses, he will, in Don Juan's slightly enigmatic terms, "be snuffed out." But if he wins, his reward is "true power" [—the ultimate desocializing of sorcery, the achievement of interpretation-free wonder].

Up to now, Castaneda claims, he has chosen to duck the final battle with an ally. He admits to an inner struggle on the matter. Sometimes, he says, he feels strongly tugged away from the commitment to sorcery and back into the mundane world. He has a very real urge to be a respected writer and anthropologist, and to use his newfound power of fame in tandem with the printed word to go on communicating glimpses of other realities to hungry readers.

APEX. Moreover, like most men who have explored mystical separate realities and returned, he seems to have reentry problems. According to the books, Don Juan

taught him to abandon regular hours—for work or play—
and even in his apartment in Los Angeles he apparently
eats and sleeps as whim occurs, or slips off to the desert.
But he often works at his writing as many as 18 hours a
day. He has great skill at avoiding the public. No one can
be sure where he will be at any given time of day, or year.
"Carlos will call you from a phone booth," says Michael
Korda, his editor at Simon & Schuster, "and say he is in
Los Angeles. Then the operator will cut in for more
change, and it turns out to be Yuma." His few good
friends do not give his whereabouts away to would-be aco-
lytes, in part because his own experience is mysterious and
he can't explain it. He has a girl friend but not even his
friends know her last name. He avoids photographers like
omens of disaster. "I live in this inflow of very strange people that are waiting for a word from me. They expect
something that I can't give at all. I had a class in Irvine that
was very large, and it looked like they were just waiting for
me to crack up."

At other moments he seems decided to be a true sorcerer or bust. "Power takes care of you," he says, "and you
don't know how. Now I'm at the edge, and I have to
change my whole format. Writing to get my Ph.D. was my
accomplishment, my sorcery, and now I am at the apex of
a cycle that includes the notoriety. But this is the last thing
I will ever write about Don Juan. Now I am going to be a
sorcerer for sure. Only my death could stop that." It is a
romantic role, this anthropological gesture across a pit of
entities which, in a different age, would have been called
demons. Will Castaneda become the Dr. Faustus of Malibu
Beach, attended by Mephistopheles in a sombrero? Stay
tuned in for the next episode. In the meantime, his books
have made it hard for readers ever to use the word primitive patronizingly again.

RONALD SUKENICK
Upward and Juanward: The Possible Dream

Everything happens and everything that happens is part
of the story and everything that everyone thinks about
what happens is part of the story and "Journey to Ixtlan" is
part of Carlos Castaneda's story about Don Juan's story
and this is my story about Carlos Castaneda's story.

My story begins as I was finishing another story a few
years ago, the very last sections of my new novel, "Out." At
that time I happened to read the first published excerpt
from Castaneda's second book, "A Separate Reality," and I
was astonished to find a number of similarities in incident
and idea between "Out" and Castaneda's story. The more
so in that the things in "Out" most parallel to Castaneda's
book came out of my dreams, on which I have come to
draw heavily in my writing. How could such a thing have
happened, I wondered, unless I were a sorcerer or Castaneda a novelist—alternatives I have good reason to think
equally absurd, Joyce Carol Oates, though I have to admit
that the possibility of Don Juan being a kind of new Ossian
presented itself strongly at first.

The mystery only deepened when I read the whole of
"A Separate Reality" and found still more similarities, as in
fact I continue to find them in "Journey to Ixtlan." Shortly
after this I discovered from Anaïs Nin that Castaneda
lived and taught in Los Angeles near which I live, and she
offered to invite him to her house so we could meet. The
fact that this happened through Nin is an important part
of the story. It was Nin who helped Castaneda publish
"The Teachings of Don Juan" when he was having publisher troubles. And it is Nin more than any other writer I
can think of who has over the years insisted on the continuity of dream and reality, as does Don Juan, and whose
theories about fiction as controlled dreaming provide such
a precise counterpart to Don Juan's ideas about learning to

control one's dreams. Isn't it interesting how in stories everything comes together but to continue?

One of the first things I talked about with Castaneda when we met was the novelistic quality of his books. I told him frankly that as a novelist the first thing that occurred to me when I noticed the similarities between our books was that he too must be writing a novel. Since Joyce Carol Oates's letter to the Sunday Times Book Review raising the same possibility, I understand this must be a natural speculation for novelists and perhaps for others.

Castaneda, when I first met him two years ago, was rather different from the way he is now, and the change in him reflects the course the books have taken. That evening he struck me as a kind of Candide parrying with a schizophrenic episode, and in fact a kind of cultural schizophrenia—parallel to what one might call the controlled pathology induced by Don Juan—has been the key to his books since the first one, with its experiential reportage in the body of the book, and its attempt at an abstract objective analysis added on at the end. His rather sturdy Indian-looking face (he comes from South America where many people, I suppose, have Indian blood) seemed split into halves and his eyes seemed to go off in different directions. He looked like someone who had been holding himself together under enormous strain.

Compounding his Candide demeanor with the signs of a struggling psyche, it struck me as impossible that anthropological forgery could have been a matter of concern for him or even of attention. He was not surprised at the similarities between my novel and his reportage, not even at the fact that my main source for them was my dreams. He said that there was a common fund of such knowledge that could be tapped by different people in different ways and that one of the ways was through dreams. He seemed to have in mind something like a lost Jungian race heritage.

He also told me on that occasion stories about Don Juan

that I have since heard him tell again, and that appear in "Journey to Ixtlan" in somewhat less intimate detail, and which have the cumulatively convincing smell of experience rather than imagination.

Finally I don't really believe Castaneda could write a sustained work of pure imagination. One of his great virtues as reporter-sorcerer's apprentice, equally apparent in his work and in his person, is his stubborn literal-mindedness, so useful as a foil in bringing out Don Juan, and in giving us a careful account of what happens between them.

On the other hand, to return to our conversation, not to further mystify what is already mysterious, grounds for a few, though not most, of the similarities between our stories can be located in my own experience, in that I had been impressed with a Sioux medicine man I met in South Dakota while I was writing "Out," and had been reading about the beliefs and practices of the Plains Indians which are in some ways like those of the Mexican Indians.

However, once having said this, I have to confess that being overly concerned with the factuality of Castaneda's account seems in itself literal-minded. Castaneda is a visionary and in what sense does one ask whether a vision is "true"? A vision is beyond the category of fact, other than the fact of its having happened at all. Like a story, it is neither true nor false, only persuasive or unreal, and I think there are few people who would argue that Castaneda's accounts of his experience are not persuasive, as persuasive in fact as the most accomplished novels. Our culture likes to think of everything as true or false—this is a way it has of fending off enormous realms of experience that make us feel uneasy, and rightly so. The unknown must be explained and explained until it is explained away and we don't have to be afraid of it any more. We have to understand everything. It never seems to occur to anybody that the unknown is not merely dangerous but also a momentous source, that it is the fertile medium in which we live, but such is the hysterical strength of our commitment to statistics.

Part of the enormous impact of Castaneda's books is due to the fact that they come at a time when this commitment is beginning to crumble in many quarters, when the empirical tradition has come to appear obviously inadequate, and the fact that Don Juan's teachings have so many similarities with Zen, with "The Book of the Dead," with witchlore, with Sufism, with various Eastern disciplines, with the Western mystical tradition, with Jungian speculations, and perhaps most interestingly with Wilhelm Reich and his followers, only indicates that it is part of an important subplot in the story of the culture, and in stories, as I said, everything comes together. A major peripeteia is about to come off: what seemed true begins to lose credibility, and the incredible looks more and more likely.

Part of this cultural turnabout is the discovery that all accounts of our experience, all versions of "reality," are of the nature of fiction. There's your story and my story, there's the journalist's story and the historian's story, there's the philosopher's story and the scientist's story about what happens in the atomic microcosm and the cosmic macrocosm (scientists have a corner on the stories of creation and genesis these days). The scientist's version can be used to affect reality, you say—but so does a newspaper story or a poem or a piece of music, and so, it seems, does the power of a sorcerer. [In "Ixtlan" Don Juan asserts that as far as sorcery is concerned, our common world] is only a description.

This is the key statement in all of Don Juan's teachings, and is also crucial, I believe, for our particular cultural moment. The secret of the sorcerer's power, it follows, is to know that reality is imagined and, as if it were a work of art, to apply the full force of the imagination to it. The alternating descriptions of reality that Don Juan works with are possible only by working through, and on, the imagination. His ordinary view of the world is only a description, Don Juan tells Castaneda [. . .]. Don Juan's whole effort is to disrupt Castaneda's description of the world [. . .], to "stop the world."

Every serious artist will immediately appreciate what Don Juan is trying to teach his seemingly unimaginative pupil. All art deconditions us so that we may respond more fully to experience, "to the perceptual solicitations of a world outside the descriptions we have learned to call reality," as Castaneda puts it. Don Juan is trying to get Castaneda to accept [the underlying assumption of a sorcerer that what we call the real world is not at all universal but very much limited to the way our culture has described it to us from infancy]. The fact, as it emerges more clearly in this book than in the preceding ones, that Don Juan uses fear, trickery, deceit, hypnotism, and least important in "Ixtlan," drugs, to accomplish this is totally beside the point.

Don Juan is Prospero. The world of the sorcerer is a stage and in Castaneda's books Don Juan is the skillful stage manager. What he is trying to teach Castaneda is not the primacy of one description over another, but the possibility of different descriptions. He is teaching Castaneda the art of description. And in so doing he breaks down, for the alert reader, that false separation of art from life, of imagination from reality that in our culture tends to vitiate both. This lost connection, which is the essence of primitive cultures, is maintained in our empiricist civilization only in the arts, where it is allowed to survive as in a zoo— in the zoo of the arts—and in witchcraft, the mystical cults, the various incursions of Oriental disciplines.

Once philosophy was stories, religion was stories, wisdom books were stories, but now that fiction is held to be a form of lying, even by literary sophisticates, we are without persuasive wisdom, religion, or philosophy. Don Juan shows us that we live in fictions, and that we live best when we know how to master the art. Fiction is the master art, Tom Wolfe, and journalism is a minor branch thereof. The sorcerer, the artist, sees beyond any particular form fiction may take to the fictive power itself, and in the absence of powerful fictions in our lives, maybe it's time for all of us to become sorcerers.

Not that I mean to imply that there's no difference between a sorcerer and an artist. Of course there is. For a sorcerer his life is his art and there is no product of it but himself.

The next time I saw Castaneda, to return to our story, was many months later when he came to lecture at the university where I was teaching at the time, and I went to talk to him for a while afterward. I was strongly impressed by a change in his bearing. He was much more together, more animated and cheerful, stronger, and there was nothing of the Candide left in him. In answer to a question, he had spoken about his fellow sorcerer-apprentices as jovial, practical, down-to-earth men, and I remember thinking how appropriate the description was to Castaneda himself. To know Castaneda is to be persuaded of the validity of his books—he is much like the consequence of the discipline he describes.

On that occasion I tried to draw him out on the resemblances between what he was involved with and the processes of the imagination in art, but his conception of art seemed a rather crude one, amounting to something like an idea of decoration. But if Castaneda's works aren't novels they're still stories, Castaneda's story about Don Juan's story, and I keep thinking of them in connection with other stories that explore similar areas for our culture.

In "Journey to Ixtlan," for example, Castaneda, wandering through the Mexican mountains amid a landscape animated by spirits and powers, reminds me exactly of the early Wordsworth wandering in the English hills that are alive with immanent spirit. Or how about another Hispanic sorcerer, Cervantes, Castaneda's Sancho Panza to Don Juan's Quijote. Except that in this version of the story all the power is on the Don's side, which leads us to the thought that maybe Quijote was right all along, that maybe the culture, not to mention the novel itself, has conceded too much to the pragmatic Sancho.

Here it is Sancho Castaneda who undergoes the conversion, who finally has to admit that the windmills are giants, and that he has to struggle with them. Here it turns out that the Don is sane after all and the rest of us are mad, or if not mad at least gross dullards. These are works of art, Ms. Oates, to answer your question directly, but works of art don't have to be novels. They are works of art compared, say, with Tom Wolfe's account of Kesey in "The Electric Kool-Aid Acid Test," not because one is factual and the other is not, but simply because Castaneda's books attain a high level of imaginative power and coherence, of precision in language, of inventive selection, and Wolfe's book does not, though it may be an exemplar of the new journalism.

Must we really wait on the testimony of anthropologists about the value of these books? If the anthropological establishment were to rise up and cry fraud—and since it hasn't by now one can be certain it's not going to—wouldn't that, in a way, be even more exciting in imaginative terms.

When Joyce writes about forging the conscience of his race, I think he means "forge" in all of its senses. Gide understood that all art is counterfeit, even realistic art; this being so, why are American artists so guilty about the imagination? We should not need an old wizard, O Humanities Departments, to remind us of its scope and power. What's happened to our faculties? Why do we have to keep on saying the giants are, of course, really windmills, when the only important thing about them, as far as we're concerned, is that they're really giants? For Don Juan truth and lies are both unreal—the only thing that's real is knowledge.

Knowledge but not understanding. Don Juan speaks of [how absurb it is for Castaneda to continue his attempts to unravel an irreducibly mysterious universe]. With knowledge one is able to create a plausible description of that mystery. For that you need what Don Juan calls "personal power." Power is a feeling, according to Don Juan, "something like being lucky." In fact, for Don Juan "the world is a feeling," so one might say that the power of a sorcerer is the power of the feeling he can invest in his description so it is felt as a persuasive account of the world. As Castaneda comes to accept Don Juan's description of the world: there are spirits in waterholes, he can turn into a crow, Mescalito lives.

What I find extraordinary here is the idea of feeling as a way of acting on the world, just as the forces we know through the physical sciences act on it. Feeling is neglected not only as a response in our culture but as an efficacious force, a power, though of course we see it acting every day and it is the effective force in the imaginative arts, in the imagination itself. It is, for example, the power that George McGovern didn't have and the Kennedys did. Feeling is the secret of power and the body is its medium: [Castaneda testifies that his body is able to grasp this secret even though he cannot conceive or speak of it]. Don Juan tells Castaneda that what he learns from him he learns with his body: "Every time you have seen me your body has learned certain things, even against your desire." It is as if what Don Juan is teaching him is the wisdom of the body, the forgotten wisdom of animals that we have put out of consciousness and must now reintegrate.

Since I read that first excerpt from "A Separate Reality" I felt I had something to talk about with Castaneda, and, as I say, in stories everything comes together. First we met, then he came to lecture at the school where I was teaching last year, and finally he came to teach at that school and we had another chance to talk. One day Castaneda was good enough to come to a class I was teaching to discuss one of his books. One thing that was apparent then was his great caution in making claims about his apprenticeship to Don Juan, or "the field work" as he calls it. He seemed to feel that the very nature of his situation as participant-observer called for great caution in his account of it. When I pointed out that his situation enabled him to do something of unique value, that is, to describe the discipline of a sorcerer from both anthropological and subjective points of view, to both experience it and write about it, he replied first of all that Don Juan could produce a perfectly rational account of sorcery if he wanted to, and second, that there might come a time when he himself, Castaneda, might no longer want to write about it.

He was stubbornly indifferent to any similarities between his experience with Don Juan and Zen or any other discipline—that wasn't his concern. He was insistent—as he is in "Ixtlan"—that drugs are not at all an essential part of the apprenticeship and he spoke of a fellow apprentice he knew who had taken peyote only once and yet was far ahead of him as a sorcerer.

At that time he had already seen Don Juan for the last time in his apprenticeship, which is where "Ixtlan" leaves off. He was a powerful presence and, also, or maybe because, he really had his feet on the ground. Nevertheless I still sensed a split, not in him this time but in his effort to bridge two opposing cultures.

There was a lot I still wanted to talk about with Castaneda, but while he taught at the university he became increasingly elusive. Part of it no doubt was that there was a kind of mob scene with the students, but I think what he was really doing was emulating Don Juan in "dropping one's personal history," as it is put in "Ixtlan." This is another strategy of the sorcerer, to increase his power: [Don Juan says that once this strategy is put into effect people no longer expect enough from a sorcerer to be disappointed by what he does; he is freed in a radical way from their preconceptions of him].

What this finally amounts to is living totally in the present, concentrating one's power totally on the present rather than wasting it on the past and future. Don Juan believes one should behave as if each act were one's last on earth. This is something that Castaneda, in "Ixtlan," is reluctant to do: [He complains there that a deep confidence in the ongoing connectedness of events in the world and in his own life is basic to his mental well-being and worth defending against Don Juan's efforts to undermine it].

Nevertheless, that is perhaps the direction in which, as a

sorcerer, he is heading. He became notoriously hard to locate. He would claim to be going one place and mysteriously end up in another. You would expect to meet him here and you would find him there. I once went to meet him for a lunch appointment and was told by his colleagues and several other people that they knew for a fact he was in Mexico—when one of them met him in the elevator an hour or so later, he thought he was having a hallucination. Another time it was reported to me that he had abruptly left a line of students outside his office and disappeared, exclaiming that he had to speak to me right away—I never heard from him. More recently there was even a rumor that he was dead.

The best way to meet him was by accident. And that, in fact, is how I met him last, a few weeks ago, in a coffee shop in Los Angeles (neither of us is teaching now) after coming from a talk by—we are apparently approaching the end of the story—Anaïs Nin. However, there was no chance for conversation because it was not the place and because, as he said, looking me straight in the eye, "I'm in Mexico." Then in explanation: "I go back and forth very fast. Why don't you get in touch next time you're in Los Angeles," he added. "We should talk." So there's still another conversation I've been wanting to have with Castaneda, and this is it.

If the way of the sorcerer lies in the direction of utter detachment then I have a final question. Don Juan and Don Genaro at the end of "Ixtlan" are seen to be magnificent but terribly lonely and isolated men. They have dropped out of the human community and their only community is that of other sorcerers. This is Castaneda's most unillusioned book and the two master brujos are to this extent demystified. But even Prospero throws down his staff.

It occurs to me that there are two ways to go about things on the journey to transcendence—either bring the human baggage along or leave it behind. As in the mystic tradition Don Juan leaves it behind. He has power but he is empty. It seems to me that it would be preferable to bring it along, and that the more you can bring along the better. That's what makes the difference between a saint and a mere ascetic, I suppose. And I suppose the greatest saint would bring along not only all his own baggage but everyone else's as well, and by the passion of his involvement with the human community would become a prophet: Moses, Christ, Gandhi.

Don Juan goes the other way: personal power, personal composure, at the price of withdrawal from the community, an awesome isolation, a contained nostalgia. Given the community maybe it's the only way out, but I hope not. Is that one single sorcerer who won the struggle with his ally and so retained his humanity the only one able to maintain a continuity with those he has left so far behind? Is even he able to do it?

What do you think, Carlos?

7

REBUTTAL

Beyond *Tales of Power*, the Controversy Continues

WITH the completion of the tetralogy in the fall of 1974, Joyce Carol Oates returned to the public argument over the books' veracity which her letter two years earlier had helped to spark. Her essay *Don Juan's Last Laugh* appeared to be her own attempt to get the last laugh on those who believed Castaneda was telling the truth. Citing the inclusion of the don Juan volumes in a review of recent science fiction to offset their anthropological authentication in the Paul Riesman review, she states her position with quiet certainty: "Perhaps it takes a writer of fiction to intuit the work of a fellow artist: at any rate it seems to me beyond a doubt that this series of books is art, not mere reportorial observation." She does not take account of the fact that fellow artist Sukenick failed to intuit a fellow novelist in Castaneda, having written of himself that he doesn't "really believe Castaneda could write a sustained work of pure imagination."

However, the careful reader of Oates' essay will notice that she never uses the term "hoax" and that she does not necessarily disagree with Sukenick at all, particularly when his extended view of story and fiction as ingredients in factual objectivity are borne in mind. "If a nonfiction work is not really fiction in another guise," Oates wonders, "why are there so many competing versions of the same events? Everyone writes fiction to some extent, but most write it without having the slightest idea that they are doing so." Granting that Castaneda did experience something "non-ordinary," she never quite says whether his efforts to convey it amount to the *unconscious* artistry of a reporter or the deliberate fabrication of a novelist.

And so, strangely similar interpretations by Sukenick and Oates transpose the debate into a new key. What seemed to be a clashing chord—"fact" *against* "fiction"—can now be heard as contrapuntal harmony. Or at least appreciated in its dissonance.

There are other issues explored in the Oates article, and her reading of *Tales of Power* should be compared with Elsa First's. However, Ronald Sukenick's observation nicely captures the movement of the controversy through letters, interviews, and exposés into *Don Juan's Last Laugh:* "Isn't it interesting how in stories everything comes together but to continue?"

JOYCE CAROL OATES
Don Juan's Last Laugh

Tales of Power is the fourth and presumably the final, book of the don Juan series: the "field notes" of an anthropology student at the University of California at Los Angeles, organized in such a way as to give the attentive reader the experience—drawn out and exasperating as no doubt it would be, were it authentic—of having undergone a rigorous apprenticeship to a Yaqui Indian sorcerer. The tetralogy consists of *The Teachings of Don Juan: A Yaqui Way of Knowledge* (1968), *A Separate Reality: Further Conversations With Don Juan* (1971). *Journey to Ixlan* (1972), and now *Tales of Power,* a voluminous work that has the feel of being three shorter books, united under a single title.

Throughout, Carlos Castaneda has presented himself as a first-person narrator named Carlos. He is a graduate student in an academic discipline and, as such, represents, with an often-allegorical simplicity, the West's commitment to rationalism and the reality that rationalism gives

us—the system of perceptions and verbal descriptions of
the world that, in our culture, is a social convention. This
"Carlos" is disarmingly frank about his own limitations; he
is likable, funny, naïve, and occasionally so dense as to be
an outrageous parody of Western Academic Rationalism,
subcategory Anthropology. Part two of the first book, *The
Teachings,* is "A Structural Analysis," a deadpan scholarly
assessment of the student's experiences in the Southwest . . . either a parody that goes beyond what Vladimir
Nabokov did in *Pale Fire* (his target being literary criticism), or the legitimate thing, for which Castaneda was evidently awarded an M.A.

NOT QUITE SOCRATES

The books are constructed around question-and-answer
sequences that are not quite Socratic, for don Juan sup-
plies most of the answers, and does not draw them out of
his pupil. At their very best they afford marvelous, concise
definitions (". . . the true art of a warrior is to balance terror and wonder") and offhand remarks that never suffer
by being quoted out of context ("There are no survivors
on this earth!"). Elsewhere, notably in *The Teachings* and *A
Separate Reality,* there are chapters that involve genuine
dramatic tension and development, and the conclusion of
Tales of Power is both intellectually and emotionally moving. In every sequence Carlos, or "Carlitos" as he is sometimes called, appears to be much younger than his actual
age, very nearly childlike, and innocent; he is an ingénue
in the tradition of Gulliver, or in the tradition of those Zen
tales that involve an enigmatic exchange between student
and master. Indeed, like any student who would attain enlightenment or satori or wisdom, he must subordinate his
ego to his master's, at least temporarily. The present book
takes Carlos to the edge of the abyss itself, an excursion
into the unknown (the *nagual*), which represents the death
of his personal, historical self (his *tonal*). Don Juan, his patient teacher, and don Genaro, his lively, acrobatic bene-

factor, must say farewell to him. They cannot help him any longer; he is totally alone, free, a warrior at last. The last words of the tetralogy are ". . . and then I was alone." Since Carlos survived and returned to write *Tales of Power,* his initiation into sorcery is evidently now complete. We are left not really knowing the fate of his fellow apprentice, don Genaro's pupil Pablito.

The best-selling don Juan books have, of course, become quite controversial; their factual authenticity has been widely questioned, and widely defended. Are these dramatic books really the "field notes" of an anthropology student? Theodore Sturgeon, a science-fiction writer, included one of them in an omnibus review of new science fiction: he was very enthusiastic, and suggested they represent something new in his field. Elsewhere, in so staid and "rationalist" a journal as *The New York Times Book Review,* a presumably qualified professor of anthropology reviewed the books as if they were utterly authentic, academic anthropology in a new and exciting form. Perhaps it takes a writer of fiction to intuit the work of a fellow artist: at any rate it seems to me beyond a doubt that this series of books is art, not mere reportorial observation. Like all art, it is somewhat self-conscious; it resists and transcends conventional categories of labeling, like Norman Mailer's poetic journalism and Truman Capote's "nonfiction novel," *In Cold Blood.* The *trompe l'oeil* technique of the first two books is part of their art.

ANGLO-SAXON ATTITUDES

Journey to Ixtlan, however, strikes a different note; and the first part of *Tales of Power* (called "A Witness to Acts of Power") seems almost to have been written by another person, or by Castaneda at a time in his life when his grasp of don Juan's conversation and character is not what it is elsewhere. (Most readers, admiring don Juan, will wince at the extraordinary number of times he collapses into giggling fits, and the odd Anglo-Saxon cliches he uses: "shenani-gans," "good show," "the real McCoy," "consolidate one's gains.") The second and third sections of the book, how-ever, are almost as good as the best parts of the earlier books—indeed, the dialogues on the *tonal* and the *nagual,* set for the most part in Mexico City, more than redeem the perplexing banality and excessive verbiage of the first sec-tion. It is almost as if a Zen koan were seriously fleshed out and experienced, instead of being posed merely in the mind. One follows with interest and occasionally with im-patience the gradual awakening of an introverted, easily bored, self-pitying young man into his maturity: the classic pattern of initiation, and no less "authentic" for being in this tradition.

Don Juan urges us, through Castaneda, to experience the world "without interpretation," to stop our "internal dialogue" so that our natural, human wonder at the world might be awakened. This is called "seeing" and is not nec-essarily connected with sorcery as such; at the end of *Tales of Power* don Juan speaks lyrically of the natural love a war-rior feels for the earth, which is, of course, not separate from him but part of his very essence. And very beautiful-ly he expresses it: [He refers to the earth as a "splendorous being" which the warrior, solitary and mortal, must learn to care for in such a way as finally to be free].

Everyone Writes Fiction

Art is usually richer than nonfiction, and more valuable, for it deals with layers of experience—emotional and psy-chological as well as intellectual—that nonfiction cannot comfortably touch. Most history books are incredibly dull, yet William Faulkner and Charles Dickens and Tolstoy were also writing "history" in the way that it is actually ex-perienced, by living, breathing, existing individuals. Don Juan is certainly right in being scornful of the official West-ern "way" of knowledge, as if, in a post-Einsteinian universe, people could still lay claim to absolute facts. If a nonfiction work is not really fiction in another guise, why are there so many competing versions of the same events? Everyone writes fiction to some extent, but most write it without having the slightest idea that they are doing so.

It is impossible not to feel, having read the don Juan books, that Carlos Castaneda did experience something terrifying, oceanic, ineffable, and finally transforming, and that these books are his sincere attempt at explaining the inexplicable, to himself and to us. No one feigns mystical experience; before having had it, one simply does not believe in it, and would have absolutely no interest in writing about it, especially not at great length. Afterward, he searches for metaphors, and our great tradition of mystical writings (in the West, nearly always non- or anti-institutional) is the result.

Castaneda is also writing in a more immediate tradition. The flooding of Western "ego-consciousness" (an awkward term, but there are few others available) by Eastern, or more "primitive" wisdom, is a phenomenon of the last decade or two. Let us hope that it will not be matched by a violent reaction in the form of primitive Christianity, with its Devil loosed once again in the world. The esoteric subtleties, the truly intellectual distinctions and respect for words that don Juan does, in fact, observe, could never be a match for Christian fundamentalism should it ever erupt. Much of don Juan's teaching is mysticism of a high intellectual quality, exactly like Zen and certain forms of yoga, and only a person who had already developed the rational side of his mind quite rigorously could make of don Juan's example what Castaneda does. Nonrational or antirational people assume that the emotions are always superior to the intellect. But don Juan teaches that one must transcend the crippling limitations of both intellect and emotion in order to attain awareness. I suggest that this teaching is incomprehensible to most people. In its vulgar form it takes on a terrifying power—"the blood" in Hitler's sense of the word is imagined as a spiritual force.

Evoking Yaqui Culture

What is unique about the don Juan books is their evocation of native American Indian culture, and the role of the 70-year-old don Juan, who is unquestionably superior in terms of personality as well as knowledge to anyone in Castaneda's "civilized" world. It is almost a too-perfect realization of the prophecy Carl Jung made somewhere, that Western one-sided consciousness would require, and unconsciously will into being, compensation from its opposite. Our archetypal Old Wise Man is, significantly, not Anglo-Saxon, nor even European. He can only be from the East, or from the Third World, or a native of our continent, long-repressed and cruelly treated, like American Indians or Canadian Eskimos. The mysterious "power" that once belonged to the West, in psychological terms, will never be experienced again in our lifetimes. Dare one predict that this archetypal drama will rejuvenate our culture, if the process of transformation is not too accelerated, and is guided by a general faith in ordinary consciousness?

There is an odor of sheer, brutal nature about the sorcerer's power, before we come to know it through the person of don Juan. In the first two books, death is everywhere, a physical possibility that must be respected almost as a deity is respected; coyotes and crows may really be *diableros* (a term used by Sonoran Indians to mean an evil person who practices black sorcery and is capable of changing himself into other life-forms). To see our ordinary world as merely one version of reality, which others, more powerful, can easily contest and invade, is exhilarating when one reads about it; but to contemplate the teachings of don Juan seriously and soberly is by no means a happy experience, as Carlos keeps insisting in the books (without convincing most enthusiastic readers, one suspects). The warrior's closeness to death is stressed repeatedly. He purchases enlightenment at great cost, for he can no longer believe in the comfortable, naive assumptions of his culture; he cannot even believe in his own "identity," because he experiences himself as a temporary unit, a cluster of experiences and perceptions. (As the Buddha taught: Man is a composite being.) Is there a deity? Of course—but this deity is sheer energy, and manifests itself as readily in suffering as in joy, in cruelty as well as in kindness. Don Juan's teachings are compatible with the revelations of most mystics, in that they refuse to differentiate between self and other, good and evil, "God" and the "Devil." To use one of his own terms, don Juan emerges as an "impeccable" man of wisdom.

Who Is Don Juan?

Yet *Tales of Power* could be a far more moving, convincing book. The first third is very weak: so much repetition of obvious truths, so much reliance upon the stereotyped stupidity of the pupil and the proverbial wisdom of the teacher . . . on every page a scattering of don Juan's unaccountable giggling fits, an insistence that Carlos is really experiencing strong emotions. He is "scared," "panicked," he suffers "convulsions of fright," [and is given to other such hyperbole]. Too much, too much. The magic seems to have gone out of Castaneda's writing in this section. And, in the last section, don Juan gives a kind of lecture to his amazed student, a five-hour recapitulation of years of teaching that is "academic" in our sense of the word, extremely helpful to the reader who wants everything summarized, as in textbooks, but damaging to one's sense of verisimilitude. One cannot help but keep asking: *Who is don Juan? Why does he speak in so many different voices and idioms?* I suggest that Castaneda is concerned primarily with teaching his readers a few general, and very important, truths, and that he will use any means possible to explain the inexplicable—in which case he ultimately honors the urgency of his vision over its esthetic forms, in the tradition of nearly all mystics.

Part Three

ANALYSIS AND APPLICATION

8

CASTANEDA AS EXPERIMENTAL FICTIONEER

AMONG those who have produced more sustained analyses of Castaneda's work from distinctive vantage points, or applied his work to issues of current intellectual concern, Jerome Klinkowitz represents a literary-critical perspective and a special interest in the history of contemporary American fiction. As co-editor of *Innovative Fiction* and *The Vonnegut Statement*, Klinkowitz is amply qualified to draw out the connections between the don Juan writings and the techniques of experimental novelists and short story writers. It happens that the particular writer he is concerned with in *The Persuasive Account* is Ronald Sukenick, whom we have already encountered as a commentator on Castaneda but whose own work stands in the forefront of fictional experimentation today.

It is a curious thing, which Klinkowitz makes the focus of his essay, that for a highly sophisticated urban novelist the traditional—not to say "primitive"—worldview of the American Indian can become a paradigm of appropriate forms, a source of renewal for fictional rationales beyond civilized decadence. Such is the case with Sukenick's development, as if the problems of imagination and reality posed for him in his work on Wallace Stevens could only be dealt with in supremely self-conscious fictions which led him to don Juan's desert. In terms of Castaneda's own role and meaning this does not necessarily entail our deciding he is a conscious or intentional novelist. However, it does show that he has shared with us experiences and insights which turn out to be surprisingly relevant to the attempts of the Western fictional tradition to survive the besetting dilemmas of modernity.

It is worth noting also that Jerome Rothenberg and George Quasha have seen fit to include Castaneda in their revisionist anthology of American *poetry, America a Prophecy,* but neither does this imply Castaneda is a poet in any deliberate sense. As we began to see in following the controversy over Castaneda's reportorial veracity, these issues run deeper than our convenient distinctions, forcing us to face the same realities our most innovative novelists and poets are confronting.

JEROME KLINKOWITZ
The Persuasive Account: Working It Out with
Ronald Sukenick and Carlos Castaneda

Halfway from the Lower East Side of New York to Laguna Beach, California, the protagonist of Ronald Sukenick's *Out* meets a Sioux medicine man, Empty Fox. "I want to write a book like a cloud that changes as it goes," he tells the Indian when asked his ambition. "I want to erase all the books," Empty Fox replies: "My ambition is to unlearn everything: I can't read or write that's a start. I want to unlearn and unlearn till I get to the place where the ocean of the unknown begins where my fathers live. Then I want to go back and bring my people to live beside that ocean where they can be whole again as they were before the Wasichus came." *Wasichus*—"fat takers"—are what the Sioux call white men, despoilers of the continent and disgusting examples of the wrong way to live. The Indian people see the land as a community to which they belong rather than as a commodity to exploit, and are ideals of ecological balance who will neither exhaust the earth nor overload themselves to the point of death. But Empty Fox does more than show a white man how to live; he

points a way of life for something else that's dying—
fiction—and provides Sukenick with a model for sustaining his novel, which is what the book is all about.

Since 1968, when John Barth declared that literature
was "exhausted" and Leslie Fiedler, Susan Sontag, Norman Mailer, and other critics cheered along that the novel
at least was dead, Ronald Sukenick has been proving that
there is a great deal of life to be rediscovered in the form.
His first novel, *Up*, followed Barth with a generous indul-
gence in aesthetic allegory, but instead of painting itself
into a corner or disappearing up its own fundament, *Up*
pointed a way out. Is the real world too ponderous and
depressingly dull to capture in interesting fiction? Is it indeed a problem for art? "'Sure,'" agrees Sukenick's
aesthetic-allegorist character, who's involved with living
the novel, writing it, and teaching literature at the same
time. "'That's what Wordsworth is talking about. He tells
how as a kid he had to grab hold of a wall to make sure the
world was really there, but when he grew up the dead
weight of reality almost crushed the sense of his own existence. It's when the world seems oppressive, dead, or to
put it another way, unreal, that I get the feeling I'm walking around like a zombie.'" To be of help, art must not describe but create reality, seeking "'a vital connection with
the world that, to stay alive, must be constantly reinvented
to correspond with our own truest feelings.'" "When,
through the imagination, the ego manages to reconcile reality with its own needs," the actual Ronald Sukenick once
wrote in a book about Wallace Stevens, "the formerly
insipid landscape is infused with the ego's emotion, and
reality, since it now seems intensely relevant to the ego,
suddenly seems more real." Insipid reality has been the
downfall of many novelists of Barth's generation, who
abandoned it entirely for self-indulgent aestheticism. But
Sukenick applies to the novel what he sensed about art in
general, and revitalizes fiction by having it do what it
should: to make reality seem less unreal.

Out moves from the clutter and hassle of the East to the

pure space of an empty California beach, leaving behind much of Sukenick's Brooklyn-Greenwich Village-Lower East Side material, and also his forms which served as parodies of themselves and were—for the '60s—the style of the time. "It's easier and sociabler to talk technique than it is to make art," Barth admitted in his "Literature of Exhaustion" essay, but as a form—*Lost in the Funhouse* in fiction, Warhol's soup cans in painting—the result was an apparent dead end. "In the late 60's innovation in general was good, now innovation in general is bad," Sukenick complained recently in *The Village Voice.* "The Pop movement, though it had its moments, was a disaster for the arts. It introduced a confusion of criteria that has yet to be straightened out. Meantime Poppers and Nonpoppers alike pay for their exploitation of the artmart in the name of avant-garde." Or as Gilbert Sorrentino explains in his novel *Imaginative Qualities of Actual Things,* in a passage Sukenick is fond of quoting:

> Art is the undoing of many a hick. I think of those twangy painters slaughtered in the floods of coin the pop art machine produced. Only people like the Pope can engage pop art and survive. I remember having lunch with one of these painters once, in McSorley's. Something about painting the pickle on my plate, my ale, etc. My face was stiff with my polite smile. I can hear that flat Nebraska speech right now. Or take the New York School. Joy of decadence. Wait till the folks in Terre Haute see this! How to put it? That New York becomes a chocolate bunny, and that they print their work, in teams. You see them together, nice young men and women, looking at that bunny. They are amusing, glib articulators of arrested development. Their noses are pointed toward the Iowa Writers' Workshop, or some other Workshop, some Seminar on Contemporary Poetry. Safe in hamburger heaven. Back home again in Indiana.

A few years before, Sukenick had reported the similar destruction of a geographical avant-garde, the Lower East

Side of New York, which as "The East Village" did as
much harm as Pop and despoiled a necessary haven, making the survival of serious American art all the less likely.
His essay "Live & Let Alone on the Lower East Side" ran in
The Village Voice the week of Robert Kennedy's assassina-
tion, and was typographically framed by memoria to the
slain candidate.

Yet Sukenick is no writer of obituaries for a dead tradition, nor is he a New York snob resenting the Midwestern
tourists invading (and taking over) his home. His art
moves West, toward a California emptiness, which he sees
as anything but derogatory since it is first established in
Empty Fox's South Dakota—a tremendous, surging sensation of freedom, of liberation from space, even from
sound, so that a resolution seems for once possible.
There's always the danger of an ersatz California clutter,
which can happen even in the Black Hills. "The Wasichus
make Disneyland of all this so they can sell it," accuses
Empty Fox; "they get the Indians to pretend they're Indians they make believe these beautiful mountains are beautiful they pretend magic is magic they make believe the
truth is the truth otherwise they can't believe anything.
There is a place with a billboard of a mountain in front of
the mountain you Wasichus can't see anything without
pretending to see anyway you don't believe it." For Sukenick imagination is an essential faculty of the perception,
but through "Disneyland" it becomes a cheap version of
the willing suspension of disbelief. "Is Disneyland really
necessary?" he asks in his contribution to Raymond Feder-
man's book, *Surfiction*. "It's as if we have to make believe
before we can work up the confidence to believe, as if belief in good conscience were the privilege of primitives or
maybe Europeans."

What the "primitives" have is a better hold on reality,
not just because they are "in closer touch" but because of
their ability to sense the totality of what's going on in the
world. "We Sioux are not a simple people," writes the old
medicine man Lame Deer in his book *Lame Deer, Seeker of
Visions*. "We are very complicated. We are forever looking

at things from different angles." Empty Fox is a man in
Lame Deer's tradition, and so is Juan Matus, through
whom Carlos Castaneda learned ways of approaching the
world Sukenick was at the same time finding appropriate
for fiction. "For a sorcerer, reality, or the world we all
know, is only a description," and in *Journey to Ixtlan* Castaneda tells of Don Juan's [attempts at getting him to assimilate this sorcerer's sense of the learned and linguisti-
cally relative nature of our worlds]. Castaneda's "mistakes"
sound strikingly similar to the failures of modern fiction-
ists to keep up with their world, too. "'Your problem,'"
says Don Juan in *A Separate Reality,* "'is that you confuse
the world with what people do. . . .'" [He goes on to call
human acts "shields" to give us the illusion of security; understood as such they are proper to us, but] "'We let them
dominate and topple our lives'"—and also our fiction.

Ronald Sukenick would revalidate our imaginations so
that we can look at our environment in a real way. For Don
Juan, it's a question of two distinct manners of perceiving.
[Beyond mere "looking," with its habituated perspective
on the world, there is a true "seeing."] For fiction, it is the
ability to transcend a mere describing of life (always a danger in this most mimetic of forms) to a revelation of the
truth of experience, which may be at odds with the popular consensus. To stop the world—to call a halt to having
one's personal, provisional view of things as absolute—
may be a key to the cultural turnabout so apparent around
us, reflected in Sukenick's new style of fiction, Castaneda's
great popularity, and the appeal environmentalist Aldo
Leopold has for such a broad intellectual audience as bi-
ologist Paul Shepard and philosopher of ethics John J.
McMahon, commenting in *The New Republic*: "Leopold
has learned that to absolutize our narrow wavelength of
perception is sheer arrogance," and a sure way to extinc-
tion.

To arrive at "seeing," Castaneda learned in *Ixtlan,* one
must stop the world. [This entailed being made aware, "by
a set of circumstances alien to that flow," of how reality is

constituted for us by a continual flow of conventional interpretations.] Don Juan's task, as exercised in *A Separate Reality*, "was to disarrange a particular certainty which I shared with everyone else, the certainty that our 'common-sense' views of the world are final." The imagination, Sukenick has said, makes reality seem more real—and Don Juan's methods are a paradigm for liberating oneself from the obstructed, unimaginative view. [Smoking the mushroom mixture, for instance, is said to free the sorcerer's body for vision-flights into nonordinary reality and back again.] The fullest possibilities of vision—not just the documentary records of what historically occurred—are what Sukenick wants for his fiction, and Don Juan is the master who can show how [many realities there are in front of our eyes.] As Walter Goldschmidt wrote in the foreword to the first Castaneda volume, *The Teachings of Don Juan: A Yaqui Way of Knowledge,* [anthropology can allow us to compare our culturally limited perspective with alien ones, thereby learning its relativity and glimpsing, perhaps, an absolute reality *in between* ours and the others].

Although such wonderful revelations of the world are the goal of art, and certainly proper business for the novel, the vitality of Sukenick's theories have made them controversial. Tom Wolfe, who asked "Why aren't they writing the Great American Novel anymore?" and answered "because the new journalists were doing it better," granted Sukenick "a curious ground in between, part fiction and part nonfiction," but other critics—notably Pearl K. Bell in *Dissent*—have cast him among "such celebrants of unreason, chaos, and inexorable decay as Kurt Vonnegut, Jr., John Barth, Rudolph Wurlitzer, Donald Barthelme, and a horde of mini-Jeremiahs crying havoc in the Western world." The real issue, as Nathan Scott lets slip in his latest essay on contemporary fiction, is that the "inward liberation" of the imagination "offers us an effective release from the bullying of all the vexations of history"—and, incidentally, that this aesthetic has been so demonstrably adopted "by the hordes of those young long-haired, jean-clad, pot-smoking bohemians who have entered the world of psychedelia." But Sukenick has critically covered himself since 1967, in his *Wallace Stevens: Musing the Obscure.* "The mind orders reality not by imposing ideas on it but by discovering significant relations within it," and even freaky old Don Juan agrees that [it is our method of perception, rather than exterior reality, which is altered]. If the teachings of Don Juan offer one cumulative lesson it is that the "other realities" bear just as much objective weight as the provisional realities we live day to day, and that the only responsible way out is "in." "Our particular moment and place is located in our heads and our bodies," Sukenick wrote for the *Partisan Review* symposium on The New Cultural Conservativism, "and at the risk of solipsism we must start there and push outward." Or as he told interviewer Joe David Bellamy in the *Chicago Review,* "I don't want to present people with illusions, and I don't want to let them off cheaply by releasing their fantasies in an easy way. If the stuff has done that, okay. It's probably inevitable in any case, but it's not really the kind of thing I'm trying to do. . . . Because what that does is allow people to escape, obviously, from reality, and I want to bang them with it." Or, as he's said in casual conversation, part of the Disneyland rap, "the less we use our imagination the more somebody else is going to use it for us—by manipulating us."

Fiction plays its tricks, but in his own *Village Voice* essay on Castaneda's work Sukenick insists that "All art deconditions us so that we may respond more fully to experience." The wealth of that response has been his aim since *Up,* through the efforts to capture the truth of experience in *The Death of the Novel and Other Stories,* and most recently *Out.* While others would let fiction die, Sukenick argues that its great advantage "over history, journalism, or any other supposedly 'factual' kind of writing is that it is an expressive medium. It transmits feeling, energy, excitement. Television can give us the news, fiction can best express our response to the news. . . . No other medium, in other words, can so well keep track of the reality of our experience." Technically, his novel *Out* proves that a novel can be a concrete as well as an imaginative structure, and offers art for the eye and the page-turning hand as well as for the mind. But ultimately Sukenick's genius rests with his discovery that the reality we know is only a description, and that "The power of a sorcerer is the power of the feeling he can invest in his description so it is felt as a persuasive account of the world." This same persuasiveness is the measure of good fiction, which Ronald Sukenick brings to life, proving what an unexhausted novelist can do.

9

SORCERY AS OPPOSITION TO TECHNOCRACY AND SCIENTISM

IN WORKING their way out of what has come to seem the *cul de sac* of modern technocratic and scientistic consciousness, many thinkers have begun to research neglected or undervalued corridors of Western intellectual history. Although the romantic poets of the nineteenth century have been enshrined as important figures in our literary tradition, few twentieth century intellectual opinion-makers have found any large and current social relevance in their notions of symbolism and nature. The rationalistic, utilitarian attitudes to which romanticism was an eloquent opposing force have largely carried the day until now. But the reassessments brought about by our current cultural dissatisfaction have begun to challenge this hegemony: Romanticism may indeed have "come of age," as the title of one of Owen Barfield's books puts it.

One of romanticism's most forceful champions these days is Theodore Roszak, whose *The Making of a Counter Culture* in 1969 outlined the motivations and ideological components of youthful protest against technocracy and its "myth of objective consciousness." In *Where the Wasteland Ends* he takes the ideas of such romantic spokesmen as Blake, Wordsworth, and Goethe as tools for thinking through the longer-range religious and political implications of the forces surfacing in movements like the counterculture of the 1960's.

For Roszak, in the chapter called "Uncaging Skylarks: The Meaning of Transcendent Symbols" from the latter book, flight and gravity are dramatic examples of inter-related experiences which the orientation underlying modern scientism and technocracy misunderstands. Such experiences, he argues, are grasped by romantic symbol-ism not just more "poetically" but—as our compulsory eco-logical perspective now reveals—more *accurately* as well. In discussing this case in point, Roszak applies the oft-quoted conversation from *The Teachings of Don Juan* about wheth-er Carlos "really" flew under the influence of "devil's weed" or only underwent a "subjective illusion" of flight. As Carlos learned to his chagrin, this is another of the is-sues which will no longer submit to the prevailing Carte-sian and Newtonian distinctions. Roszak's chapter sets forth *how* those distinctions came to prevail over the ro-mantic orientation (one in keeping with Don Juan's sor-cery) and indirectly produced the attitude Carlos had to *un*learn in his apprenticeship.

Along the way Roszak refers back from his specific illus-trations to the larger issue of what he calls "the loss of root meanings," the sundering of connection between primal experience and its "universally compelling" symbolic ex-pressions. Significantly, he supports the claim that the symbolism in root meanings is universal by demonstrating that this symbolism treats natural objects as "found po-ems": "The skylark is a symbol of the vision-flight, but in its own right as an object perceived, it is also an occasion for the experience which generates the symbol." The fact that this is remarkably close to the way bodily and environ-mental details function in don Juan's teachings as "physio-logical metaphors" or "natural parables" is probably no accident, as becomes clear when Roszak concludes the ex-cerpted selection with a discussion of "seeing and 'see-ing.'" Here he compares the visionary imagination of a romantic poet like Wordsworth (mentioned also in the Ed-mund Leach and Ronald Sukenick selections) with the nonordinary perception don Juan and Carlos employ to recognize concretely that "it is in the nature of a thing 'in itself' to be a symbolic presence."

While the members of the Technology and Culture Seminar who assembled at MIT on October 26, 1971, were not directly concerned with Roszak's romantic poets, they were intensely caught up with similar problems of politics and the history of science. More important for our purposes, the Seminar participants came together to hear and discuss an address by Carl Oglesby, former president of Students for a Democratic Society, a probing writer on issues of political change in literature and society, and at that time an MIT lecturer in humanities. Portions of the talk and responses (published here for the first time) reveal that for Oglesby, as for Roszak, "a Juanist way of knowledge" can be an antidote to the cultural poisons infecting post-industrial society: technocratic alienation, scientistic reductionism, the general separation of object from subject and fact from value.

After an introduction by Merton J. Kahne, psychiatrist in chief at MIT, which stresses the process of socialization as a determinant of the real—a point made by Sam Keen— and science's role in that process as it occurs in the modern West, we pick up Oglesby's lecture at the point of his relating C. P. Snow's "two cultures" thesis to the political climate of the 1950's and 1960's. Whereas in the Cold War period the humanities were felt to need the objectivity of the sciences, by the middle of the sixties the humanities began to exert a critical moral pressure *on* the sciences, revealing that the objectivity of the latter had in fact served the all-too-subjective purposes of the Cold War. From his review of these factors Oglesby asks, "Is science the potentially universal method of knowing all knowable reality, inner and outer alike, or is it culturally and structurally bound the way all other human activity is?"

This question is obviously one to which Castaneda's writing speaks, and in a section on "a Juanist science" Oglesby explores the implications of a "rigorous savage" method of inquiry which leads to the heretical definition of subjectivity as "the creator of its own nature, its own experience." One of the many features he lists for this Juanist science is that it would be "determined in the social or cultural or political world where people make decisions in permanent conflict and doubt."

Responding at length to this politically attuned portrait of a science modeled upon don Juan's teachings, Harvard historian of science Everett Mendelsohn stresses the "personalized" nature of Juanist knowledge and wonders whether we really understand the relation between this personal knowledge and scientific knowledge. He asserts that early modern science, like Oglesby's Juanist science, had to win its place in the social structure against entrenched ways of knowing and was experienced as a personally liberating perspective. But now, Mendelsohn continues, our civilization expects orthodox science to explain subjective experience. This expectation stretches Western science "far beyond the bounds which it was socially constructed to deal with." In a sense Mendelsohn is defending standard science by clarifying its social limitations. At the same time he is challenging the ability of Juanist knowledge either to provide a single, all embracing meta-science or to generate an ethical system which transcends the isolated psyche of the individual sorcerer.

MIT political scientist Christopher Schaefer then notes briefly that "the relationship between the observer and the phenomena must be clarified in some way" and that the phenomenological orientation of Castaneda's work can aid in that clarification. Adopting such an orientation would allow social sciences like political science to develop methods which are independent of the natural sciences, more suited to the study of man as a "symbol-maker and meaning-giver."

Oglesby's reply to Mendelsohn and Schaefer follows, touching upon the experiential-experimental overlap in Juanist technique, the freely chosen or non-necessary character of the Juanist ethic of "heart," and the possibilities for understanding the social formation of Juanist knowledge in one culture and its adoption by another as entailing "a massive social re-conception of reality."

The discussion between Carl Oglesby and his fellow seminar members is often difficult to follow, but in its complexity it complements Theodore Roszak's use of don Juan's sorcery. Both Roszak and the technology and culture seminar welcome the don Juan writings as subversive of a Western scientific knowledge which, in technocracy and scientism, encourages a Faustian overextension we can no longer afford.

* * *

THEODORE ROSZAK
Uncaging Skylarks: The Meaning of
Transcendent Symbols

THE VISION-FLIGHT: EXPERIENCE AND SYMBOL

The Divine Being Himself cannot be expressed. All that can be expressed are His symbols.

—Gershom Scholem

There is a remarkable passage in Carlos Castaneda's *Teachings of Don Juan.* At one point in the narrative, Castaneda, a young anthropologist acting as apprentice to the Yaqui sorcerer Don Juan, has fed on "devil's weed" (the *Datura* plant) and has experienced the vivid sensation of flight while in a state of trance.

[He asks afterward whether he had "really" flown—"like a bird"—and whether his friends, if present, would have observed him in flight. Don Juan, however, will neither confirm *nor* deny with his answers the objectivity of Castaneda's experience: someone on datura "flies as such," he replies. And the response to the second question is no less enigmatic]: If the friends knew the power of the devil's weed, they would have seen the apprentice fly. But, asks Castaneda, suppose he tied himself to a rock with a heavy chain; would he then still fly? "Don Juan looked at me incredulously. 'If you tie yourself to a rock,' he said, 'I'm afraid you will have to fly holding the rock with its heavy chain.'" And there the discussion ends.

Modern philosophy gives us a convenient rule of thumb for dealing with such a tangle of cross purposes. We revert to Descartes and simply slice the discussion down the middle. We say there is an objective realm and a subjective realm. (Freud's Reality Principle again.) The apprentice is talking about objective behavior. The sorcerer is talking about subjective feeling. The apprentice is talking about *real* flying. The sorcerer is talking about the *illusion* of flying. Reality is objective and happens "outside." Illusion is subjective and happens "inside." In this case, the illusion is a mental reflection (a hallucination) of real flying. So it is unreal.

How utterly sensible. But why does the old sorcerer not see it that way? Why does he not agree that his flying is an illusion of flight and therefore unreal? It is not because he cannot distinguish between the way a bird flies and the way a person flies. That is as obvious to him as it is to us. He is neither feebleminded nor mad. What he sticks at is the ontological priority of the distinction: which is more real than which? "Did I *really* fly?" It is the prejudicial adverb that makes the trouble. The dispute between the two men leads us back to Plato's cave, where all significant philosophical controversy must return sooner or later. Which reality is the substance and which the shadow? The old sorcerer is at the same disadvantage as the sun-stunned philosopher who must explain daylight to those who have lived all their life in darkness.

For Don Juan, the real experience of flying belongs to an old and formidable tradition. He brings us back to the shamanic vision-flight, one of those supreme symbols of human culture which has been elaborated into thousands of religious and artistic expressions, embedded in the foundations of language, driven like a taproot into the bottommost stratum of our consciousness. Because we are used to dealing with *mere* symbols (ciphers), we ask auto-

matically: what is the vision-flight a symbol of? But there is
no answer, except to say that this symbol belongs uniquely
to an ubiquitous experience of enraptured awe which is to
be *lived*—whether suffered or enjoyed—but not in any
sense "explained." The experience is transcendent. The
symbol is as close as we can come to expressing its reality.
All discussion of whether the symbol means to say "I flew,"
"I felt *as if* I was flying," "I did something that was a kind
of flying," "Metaphorically speaking, I flew," etc., is totally
beside the point. The symbol *means* the experience. The
experience is non-verbal bedrock; the symbol lies next
against it as its universally compelling expression. No
words can delve below the bedrock; no words can impose
themselves between the bedrock and the symbol without
distorting meaning. We can only work away from experience and symbol by way of abstraction or metaphorical extension.

Experience and symbol taken together are what we
might call a *root meaning:* an irreducible sense of significance, a foundation the mind rests and builds upon. For
thought must begin somewhere, with some rudimentary
material. These are the root meanings. The task of human
culture is the elaboration of root meanings in the form of
ritual or art, philosophy or myth, science or technology—
and especially in the form of language generally, by way of
progressively more attenuated metaphors drawn from the
original symbol. Root meanings cannot be explained or
analyzed; rather they are what we use among ourselves to
explain—to give meaning to—lesser levels of experience.
They are the diamond that cuts all else.

In the case of flight, all language that associates height,
levity, loftiness, climbing, or elevation with the qualities of
superiority, dignity, privileged status, worthiness, etc., is
an extrapolation from the original symbol of the shamanic
vision-flight. Hence the "highness" of kings, the majesty of
mountains, the prestige of being "upper" class. Converse-
ly, lowliness comes to betoken inferiority, sinfulness, igno-
bleness, etc. We are drawn "upwards" to God, and "fall,"

"slide," or "plummet" into hell; we "climb" to social heights and are dragged "down" into the gutter. The same symbolism can be extended into other forms of expression: music, architecture, dance also have their soaring and falling gestures. The dancer's *jeté,* the singer's high note, the Gothic vault fly with the mind like the poet's lark. The symbolism is universal and hardly arbitrary; the same root meaning lies behind all these elaborations, mined out of a primordial experience.

A great symbol—like that of the vision-flight—is a prodigious human invention. It is the substance from which human understanding is fashioned. As imagination stretches form and language away from root meanings toward ever more distant associations, the power of thought grows potentially richer and more subtle. I say "potentially," because there is always the risk that root meanings will be lost amid their multitudinous and increasingly remote reflections. That is Castaneda's problem in the encounter with Don Juan. Castaneda lives amid abundant reflections of the vision-flight, but, like most of us in the modern west, he has grown hopelessly away from the root meaning. So when Don Juan takes him back to the source, he fails to recognize it for what it is, and asks, "Did I *really* fly?" When we become so estranged from the meaning of symbols, language loses touch with experience and goes into business on its own, becoming a collection of perplexing abstractions. And then all sorts of absurdities and pseudo-problems ensue. For example, the root meaning of the vision-flight associates divinity and the skies. But when the experience that underlies the root meaning is lost, we are left with an absurdly literal proposition which seems to locate God in physical space above the clouds. Then, when the Russian cosmonauts fail to find the old gentleman there, village atheism holds itself vindicated.

Few pagan or primitive peoples, grasping intuitively as they do the true ontological status of myth and symbol, would ever be so foolish. Their reality is polyphonic: it has overtones and counterpoints and resonances—which is exactly what we, with our two-value, objective-subjective sensibility, are inclined to call "superstition." Only Christians, especially Protestant Christians, have ever been so far gone with the disease of literalism as to produce a monstrosity like Biblical fundamentalism. The irony is, of course, that the fundamentalist and the scientific skeptic share the same single visioned consciousness. They stand or fall together by the same Reality Principle.

THE LAW OF GRAVITY

God keep me . . . from supposing Up and Down to be the same thing as all experimentalists must suppose.

—WILLIAM BLAKE

Let us consider another, rather more complex transformation of vision-flight symbolism—in this case one that has played a critically important part in shaping basic scientific thought. The argument is a circuitous one, but by the time we reach the end of it, we shall see how single vision borrows from the traditional symbolism of human culture, but then loses the root meanings of things.

From the shamanic vision-flight we inherit the religious and mythic connotations that cling so stubbornly to all thinking about rising and falling, up and down, light and heavy. The vision-flight asserts levity as the prime orientation of the soul. The notion of gravity—"weighed-downness"—comes into existence as a companion idea, almost by negative definition. Gravity is the shadow side of levity; in the shaman's experience, it becomes symbolic of what one feels when the soul drifts from the sense of buoyancy that keeps it close to the sacred. Gravity in any other sense is not a fundamental preoccupation at this cultural stage. That is why—and the fact is remarkable—gravity traditionally played no important part in human thought prior to late Greek speculation. There is simply no body of folklore or mythology dealing with the creation of a force or substance we would recognize as physical gravitation. And yet gravity is such a (seemingly) basic, simple, inescapable notion. Why did no one "discover" it until so late in history? Because—so the conventional wisdom reasons—people did not always enjoy a *realistic* relationship to nature. Before the modern western era, they had not paid rational attention to the world around them, but had distracted themselves with speculations about angels and devils, animistic figments and mere secondary qualities.

And in some respects the conventional wisdom is not far wrong. The intellectual slot we reserve for the physics of gravitation is taken up in non-scientific cultures by the spiritual experience of "fallenness," the loss of visionary levity. The concept is moralized and mythologized. From such a viewpoint, to take on weight is not primarily a physical fact; it is first of all a symbol of having descended from a normal and proper condition of grace. Thus, in cabbalistic philosophy, the quintessential body of Adam Kadmon, the primal human being, is weightless, just as the crystalline spheres of Ptolemaic astronomy—being in a state of original and eternal perfection—are without weight. Gravity becomes an important and isolated concept only after weightiness (fallenness) begins to seem like an irresistible fact of life needing to be accounted for. This happens as the sense of levity ceases to be a readily accessible, normal experience and becomes more and more exotically mystical—or perhaps evaporates from the mind altogether. Only then does gravity remain as a thought-provoking "something" that demands explanation.

It was not until the time of the later Greek philosophers that the transcendent symbolism of lightness and weight gave way to a more strictly scientific discussion of two physical forces of nature called "gravity" and "levity." In Greek and medieval European science these forces were still faintly embued with the sort of animism that Galileo and Newton would later eliminate. There was still the sense that ascension moved an element or object closer to divine perfection, and that things strove or willed to rise and fall depending on their degree of worthiness. This way of thought was, however, well on its way to becoming a mere convention, no longer deeply felt as part of a comprehensive religious worldview. The ideas had become *explanations,* not experiences. It is significant that as this happened, gravity was upgraded to the point of becoming coequal to levity in Greek and medieval natural philosophy. The sense of a levitational norm had weakened as the symbolic significance of the concepts faded.

But it was not until the age of Newton that gravity finally exiled levity entirely from the scientific mind and became a domineering concern of natural philosophy on which much thought had to be expended. Indeed, the universal law of gravity holds a special place as the master concept that inaugurated the scientific revolution—as if the first thing modern science had to do was to destroy the symbol of the vision-flight. Bacon very nearly says as much in the *Novum Organum* as part of his open warfare on imagination. "The understanding," he insists, "must not be supplied with wings, but rather hung with weights to keep it from leaping and flying." To mistake these for mere metaphors is to miss the very role symbols play in the creation of language and the molding of the psyche. A society that decides it must keep its thinking "down to earth" is a society that begins taking the phenomenon of gravity seriously.

Significantly, this new concentration on gravity as a basic and universal fact of nature corresponded to the growing obsession with human fallenness in the religious thought of the sixteenth and seventeenth centuries. As the sense of human degradation before God increased and as the soul took on an impossible weight of sin, the problem of gravity began to tease the mind. Up to this point in history, we have been dealing with perceptions of morality and nature derived from an ancient symbolism that united the experience of weight to the experience of ungodliness. But now something of supreme importance happened; the two lines of thought—spiritual and natural—parted company to become separate realms of discourse. The scientists took up the discussion of gravity as if it were without a spiritual meaning; they cut the natural phenomenon away from its primordial religious connection. They demythologized it. They could simply no longer feel gravity in their understanding as symbolically related to an experience of transcendent significance. What is ironic, of course, is that their very loss of this dimension of experience was itself a sign of ultimate fallenness. They—and their society generally—were losing their capacity to perceive the universe about them as a repository of spiritual meanings. In the new science, there was to be no trace of sacredness left in nature. What is this if not the very state of cosmic abandonment that provides the basis for Protestant Christianity?

Essentially, gravity finds its place in the human understanding as the experience of fallenness, the loss of spiritual buoyancy. That is its root meaning. But the single vision of the scientific style required that this experience, being "merely subjective," being part of a failing mode of consciousness, must be eliminated. With Newton's speculations on gravity, we are at the beginning of a natural philosophy grounded in alienation, the measure of alienation being the degree to which the symbols used by a culture to achieve understanding have been emptied of their transcendent energy. Of course, from the standard scientific viewpoint, this is the whole value of Newton's thought. He at last objectifies and secularizes the phenomenon of gravitation. He "liberates" all thinking about up and down, rising and falling in nature, from its mythic and religious connotations. That, says the conventional wisdom, is what makes his approach "realistic."

"OCCULT PROPERTIES"

. But to objectify gravity was to separate it from the experience that had always provided its meaning. As the scientist's derivative conception of fallenness, gravity could

no longer be attached symbolically to a religious significance. This made scientific discussion of gravity strangely
abstract—even for Newton himself, and he became much
troubled. Yes, he could express gravity mathematically as a
behavior of things in nature. But he could not help wondering if this thing he had now so ingeniously measured
must not have *some* sort of substantial reality to it, something solider than mathematics. What *was* gravity besides
an algebraic equation?

Newton finally contented himself that it was a "force"
that acted at a distance. But this only took him into deeper
waters. Instead of giving him the sort of tangible, material
thing his science seemed to require, it gave him another
deracinated abstraction. For the kind of ultimate cosmic
force Newton invoked was also a symbol. As Durkheim
recognized, all the strange, elusive, but seemingly indispensable "forces of nature" that haunt western scientific
theory trace back to the original religious experience of
mana, the sacred power. "The idea of force is of religious
origin," Durkheim reminds us. "It is from religion that it
has been borrowed, first by philosophy, then by the
sciences." No primitive people acquainted with *mana*
would have any difficulty grasping the idea of a force that
acts magically at a distance; though of course they would
translate the idea into a religious experience, an action of
the divine. That would carry the idea of force back to its
root meaning.

But Newton's fellow scientists, being objective in their
approach to nature, could no more find the root meaning
of force than they could of gravity. The notion therefore
looked suspiciously meaningless. Was such a force there at
all? If so, what was its cause? And how could it possibly act
at a distance? Newton was hard pressed by such questions—but when it came to the "suchness" of gravity, he
had no answers. His critics, even those who accepted his
mathematics, accused him of inventing "occult properties." A major part of Roger Cotes's preface to the second
edition of the *Principia* is spent fighting off these charges

of obscurantism. Newton bridled at the challenge, but finished by giving up the problem. A "force" of gravity must exist, because how else to explain the behavior of the objectified universe? But, he confessed, "the cause of gravity is what I do not pretend to know, and therefore would take no time to consider it." On this point, said Newton in a famous remark, "I frame no hypotheses." Gravity was simply left as a measurable behavior of things.

In effect, this was to leave the key concepts of "gravity" and "force" suspended in a vacuum of abstraction. The only experiences that could restore their original meaning to these words lay on a transcendent level which was no longer in the repertory of western consciousness. So the terms finish as mere words tenuously linked to mathematical formulations. The same might be said of that other, even more critical term in the Newtonian synthesis, "law"—the most obviously metaphorical borrowing in science and probably the most important notion involved in launching the scientific revolution. It too traces back, even more obviously, to origins in religious experience. But as all these concepts have been drawn away from their root meaning by the demands of objectivity, they have come to seem more and more dispensable—like many another substantive noun in science. Until at last they are so much excess linguistic baggage loosely attached to the *real* thing—which is the mathematical description of behavior.

THE NEWTONIAN PHANTASM

Let us make one final observation about the idea of gravity as it comes down to us from the scientific revolution. As we have seen, objectivity demanded that Newton strip his scientific vocabulary of its symbolic resonance; one was no longer to talk about nature in animistic or visionary ways, lending transcendent meanings to natural phenomena. But the result was not, as one might expect, to make nature more physically real. True, from Newton onwards, there is a growing ethos of what we call "materialism" in western culture, carried mainly by the scientific tradition. But—paradoxically—that materialism is remarkably abstract; it is more an idea than an experience. We find more and more people thinking about matter and its attributes, but—as our discussion of the Romantic poets has suggested—with very little enrichment of sensory experience.

For example, Newton never once discusses the physical sensation of gravitational pull. He never explores gravity as a feeling—something that tugs at the body, shaping its movements, sculpturing its structure, grafting it onto the natural continuum. There is no sensory awareness to his theory, only linguistic and mathematical conceptualization. Nor has physics since Newton paid any greater attention to the living experience of gravity on the organism and within the organism. It has not seen this in the least as an interesting line of inquiry.

Instead, Newton treated gravity as a relationship *between* bodies; it is a force acting at a distance that affects only the hypothetical mass-points of bodies. It does not physically permeate them. In short, the idea has been totally alienated—turned out and away from human participation. It is Out There, in the universe . . . an objectified something. As we observed in Chapter 3, single vision is as anti-organic as it is anti-symbolic. It has done nothing to deepen the quality of our sensory experience. Only now, three centuries after Newton, do we learn from our astronauts that gravity is as much in the body as oxygen is in the lungs and bloodstream. When it is subtracted, the organism deteriorates.

This astonishing neglect of the organic phenomenology of geotaxis happens not because there is nothing there of importance to learn. Modern dance (especially the work of Martha Graham) and Structural Integration therapy (the work of Ida Rolf) have made extensive explorations of gravitational dynamics within the body. Along these lines, we arrive at a deep physical knowledge of gravity that scientific empiricism has wholly ignored. But then Newton was a scientist—a *good* scientist; and science diets on abstractions. What he wanted was a quantifiable, conceptual model and only that. So in his work, we are left with a word, "gravity," no longer understood to be a symbol but only a cipher, no longer related to visionary or organic experience, no longer accompanied by its once dominant counterpart, levity. To this word Newton then attached various mathematical generalizations in order to describe the behavior of mass-points influenced by a mysterious force. In this way, he achieved an operationally efficient conception of gravitational phenomena. But his thought no longer had any conscious connection with experience or with symbol. We are a long way from root meaning. Perhaps we can now begin to see how revolutionary the scientific revolution was.

Thus the paradox of physics, the "basic" science on which all others build. The more determined the physicists become to be hardheadedly empirical, materialistic, mechanistic—"realistic" in every tough-minded sense of the word—the more cluttered their science becomes with mathematical abstractions, statistical generalizations, and purely theoretical, disposable models. Blake referred to the scientist's nature as a "Newtonian Phantasm." Why does it become so? Because scientists (like their culture as a whole) can no longer consciously relate symbol to transcendent experience. Nor have they that openness to the sense life which will allow them to perceive a symbolic presence in the nature they study. For such a sensibility, even so basic a symbol as the vision-flight, which undergirds all thought about gravity and levity, comes at last to seem "unreal". . . "merely subjective." And since it is held to be unreal, it cannot be used to help us find meaning, because only what is *felt* to be real by people can be meaningful to them. So we are forced to search for meaning and reality elsewhere: in something conceived of as external and independent of mere subjectivity, something that is fact and not fantasy.

But once this inside/outside dichotomy has gained control of our experience, once we forget that a root meaning derives from an experience which is *at once subjective and universal,* the project becomes futile. Science and sound logic construe the traditional symbols as so many "propositions" about an "objective reality" and then proceed to "prove" them "meaningless." We are left to conclude that the entire human past was inhabited by simpletons and madmen hopelessly out of touch with the Reality Principle. Yes, they generated much interesting culture, but they were mistaken about its real meaning, which is to be found in class interest, Oedipal drives, tribal cohesion, legitimization of authority, etc., and which only our psychology and social anthropology can understand. Yes, they invented language—but having no linguistic sophistication or logical precision, they clearly did not know what they were talking about.

Meanwhile, as this self-congratulatory ethnocentrism makes a shambles of human culture, inevitably a philosophy and literature of despair grows up which has but one sad message to deliver. "Very well: if the Old Gnosis is meaningless, then life is meaningless."

After this fashion, the ontological priorities are inverted; we stand the world on its head as we secularize the cultural repertory. Or, as Blake put it:

> The Visions of Eternity, by reason of narrowed perceptions,
> Are become weak Visions of Time & Space, fix'd into furrows of death. . .

The shamanic vision-flight becomes an illusion; the airplane becomes the real thing. Then what is the old sorcerer who works by another priority of things to say when his apprentice asks, "But did I *really* fly?"

A symbol torn away from the transcendent experience that generated it is a morbid thing. It has died as surely as the body dies once the heart is torn out. The world we build from such cadaverous symbols is the world of the dead—Blake's Ulro. The symbols are still with us; they must be as long as there is human culture—language, art, thought, all are crafted symbols. But dead symbols are counterfeits, in the same way that a well-embalmed corpse counterfeits a live body. And just as a corpse becomes more grotesque the more it is painted to imitate life, so a defunct symbol only grows ghastlier the more desperately we labor to disguise its death with the pretense of life.

This, I think, is what it means, most basically, to charge science with being reductionistic. It is the effort to make up a reality out of morbid symbols, symbols from which, in the name of objectivity, all sacramental vitality has been drained away. This ghoulish project cannot be *blamed* on science. That would be to mistake symptom for cause. The symbols have died in our culture as a whole. The activity we call science is what passes for natural philosophy in a culture that has collectively lost its sense of transcendent symbolism. It is our peculiar, crippled effort to understand nature as best we can by way of the lifeless symbols we inherit.

SEEING AND "SEEING"

The myths, rituals, linguistic metaphors, and artistic motifs with which the vision-flight adorns itself are of human making. But where experience chooses a bird or a mountain height as its symbol, it takes to itself a part of nature already there. The skylark is a symbol of the vision-flight, but in its own right as an object perceived, it is also an occasion for the experience which generates the symbol. The living bird can assume a transparency to the imagination, as if it were a "found poem." The poet who appropriates the skylark has borrowed his symbol from nature and incorporated it in the human cultural inventory. Was this perhaps how people learned the art of symbolic transformations, by discerning in the objects of nature around them that transparency which allows an object to act as the window for deeper meanings? "All spiritual facts," said Emerson, "are represented by natural symbols."

Here is a special magic which imagination works. It does not only project symbols, but *finds* them in the world. For the world is indeed filled with natural symbols that can assume an absolute transparency. Where the visionary powers are robust, such symbols can appear anywhere and everywhere, in every pebble, shell and leaf; they can illuminate the humblest objects. So Wordsworth tells how, as his visionary imagination strengthened:

> . . . then and there my mind had exercised
> Upon the vulgar forms of present things,
> The actual world of our familiar days,
> Yet higher power . . .

For those who have the eyes to see ("the spiritual eye," as Goethe called it) all nature can become a script of root meaning wherein everything is simultaneously ordinary and sacred, at once itself and yet invitingly transparent. Where this happens we have that magical or sacramental vision of nature which is the antithesis of single vision.

"There may be," Goethe said, "a difference between seeing and seeing; so that the eyes of the spirit have to work in perpetual connection with those of the body." How effortless this second way of "seeing" can be for the well-developed imagination is nicely expressed by Don Juan, who, at one point, tries to explain to his apprentice about the visionary ambiguities of the world he sees about him. [Don Juan points out that learning to "see" will reveal to Castaneda a whole new world, and when asked whether he retains an ordinary vision of objects he says that he can see either way. This pushes Castaneda to probe further about the value of nonordinary "seeing." Don Juan tells him that the value lies in an increased power to discriminate between things, in being able to] " 'see them for what they really are.' "

For the pagan and primitive peoples whom Jews and Christians alike have always reviled as idolaters, the moving air, the fire on the hearth, the rhythm of the seasons, the bird on the wing, the markings and movements of beasts, the streaming waters, the circling stars . . . all these, and the works of man's own hand are alive with an intelligible presence. They are symbolic doorways that invite the imagination through to high experience. Nothing in heaven and earth is without its transcendent correspondence. In Goethe's words, "Nature speaks to other senses—to known, misunderstood, and unknown senses. So speaks she with herself and to us in a thousand modes. To the attentive observer she is nowhere dead or silent." Similarly, Kathleen Raine has remarked that as we probe the symbols of nature more and more deeply "we are asked to make increasingly animistic assumptions about the world."

But there has occurred in our culture—peculiarly—a strange and tragic process: a *densification* of the symbols, by which they lose their subtle nature. They survive for us, if at all, by hardening into purely secular things, historical projects, objective formulations. They are real for us *only* at that level. We are indeed like the prisoners in Plato's cave, transfixed by the shadows we see, sealed off from the sunlight. Even to mention the notion of transcendent correspondence would perhaps sound mystical in the most outlandish sense to the great majority of people in our society. Yet it is only to speak of what has been in other cultures a daily commonplace—and within our culture as well for an exceptional few. For the Blakes, Wordsworths, Goethes, and those who share their powers, it has been as natural as breathing to read the meanings of the world's symbolic script; one just does not see anything as a "nothing but," but rather as a "both/and." Which does not for a moment deny the reality of the natural object "in itself" or of any human artifact or project. Instead, the other "seeing" recognizes that it is in the nature of a thing "in itself" to be a symbolic presence.

The plant was, for Goethe, as real a thing as it is for any botanist; but also, it was the unfolding saraband of its growth, fertilization, flowering, and decay—a choreography of symbolic gestures. Its reality was on both these levels—indeed, the two realities were locked together hierarchically. To encounter the world in this way is to abolish the alienative dichotomy so that the distinction "In Here," "Out There" no longer obtains. That dichotomy cannot sensibly cope with the question, "Where do we find the plant's symbolic meaning?" For what is "Out There" only acquires its naturally transcendent meaning when it has entered "In Here." Nothing can be a whole reality until it enters and mingles with what we call "subjectivity." This need not be an explosive psychic upheaval, an annihilating revelation that wipes out the personality and absorbs all things into "the godhead"—though this is the way the more dramatic mystics often describe the experience of a root meaning. But it is especially remarkable how in artists like Goethe and Wordsworth the experience is one of great calm and normality that seems only like a homecoming of the spirit. And in such a surrender to quiet rapture there is, I find, more conviction than in strenuous ecstasies.

Because our orthodox consciousness has become objectified (alienated) to the point of freakishness, there is much misunderstanding of what it means to "overcome the subject/object dichotomy." The usual academic reading of the experience takes it to be some sensational obliteration of identity—the dazzling effect many people seek in the psychedelic drugs. But sensitive reflection might best reclaim the experience from our "normal" state of alienation by small exercises in self-awareness which show up how meaningless the alienative dichotomy is. For example, Owen Barfield, in his *Saving the Appearances,* asks us simply to consider where a rainbow is. In Here? Out There? The answer also tells us where the transcendent symbolism of natural objects is.

CARL OGLESBY ET AL
A Juanist Way of Knowledge

INTRODUCTION
Merton J. Kahne

Carl Oglesby is about to speak, and I would like to try to set the stage a little bit in a rather difficult area. From the standpoint of the sociology of knowledge, the social construction of reality is conceived of as a never-ending process repeatedly constructed, reconstructed, reaffirmed, or transformed in the exquisite interplay of communications taking place between people. That is to say, while the reality of everyday life is experienced as existing independently of ourselves, attention to the details of the moment-to-moment transaction occurring between people is rewarded by an increased awareness of just how man creates the social order which gives substance and meaning to his experience. The importance of a social consensus in delimiting the beliefs of man, as well as a structure for adjudicating the legitimacy of an event and the legitimacy as well of the arguments used to justify an assertion, were very early recognized as crucial concepts to any analysis of just what men mean to say when they say what they mean.

More recently, and with increasing clarity, the part played by language, as the envelope within which all the categories of a person's experience which can be communicated to another are contained, and in its role as a pre-existing structure of shared behaviors through which any newcomer must pass in the process of socialization, has also emerged to lay claim for some consideration in any searching analysis of that which is to be called real.

Finally, the repetitious validation of one's sense of reality, of the reality of one's experience, would appear to be sustained by rather trivial features of the social scene, by small talk and banter, by the appearance and demeanor of other persons, and even by such otherwise distracting background features as the setting, the nature and the quality of the physical arrangements. All of this, of course, is orchestrated through a more or less systematic world view, each part of which serves as evidence for the supposed independence and objective existence of particular events.

Now the crucial role of science as the major legitimizing agency in the modern life, both in the larger socio-technological and political arena as well as in the more mundane exchanges of men in the street, is, of course, one of the concerns which actuates this seminar. Critics of the present state of affairs hold that a scientistic image of science is the fundamental source of the human difficulties of our times. This scientistic image emerges, in their view, from the domination of science by positivistic philosophy which, in turn, they believe, holds that knowledge is inherently neutral, that there is a unitary scientific method, and that the standards of certainty and exactness in the physical sciences is the only explanatory basis for scientific knowledge. Its consequences, it is asserted, are to place undue importance on instrumental effectiveness and efficiency in decision-making at the expense of a broader, more expressive participation and individuation of affected people.

Carl Oglesby will, I suspect, catapult us into the middle of all of these issues, and more, as he undertakes a discussion of the experiences of a gifted anthropologist with a sorcerer, an aged Yaqui Indian's experience of life, and its possible implications for our future directions.

* * *

CARL OGLESBY
C. P. Snow: The Alienation of Fact and Values

Snow's famous two-cultures thesis implies Kant's distinction between the two reasons—crudely, between a scientific method of reasoning about nature which proceeds experimentally from doubt toward certainty, and an intuitive method of reasoning about moral cuture which circulates between notions of indeterminacy and constraint. Ancient, traditional, and modern arguments try to establish the irreducibility of this distinction.

But the West-modern temperament is characteristically dissatisfied with an epistemology that detaches the scientific discussion of nature from the moral discussion of culture, giving us a world reality divided into structurally incommensurable pairs, a domain of objects and another of meanings, a domain of facts and another of values, a domain of words and another of sentences, a domain of surfaces and another of textures, a domain of body and another of mind, each unreachable from each. As it was understood by the discourse community that employed it, Snow's observation that a breach had arisen in the body-mind continuum was taken as implying, first, the desirability of its being repaired, and second, that in order for this to happen, the humanities more than the sciences needed modernization. Snow did not say that social values could be scientifically derived. But compared to the sciences at that moment in the fifties, the humanities looked inert. All the sciences were getting results at a rate and of a quality previously unimaginable and all the humanities were still bewildered by the A-bomb and had produced no answer to this dreadful challenge to reason. People complained about the Silent Generation, and proposed faster moral progress. In that setting Snow was taken to be suggesting approximately that the method of positive validation and experimental evidence might be useful to the humanities: to the ancient and current search for meanings and values, the application of the scientific method might impart new energy.

This idea has faded, to be sure, *pace* Skinner's best seller, but it is only lately and tentatively that one can say so. Industrial world orthodoxy still represents the scientific way of knowing the material world as the realest way of know-

ing the realest reality. (Moreover, contrary to a current po-
lemic which gives all the facts to scientists and all the values
to scholars, recall how slight a chance at sinning with Faust
their fate offered the scholars to begin with, owing to the
political uselessness of their kind of knowledge; and once
the chance did come, recall how eager were large components of psychology, sociology, anthropology, and "political science" to be elevated to the status at which that kind
of sinning could be a way of life.)

The ascendency of positivist scientism in the social status
must somehow be tied in with the diffuse national demand
for unity and power in the Cold War. Even before Sput-
nik, the choice of a scientific or technological career—a career, so to speak, in the "objectivities"—was regarded as
the optimization of self-interest and patriotism. I am talking about *zeitgeist,* not conspiracy, when I say that the An-
glo-American and Soviet philosophical attacks on subjectivity served the convenience of the Cold War state. This is
because it is the very method and quintessence of internal
political criticism that it is intuitive, personal, presump-
tuous and rigorously unquantifiable. When subjectivity is
objectified and rationalized, it, of course instantly disinte-
grates, becoming a thing. Disintegrated or quantized subjectivity has no way to criticize the state; preoccupied with
disintegration, it abandons politics, in which the discussion
of national-tribal purpose reverts to cant. The silence of
the fifties and the dominance of positivism in the sixties
are connected. What of now?

As long as the main alternative to normal American life
was plausibly defined as national subjugation to Stalinized
Soviet communism, the normally critical humanities accepted privatism as a code if not scientism as a practice,
and as public professions, as callings, disappeared behind
the mountain to console melancholy with technique (as
with the New Criticism, which in its rejection of intentions
and affects—*i.e.*, of subjectivity—isolated even an obviously critical poetry like Eliot's from the world of ·motivated,

transactional reason; purified it of its idea). But once Stalin had passed from the foreground and Berlin had been displaced by Selma and Saigon, the critical spirit proper to the humanities began to reappear. In a matter of a few years, the current movement of academic "revisionism" was challenging the representation of reality in American policy and, ultimately, the whole apparatus of normal American thought and life. When critical revisionism returned to Snow's challenge, then, it was not in order to secure for the humanities, at last, their long-awaited fulfillment as sciences, as if everything would be science if only it could be. "Scientific" is no longer so intimidatingly absolute a standard of thought. The purpose is to see whether or not the domination of ideas by the model of normal physical science is not an aspect of a much wider predicament.

The question is easy to muddle because it moves the passions and because it poses so many basic problems of knowledge and action in unfamiliar ways. The passions arise, I suppose, from the invidious-seeming treatment of contemporary science as Cold War science. American science seems so wrapped up in its perhaps trivial claims of objectivity and at the same time so nervous about its role in everything horrifying about the twentieth century from ovens, Hiroshima and Vietnam to the perhaps forthcoming apocalypse that one has merely to hypothecate its complicity and like magic the whole dispassionateness goes overboard. The basic philosophical issue boils down to the universality of science, or to turn this around, to the question of "realities" beyond those perceived through the common classical senses. Can or cannot the method of science lead to the discovery of the laws governing the behavior of the universe as a whole, the behavior we simple-mindedly call subjective, along with objective, the cultural world as well as the natural? I say this issue is posed unfamiliarly because we are used to asking this question in order to continue the modern struggle against subjectivity; but now we are asking this question on behalf of subjectivity and with a view toward establishing the limits or the nonuniversality of science (which I will argue will be the emancipation of science, too, as well as art, from the curse of modernity).

In sum: is science the potentially universal method of knowing all knowable reality, inner and outer alike, or is it culturally and structurally bound the way all other human activity is? Is the method of objectivity not a project of subjectivity? Or does this conventional dualism fail us altogether?

CARL OGLESBY
A Juanist Science

Don Juan Matus is the attributed literary name of a Yaqui Indian sorcerer, contemporary with us, who lives in central Mexico with friends and relatives in a withered but not-about-to-die band of Yaqui Indians. Don Juan continues the ancient Yaqui practice of sorcery as a means of knowledge of another order of reality from the ordinary.

A young anthropologist by the name of Carlos Castaneda (also an assumed name) in about 1960 discovers Don Juan, announces that he is interested in learning more about the peyote cultists among the Yaquis. One thing leads to another, and finally Castaneda has written two books describing his apprenticeship: *The Teachings of Don Juan* (1968), and *A Separate Reality* (1971).

The books were noticed by the youth culture, but in order to disapprove of Castaneda as fervently as they approved of Don Juan. Castaneda writes everything down in order to be able to repeat to us what happened in his conversations with Don Juan, and Don Juan finds it amusing that rather than giving himself unreservedly to the experience into which Juan is leading him, Castaneda always pauses to take notes. Juan wonders how much he can really be learning. . . .

Experimental Knowledge Superimposed
Upon Experiential Knowledge

Castaneda's books are a careful record of an experimentalist approach to an internal experience which affirms a separate reality which is structurally set over and against the ordinary reality that we ordinarily inhabit. My reading of Castaneda's report on Juanism is that realities, although they be various, are not discontinuous, are *not* separate from one another. That is, in order to confront Juan directly, we have to try to expand our conception of subjectivity as a sphere of practical knowledge.

For example, there is an argument that says, "That is just happening in his head. The sense of flying as a crow, or of meeting spirits is induced by the psychoactive mushrooms and cactus buttons that Juan uses in his sorcery." This argument may remain apposite, relevant, interesting, even decisive on its own terms. But Juan puts us in a context in which this is not enough. We are trying actively to transcend the current general conceptions of domains of being. We are trying to posit subjectivity itself as an uncharted wilderness that includes itself. "It's all in the mind." We know this is true, but we no longer know what it means or even where it puts us.

The beginnings of an incursion into that wilderness may be offered in the rigorous savage science of Don Juan Matus. We may even be in confrontation with some form of creative indeterminacy. We can already see, before eating a single peyote button, that Juan's approach to subjectivity embodies a *practical*, indeed a *technological*, mysticism whose main thesis is that subjectivity, just as with the external world which subjectivity somehow resumes and continues, is a "domain" which can be explored by means of a method which is like that of normal science in that it is experimental, but unlike it in that it is at one and the same time *experiential*.

There is a tendency in Western epistemology, as I have said earlier, to divide ways of knowing from each other.

We know some kinds of things by experiment: that is science. We know other kinds of things by experience: that is intuition. But there is rarely a convergence. In fact there is no methodological attempt to produce convergence of two means of knowing. But if subjectivity is a domain about which it is possible for subjectivity to have knowledge, then we might be able to imagine a knowledge whose most fundamental component is the act of free self-creation, a knowledge looking beyond itself to its forthcoming experiential creations.

That is what I take to be the underlying claim of Juanism; that is, the direction implicit in it. The use of psychoactive drugs is interesting technological apparatus, but what is basic about it is the resulting definition of subjectivity as the creator of its own Nature, its own experience. From the standpoint of modern Western science, however, this new definition of subjectivity is one that *may not be explored.* It is a new territory for us and requires a post-rational science.

Features of a Juanist Science

To make some of this somewhat clearer, I want to list a number of general features of what I would take to be a Juanist science. These are in no particular order, and I do not believe they constitute a system. Apologizing no longer for conspicuously loose language, I will try simply to suggest the quality of some possibly interesting features of a Juanist science.

(a) First, a Juanist science would decisively affirm the integrity of subjective experience. The possibility of knowledge independent of experimental methods arises on the site of subjectivity, and the possibility of then superimposing an experimental technique means that within a Juanist psychology there could be a knowledge which is both experientially and experimentally derived.

(b) Second, Juan has not only a methodology and technology but also a value system. It is very simple. Juan says you must have "heart." If you have "heart," you will know what is right. If you don't have "heart," then what you are trying to do probably will be done "heartlessly." To do science without "heart" is like doing sorcery without "heart," or concern for the results of the activities in the lives of other creatures. So a Juanist science would be specifically and aggressively committed to the *active defense* of being, of life, of consciousness. It would regard itself as an active partisan in the struggle to augment the prosperity of all things that make life live. A Juanist biology, for example, might assume that consciousness always forms a whole relationship with reality no matter what species it is situated in. For example, the whales that Roger Paine teaches us about, the dolphins that Lilly teaches us about, and so on, are presumed to experience a whole reality as completely from the standpoint of their species' window on reality as we human beings experience it from ours.

(c) Third, from this comes the experimental presumption that consciousness is everywhere like flora and fauna exfoliant with separate realities. Cockroaches are philosophers who begin with different givens!

(d) Fourth and very important, a Juanist science would want to disjoin itself from a Faustian quest for an absolute comprehension of the limits of the universe or of the elemental root of being. It seems to me that it is the Faustist enthusiasm for totalizing knowledge in a series of definitive and absolute equations of motion that lies close to a good many of our social and ethical problems. We need rather to be chastened by Pascal's sense that if you show him the smallest thing you can discover in your world, he will open up the abyss within it. Juanist science would be metaphysically more modest than the sciences we know.

(e) Juanist science would understand its program as not being determined by the nature of Nature. When Juan says that a "warrior" selects the items that make up his world, he points to the possibility of choosing an array of sciences that would be more congruent, more correspondent with our real social and personal exigencies. Science, as we have it, is conventionally explained and understood as somehow given in the inner structure of reality. Juanism says that this science is instead determined in the social or cultural or political world where people make decisions in permanent conflict and doubt.

(f) Juanism embraces more than a determinant knowledge, goes beyond positivism or the moral sovereignty of fact. In the debate that goes on now about the sciences and the humanities, an all too familiar assumption is that the sciences have "harder" knowledge than the humanities. What that means basically is that there is less ambiguity about propositions which science unhesitatingly affirms, whereas in the humanities there is hardly anything that is affirmed without hesitation. That is to say, the humanities have a greater familiarity with an ambiguous, intractable, sometimes unreachable (moral) world that won't reduce itself to any correspondence with the symbols by means of which one might try to measure it. There is a world that stands apart from all efforts of historians to reduce it to the laws of history, a world which defies all efforts of artists to understand its basic laws of beauty. Similarly Juanist practice would involve itself with softer than scientific knowledge. And I am suggesting that not as a retreat but as an advance.

(g) Another virtue is chastity. I wonder if there should not be monasteries and convents set up for science! It seems to me that there is something inconsistent in the materially-well-rewarded practice of science. Science's dependence upon elaborate instrumentation is today the measure of its dependency upon the state, and almost the measure of our servitude to data and results. It ought to be possible to connect the life of scientific activity with the vow of poverty without looking like a fool. And it seems to me that things would be better if that could happen.

(h) A Juanist science would want to be much more self-explanatory, much more forthcoming, to ordinary people. That is, it would go into the streets, would have an evangelical mode, to help people understand better what science understands and a surer grasp of what science does not promise ever to understand. This dialogue of science with ordinary people now gets increasingly closed off by specialization which is used only for isolating different experiences from each other. If science could somehow reconceptualize and activate in society our knowledge of ourselves as creatures, as animals, as bugs wriggling around with other creatures on a divine ball, it would perhaps then concretely address the question of the species-variety of consciousnesses and their means of reunification. Science has not characteristically striven to make clear this connectedness, this potential unity of being, and I think this is something that could be definitely and concretely turned around.

A Juanist Psychology

Now for some possible features of a Juanist psychology.

(a) First, a Juanist psychology would not be just a therapy, a way of curing illness. It takes itself seriously as a science of subjectivity elaborating the modes of subjectivity and extending the boundaries of subjective experience. And as it is also a therapy, Juanist psychology would also want to confront the diseased consciousness in the world in which it encountered its sickness and learned to be sick, instead of tending, as our current practice does, to isolate the individual in his consciousness with the means of his cure, the psychiatrist. That is to say, if the tendency of a Freudian materialist science is to bring things into a closet for discussion, the tendency of a Juanist science is to project images and experiences of madness back into the world where they were first necessitated by elementally destructive relationships between persons and social forces.

(b) I have already said it would want to be committed, evangelistic. It would move freely and actively in the street, which it will seek in fact to redefine over and over.

It would try to take an active role in the real, daily, routine life of men and women. (The Diggers are familiar examples.)

(c) The most sensational feature of Juanist science is probably its use of psychoactive agents in the elucidation of consciousness. Juan elaborates a mind technology based on plants. There are no doubt other ways of interior knowledge, some maybe lost in antiquity, others visible and available to us in re-emerging Oriental modes of thought, or whatever. These are all being restored. A Juanist psychology actively pursues this immense work of the restoration of humanity's lost worlds; even if this means forcing the so-called drug issue.

(d) Juanist psychology rejects a scarcity-model of spirit and in that way departs from Freudian materialism, which believes that for civilization to exist, Eros must be deprived and denied. Freudianism, like the capitalism which it represents in the realm of the spirit, is based on structural scarcity, conflict, and concealment. Wilhelm Reich gives us an almost complete philosophical apparatus for a Juanist psychology which would affirm on the contrary that the greater the liquidity of spirit in one respect, the greater the liquidity in all respects; the greater the creativity of the spirit, in one respect, the greater the creativity over all. By the same token, the greater the suppression of one faculty of society or the person, the greater the servitude of all avenues of human activity.

Conclusion: On Politics

I have said nothing about the political implications of all this. For what it's worth without explanation and defense, my belief is that a change in consciousness is a necessary co-condition of a change in polity. But I am aware that both ultimately and soon, the emergence of a new critical-creative consciousness in some sectors of the world must be seen in terms of its steadily more violent suppression in other sectors: Vietnam and the rise of Connally, in other words, must be clearly situated in any new Juanist map of reality.

* * *

COMMENT
Everett Mendelsohn

*Juanist Knowledge Is Personal Knowledge, But
Oglesby Did Not Speak That Way About It*

If I were to cast myself in the mold of what you have just described as a Juanist man of knowledge, I wonder how I could make an exegesis of any way of knowing. That, I suspect, is exactly what you would say a Juanist man of knowledge would not want to do. He would want to experience it; he would not want to argue it. A Juanist man of knowledge in this sense would be at logger-heads with a Jesuit, at logger-heads with a Talmudist, certainly at logger-heads with a rationalist. I'm not quite sure where that leaves me.

And if I were to put myself in another sort of position and ask whether there are ways of familiarizing or communicating my world to the Juanist world, whether it can, for instance, be done analytically, I suspect we could agree that it probably cannot, that an analytical way into the Juanist world would be a contradiction in terms.

Thinking about this, brought me back to experiences I have had, which you can feel and know in part only by personalizing them. And I am surprised that you did not do that. The one thing upon which I would have thought a Juanist way of knowledge would have insisted is a personalizing of experience. I may misunderstand, but certainly as I read the first Castaneda volume, and as I listen to this way as a system, it seems to me that this is the thing that differentiates a Juanist way of knowing from any other rationalist sort of knowledge; you personalize it. You called it a "subjective" way of knowledge, and yet in a sense your presentation stayed far away from that. Only in your last

comment about your own view of how a revolution in polity might be brought about only through a revolution in
consciousness did you personalize your remarks and become "subjective."

Let me now personalize my own response to you. About
twenty years ago I married a Quaker and have lived
through twenty years of close relationship to a believer
and a family of believers, in what can only be called a continual sort of "mystic experience." And I have been struck
by many similarities to categories you draw: the Quakers
would talk about "the experience of truth," "the experience of love," "experiments with truth" they called them:
an attempt to transcend both polity and theology and to
enter into an experience of God, an experience of personal relationship which transcends the categories that they
know, essentially (in their view) leaving themselves open to
some Spirit to move them. The notion of there being a
universal consciousness, as you put it, would be familiar to
them, though they might put it in slightly different terms:
they talk about the notion of God within every man or the
light within every individual. In fact, some went even further and spoke of the light of God within every living
thing, not quite willing to draw the line at light being only
in human beings. It depends, of course, on who they were
and from what period of history they came.

All of this adds up to a question: what do we do with this
understanding? (I have sensed some of this in a period of
personal relationship within a family.) Where does it come
from? In what way are we to assimilate it? Where is it going? After all, the Quakers were and are a group within
modern human history, the same human history of which
science is a part. They are not as separate from that history
as a Juanist man of knowledge or Don Juan must be. What
was it that the Quakers have been doing that is different
from what science has been doing? And what is the difference between where the Quaker way gets you and where
science has gotten us?

Juanist Knowledge and 17th-Century Scientific Knowledge

As I listened more and followed your categories of the Juanist way of knowledge, I began to ask myself whether your description would not fit rather closely (with several important exceptions) the late 16th or early 17th century man who thought that knowledge of nature could be arrived at both rationally and experientially, who broke with the notion that knowledge of nature or other things can be arrived at only through revelation. After all, the man of knowledge in the 16th and 17th centuries grew up in a world where the final arbiter of any statement of truth was thought to be that which was revealed: whether it be revealed personally, through the mystic, or through the Church, which was in this sense the Body of God, the Body of Christ on earth. In many ways the image that the scientist had in those days and the direction he was headed in are not dissimilar from those of the Juanist today as you describe him. And I can see the point. Here is a 17th century scientist up against a way of knowledge which came through revelation. What he is looking for is something which will break with the sterileness of this way of knowledge, something which will allow for greater personal experience, greater personal involvement, which will allow him to be in some way the judge of what is real and what is unreal, what is true and what is untrue. And what he does is find a new method of truth, and he calls it experience, or he calls it experiment. And he used these interchangeably. (They were not always the same: they grew further and further apart as science came to develop, but certainly at their earliest period they were interchangeable.) And think of the names that some of the early scientific societies gave themselves: the Academy of Experience, the Academy of Experiment, in the 17th century post-Galilean society in Italy. They thought of themselves as breaking with a previous way of knowledge which certainly enslaved men

to systems of truth which they could in no way affect. They
wanted to be able to affect the systems of truth, and by re-
lying on experience and experiment, they gained just that:
everyman, when it comes to experiment or experience, is
as good a priest as the man at the altar. This they fought
for very, very hard. They had to break with the authority
of the Church and revelation.

Ways of Knowledge Spring From Social Formation

In this process we can see the *social forming* of a way of
knowledge. Think, for instance, of the people who remained on one side of the breaks that were being made
and who remained on the other. Giordano Bruno, a late
16th century figure, assassinated in 1600, attempted in his
way of knowledge to include within a system of natural
knowledge everything which we would clearly recognize as
miracles. He wanted those to exist within a system of
knowledge which would be experimentally and experientially dealt with. We know that he was castigated not only
by the Church which was afraid of losing its hegemony
over miracles, but also by science, which was afraid of
where its system of knowledge would take them. It was
taking them obviously into direct conflict with the religious
and secular authority of the day. If the Church had not
finally gotten Bruno and burned him, his scientific colleagues would have, in as devastating a fashion. And indeed, we know that Father Mercé, a figure of scientific
piety in the mid-17th century, took out after Bruno and attempted to draw a line right down the middle and say that
science is going to deal with certain forms of truth, and it is
going to leave other forms of truth to someone else.
Science essentially entered into a social contract with the
social structures of the day and said, "If we leave the forms
of knowledge which you call the Church alone, will you in
turn leave the forms of knowledge which we call nature
alone? Let us deal with ours, you deal with yours." And

when you look at the charters of every one of the early
scientific societies, they all say, "This society shall not deal
with dogma, with rhetoric, with religion, with metaphysics,
with politics." They drew the line, the positivist line, which
you [Oglesby] pointed out.

The only point I make out of this is that the way of
knowledge of the 17th century man of science, which is the
direct heritage to today's man of science, was socially
formed. That way of knowledge ruled out dealing with
certain phenomena because of the social situation in which
these men of knowledge found themselves. Here then is
part of the social forming of our way of knowledge. This
leads me to ask about the social forming of the Juanist way
of knowledge, because knowledge, at least as I understand
it, does not spring from nowhere but springs from some
sort of social formation.

Our Crisis Is a Crisis of Authority:
Science Is Extended Beyond Its Proper Limits

But to return to where the scientific way of knowledge
has gotten us:

What does it do for us? Where does it leave us? Clearly,
it leaves us today unable to deal with some of the very sub
jective experiences which science in the 17th century said
it would not deal with. The crisis which you [Oglesby] al-
lude to is not a crisis of science in this sense. Science itself is
involved in no crisis; rather science is involved with a crisis
at its borders. With a decline of both secular and political
authority, with the decline of the Church as the giver of
law in areas which it previously had, with the decline of political bodies which could give law, men now want to treat
knowledge which you call "subjective" (things which we
generally think of as subjective knowledge, knowledge of
good and evil, knowledge of right and wrong) with the
same form of manipulation, the same form of juxtaposing,
with which they treated natural knowledge. This means

that it is not science which is in the period of crisis; it is the civilization which has lost alternate strong ways of dealing with knowledge outside of knowledge of nature, and finds itself unable to come to grips with these.

And what we see once again is an attempt to extend the boundaries of what is called science. We have watched them slowly extended over the years. You talked about a Juanist way of psychology! The 17th century scientist would have been aghast at the notion that his knowledge of nature, his approach to nature, would deal with what we now include within psychology, yet this is roughly now thought of as within something we call "behavioral sciences," which are certainly being patterned and modeled after the physical sciences. People think that the image of science has got to come from the physical sciences rather than elsewhere, and it is here that the kind of crisis we talk about lies. It is in the failure to recognize that the kinds of knowledge you want to deal with cannot be handled by the system of knowledge which was constructed to deal with another form of knowledge. What do you do?

You either talk about crisis, or you begin to construct an alternate way of dealing with these phenomena. I would agree with you (if I may rephrase what I think you are saying) and say that a way of dealing with human existence which is unable to cope with subjective experience is no way of talking about human beings; it is no way of having knowledge about human beings. To rule these out of a science of man (we might not want to call it that, although the older word of science might be good: a *scientia* of man) is a mistake. But to expect knowledge, in the very limited sense of knowledge that we have now embodied and call science, to be able to deal with subjective man is to stretch it far beyond the bounds which it was socially constructed to deal with and bounds which it has been socially forced to maintain in very large measure. This is the kind of travail I would say science finds itself in.

Should There Be a Single Knowledge of
Man, Nature, and Subjective Experience?

Two more responses and questions. In your outline the
Juanist way of knowledge is certainly not unsystematic.
What you are attempting to do, as I see it (and I am in full
sympathy with what you are attempting to do), is describe
a meta-science, something which goes beyond our knowledge of nature. What I am not sure of (and in a way it is a
prime question in my mind) is whether you are really saying that the same system of knowledge that we have for
manipulating a rational material world should also be used
as a system of knowledge to deal with subjective experience. Should we expect there to be a uniformity? Or can
we expect there to be different ways of knowing for different human activities and different experiences? You imply
that you want a unity. Do we? I don't know. Human history has not had them in the past except when they have
been tyrannical. Remember, the last time we had a unity of
knowledge was when the Church had hegemony over
knowledge of man, body and soul, and nature. Is this
where you want knowledge to be again? Do you insist on a
uniform system? Or can we recognize qualitatively different ways of knowing? Are we willing and able to do it? I
think we might want to.

Even in talking about the Juanist way of knowledge, in
using the term "knowledge" in the way that knowledge has
come to be used in our vocabulary, we have a problem. I
don't know what its earliest forms were, but certainly from
the modern period, the 17th century on, knowledge has
come to mean those things which are cognitive, those
things which can be known through experience, those
things which are repeatable, in a sense those things which
are non-subjective. Now I know that you are using it metaphorically, and I am not quibbling with the word, but are
you not actually using it in a way that is more than metaphorical? Do you mean that there should be a single

knowledge of man and nature and subjective experience
which uses knowledge in this cognitive sense rather than in
this more metaphorical sense?

What are the Social Roots of the Ethos of Juanist Knowledge?

Another question. You talked about the built-in ethic
that the Juanist way of knowledge has. You said that within a Juanist science you would need "heart." I assume you
are saying that within this system of knowledge there is an
ethical system built into the very way of doing and using
the knowledge. There is also an ethic built into modern
science. It is not the ethic which is good for dealing with
subjective experience; indeed it excludes subjective experience from its realm, but modern science has a very
strong ethos. Follow any student, for instance, though his
experiences and watch him be socialized to the process of
doing modern science. There is a very strong ethos which
guides the things he does and does not do. Try to slip by
an article into print which goes against the canons of what
the community of science has agreed is a way of doing
science; try to falsify data, and see the way in which the
community treats its members who do that. All these
things are dysfunctional, for science is a way of living, of
breathing, of acting.

Maybe what you are asking is that knowledge of nature
have in it an ethos for knowledge of polity, for knowledge
for subjective experience. Again, I wonder if you are not
asking too much. It may be that we need a Juanist way of
knowledge to deal with the polity. I have always been very
suspicious of the notion of political science which makes
believe that it gains its ethic from the natural sciences
when it certainly cannot. The ethic of the natural sciences
is inapplicable to an area in which there are large noncog-
nitive features, in which there are large normative or value
features. And I guess what you are pointing out is just that
problem, and I am sympathetic to it. I could not tell, however, what the source of the ethic or the ethos in the Juan-

ist way of knowledge is. We know what the source is in the way of knowledge that science now uses; I traced it in part to its social roots. And this ethos is not going to be radically changed without changing the very nature of science itself, that is, knowledge of nature itself. What about the Juanist way of knowledge? In what social form, in what social experience or social processes is it rooted? I am suspicious of an ethos that has its only source inside man's psyche. I am suspicious of one which does not reflect relationships that individuals have, relationships of man to the things he produces, of man to the way he lives, of man to the way he reproduces. It is this kind of specification that I look for. Where does the ethic come from? As you described it, could not evil be substituted for "heart" in the Juanist way of knowledge? Certainly the sorcerer can do so, as I understand the sorcerer historically: he can substitute an alternate form, an alternate ethical system, for one which he might describe to you. I worry about how in this way of knowledge, you derive an ethos for dealing with problems which have to do with justice.

KAHNE: I am not quite clear where you stand on the necessity for continuation of the bifurcation of knowledge. If I understood you correctly, it wasn't initially a political issue that the separation was intended to deal with.

The Social Roots of Science Limit It and Separate It From Other Ways of Knowing

MENDELSOHN: All I am saying is that the womb in which our way of knowing nature was born was one which bifurcated itself from polity, from theology, from subjective experience. For that reason the way of knowledge we have developed grew up in a framework very different from other ways of knowing. It is not that I want to perpetuate the bifurcation. I am saying that the social forms that science adopted were limiting ones. They were limited by the framework in which science established itself. It isn't as though there were a scientific way of knowing nature, a scientific method, which stood out here in a vacuum which we found and put down here in society and said was going to work, but agreed that we would not deal with politics or religion. It happened that we began to want to know nature, and we decided in the process that if we were going to get the freedom to know nature, and use experience as the arbiter of statements of truth to replace revelation, we were going to have to stay clear of places where religious authority still had very strong sway or where secular authority had very strong sway. So the state and religion were ruled out, and the system of knowing nature we developed in no way had to contend with those.

COMMENT
Christopher Schaefer

Perception Is an Active Process and Science Must Address the Subject-Object Problem

The comments I want to make will be very brief. I fully accept the implied criticism of political science. It seems to me that the mode of knowledge applicable in the natural sciences may well not be applicable in political science or in social science generally. That is, it seems to me, the lesson of Carlos Castaneda is that perception is an active process, that man is a symbol-maker and meaning-giver and that at least one of the tasks of social science or political science should be the elucidation of meaning and the context of meaning.

It is interesting in that regard that Castaneda had as an advisor Professor Garfinkel, who is associated with a very small group of social scientists who are working in an area called ethno-methodology which is an extension and elaboration of phenomenology. And phenomenology as a philosophical movement is particularly concerned about the subject-object relationship. So there are interesting relationships here which we should notice, beyond simply the description of experience.

It seems to me, however, that the kind of experience described is one that suggests that the use of plants or drug-substances is not necessarily vital, that the training may be vital, and that the result appears to indicate, as other people have shown, that perception is indeed an active process. And if that is the case, then I would suggest as a challenge for science as well as social science: science will have to be more than a methodological principle, as the phenomenologists argue it is; it will have to address itself to the subject-object problem in some fashion. And it cannot simply say there is a distinction. The relationship between the observer and the phenomena must be clarified in some way. I think that is a fundamental and very basic issue on which very little progress has been made since the late 19th and early 20th centuries.

REPLY TO COMMENTS
Carl Oglesby

The Convergence in Juanist Psychology of Experiential and Experimental Technique

Just a few observations in response to these comments which I found interesting and helpful. The question of the subject-object relationship strikes me as one better left until after dinner, because it takes so much energy to focus the terms that have to be employed. I would think, as a provisional observation, however, that it is important to remember that the space within which the phenomena of a Juanist psychology materialized is (in one important aspect) the subjectivity of the experimentalist. It was the possibilities for the convergence of an experimental technique with an experiential technique of knowing which I thought were the interesting features of a concrete Juanist psychology, although I would not want anyone to think that I thought I had seen the practical meaning of this.

Having Heart Is a Matter of Pure Ethical Freedom

I might respond by clearing up a few confusions I sense in Everett Mendelsohn's remarks. One important thing about the Juanist is his plea that people should have "heart." Juan does not think, however, that he can *prove* to anybody that he should have this "heart." He sees no way in which a commitment to a generally pro-species or pro-life position can be shown to be practically or logically necessary. Nothing necessitates "heart," according to Juan, not even the craft of sorcery, which rains on the pure and impure alike. What is peculiar about the Juanist ethic of "heart" is that it is necessarily chosen freely and freely sustained. Juan does not pretend that a choice can be defended on some more imposing grounds. For him, material or logical *necessity* has no ethical meaning.

Analysis of the Social Formation of Juanist Knowledge and of the Response to It Among the Youth Is Possible

More difficult is the question of the social formation of Juanist knowledge. We would perhaps agree that it would be possible to make an external analysis of Yaqui culture that would be valid on its own (conventional scientific) grounds. Such an analysis might show how the way of knowledge that we associate with Don Juan materialized in the Yaqui culture.

At the same time, if there is an increasing incidence of curiosity among the children of rational-material-progressivism about these "birds of paradise" like Don Juan, that is also a fact which has its social and historal architecture, and it would be possible to carry out an analysis of that.

It seems to me that there are also possibilities of an analysis of the sociological formation of a new science, even of a massive social re-conception of reality. At least we think we know that the current fashion in exotic paradigms is related somehow to the things that really happen to us: Vietnam, the moon, etc. We know that we cannot impose upon a culture a way of thinking about reality or way of dealing with moral questions that is not organic within it. Nor can we impose a way of thinking which does not emerge as an authentic experience of a culture's selfhood. The gradual unfolding to itself and others of its way of seeing things is, in fact, what a culture's experience of selfhood is all about.

10

DON JUAN AS MESSIAH, BUDDHIST MASTER, PHILOSOPHER OF THE UNKNOWN

CARL OGLESBY commented that the Castaneda books were "noticed by the youth culture, but in order to disapprove of Castaneda as fervently as they approved of Don Juan." We have read enough by now to know that Castaneda's literary activity—whether as the failure or the success of Carlos' apprenticeship—cannot finally be separated from don Juan's "system." As with the New Testament, we may have to settle for the "kerygmatic Christ" of the early Church's belief and expression rather than the "historical Jesus," the actual factual man behind the no doubt "distorted" portrait. That is, Castaneda's *picture* of don Juan is as close as we can get.

Still, it is the main figure in that picture which fascinates, and for at least one writer don Juan is comparable to what the New Testament shows us of Jesus. In his *The Crack in the Cosmic Egg,* Joseph Chilton Pearce details how both figures foster a break with ordinary consensus—to translate his metaphoric title into terms suggested by the "structural analysis" of *The Teachings of Don Juan.* Although Pearce has more recently moved on, in *Exploring the Crack in the Cosmic Egg,* to other "constructs of mind and reality," it is impressive how many of his insights on the first Castaneda book still seem to hold. (One of them is more provocative for the possibility that it does *not* still obtain: "Can you imagine Richard Nixon becoming an apprentice to don Juan?" Pearce asks, at a time when the former President's world was yet to be stopped.)

Pearce's chapter on don Juan and Jesus is long and complex, and no summary can do it justice. It is possible, however, to point out the major *difference* Pearce sees between two figures who *share* the uniquely radical vision of "seizing the very process by which reality *organizes*." Several times Pearce stresses that where don Juan is "a kind of hedonist of the psyche," creating "private but equally-real worlds for personal adventure," Jesus is "concerned over his fellow man," so that "his system works only in relationships between people." This diagnosis of don Juan's comparatively privatistic use of his way of knowledge recalls Ronald Sukenick's essay, with its parting question to Carlos about the necessity and desirability of withdrawal from the human community. Of course, Carl Oglesby has described how the development of a "Juanist science" might have very large and positive sociopolitical effects and the reader will have to decide upon these issues of ethical application for herself or himself.

An additional challenge to the reader's discernment is to determine whether Pearce's notion that don Juan and Jesus require "single-vision, or non-ambiguity" is in conflict with the analysis of a Theodore Roszak, for whom single vision would be a Newtonian contradiction of don Juan's way, or with the sense of other writers on Castaneda that a fruitful ambiguity is just what don Juan wants to produce. Another of Pearce's emphases, that "both don Juan and Jesus were figures for transference" seems to play into the hands of Weston La Barre's denunciation of the authoritarianism he finds implicit in Castaneda's books. But this may lose sight of the overriding weight Pearce's chapter places upon don Juan and Jesus identifying themselves with the "way," the *process* of reality-formation, so that their followers would eventually "see the transference function as itself the crack in the egg."

And perhaps Roszak and Oglesby could agree with the concluding thoughts of Pearce's extensive analysis. "Ultimate allegiance to a symbol of openness," Pearce states, "really does open things"; moreover, only by such allegiance will "the broad social drift . . . ever be changed for the better."

Many of Castaneda's commentators have noted apparent similarities between don Juan's teachings and the tenets of Asian religious thought. Philosopher James W. Boyd of Colorado State University actually takes the trouble to apply classical Buddhist categories to the first three Castaneda books in an attempt to test out the impression of significant parallels. He finds this impression largely confirmed by a close comparison: Methods for stopping the world in don Juan's way of knowledge and for turning back the wheel of life in the Path of the Buddha are based on congruent appraisals of the situation facing selves in the world. Both Buddhism and the teachings of don Juan view the world as an impermanent "mental tapestry" and the self as a temporary and all-too-mortal grouping of components. Boyd notes further that it is the anxiety of the ego at facing such a fleeting reality which provokes the socially sustained invention of a delusively stable "nature" outside us and a "personality" within.

Through Indian Buddhism's "dharmic analysis" or the creative quietude of Taoism, Ch'an Buddhism, and Zen, the disciple is forceably taught to confront the ubiquitous emptiness he had denied. "Don Juan's techniques for stopping the world," Boyd insists, "are shamanistic variations on those of the Buddhists and Taoists," and he supports this with a discussion of the "not-doing" exercises urged upon Carlos in *Journey to Ixtlan.*

The two systems share as an aim the knowledge that everything is insignificant—including the teachings, in both cases, which had effected the realization. Boyd labels this final focus on a transcendent goal "the way of mysticism." But by injecting the Buddhist formula "Nirvana *is* samsara" and using the term "bodhisattva" he also implies a leaning toward the paths of ordinary life which accords with Joseph Chilton Pearce's nonmystical perception of don Juan and Jesus.

While Pearce and James Boyd have compared the figure

of don Juan with founders or foundational doctrines of
the Western and Eastern spiritual traditions, Joseph Margolis is interested in analyzing don Juan in light of secular
thought, particularly the writings of Ludwig Wittgenstein,
perhaps the foremost spokesman for modern Western
philosophy. In an essay prepared especially for this volume, Margolis, a professor at Temple University and the
author of numerous works on esthetics and other areas of
philosophy, centers his attention on *Tales of Power*. In this
book, where many of don Juan's most baffling concepts
and his apprentice's most enigmatic experiences are described, "*our* apprenticeship to the magic presence of Don
Juan through the sorcery of Carlos himself" comes to an
end. When we do complete the fourth book we realize,
with Margolis, that the tetralogy has comprised what he
calls "a setting for the contemplative exercises of a reader
at a remove from the necessary site of full discovery"—that
is, a "place of power" for us.

And Margolis makes plain that it is the power of *don
Juan's* magic presence in the books which has led us progressively deeper into an involvement paralleling Carlos'.
He implies further that where "it makes no difference
whether the books are a record of an actual encounter or
whether Castaneda is the author of a clever fiction" is precisely within this involving sway of magic, the imaginative
identification of the reader with the process of the apprenticeship. But Margolis' repeated reference to our
"remove" from acts of power must be remembered: We
are not only not warriors performing such acts; we do not
even witness them. We are witnesses to "tales" only, so that
some of the magic at least is literary. It is just that the magic is so efficacious that, as Margolis comments, the discipline don Juan imparts becomes "oddly plausible and convincing in spite of merely reading about it."

With this valuable background on the reader's relation
to don Juan behind us, we plunge into an examination of
the central theoretical distinction toward which the four
books drive: the concept of the *tonal* and the *nagual*. Mar-

golis first compares don Juan's theory with the pre-Socratic philosopher Anaximander's notion of "the Non-Limited," arguing that "there is in both a contrast between an indeterminable source and determinate and therefore limited things that exist for an interval." Although it is illuminating to see this similarity between don Juan's concept and that of a thinker who stands at the beginnings of Western philosophy, the problem of explaining the *tonal-nagual* relationship has not really been resolved. "If the *nagual* is inexpressible what is the status of our attempt to identify it and to contrast it with the *tonal*?" Margolis rightly asks, and here he invokes the statements of Wittgenstein as a helpful resource. Especially striking is Margolis' quotation from Wittgenstein's *Tractatus Logico-Philosophicus* which begins "My propositions serve as elucidations in the following way: anyone who understands me eventually recognizes them as nonsense, when he has used them—as steps—to climb up beyond them." Not only is this reminiscent of Boyd's discussion of the final Buddhist step of "discarding the raft" so as to see the unimportance of it all, it suggests Wittgenstein's concern—one of particular relevance to the "apprenticeship" quality of reading Castaneda—to show how his concepts should and can be assimilated by his readers rather than just stating what they are. Perhaps this means that understanding Wittgenstein, too, is an apprenticeship akin to the religious discipleships described by Pearce and Boyd.

In any case, the problem of the ultimate conceptual boundaries pondered by Wittgenstein seems to be one which Carlos actually embodied in his long quest to explain experiences which called into question his every category of explanation. When, in *Tales of Power,* we are finally allowed to enter with Carlos into the concept of the *tonal* and the *nagual,* we are given a dramatic enactment of Wittgensteinian dilemmas. Gaining don Juan's logic of limits as his reward for repeated collisions with the limits of logic, Carlos is able to make sense of this "sorcerers' explanation" only through a culminating series of concrete,

though nonordinary experiences. Wittgenstein wrote that
"the sense of the world must lie outside the world," and
Carlos' physical awareness, closing out the fourth book, of
the imminence of death, of the "totality of himself," of his
being "a cluster" (echoing the Buddhist idea James Boyd
outlines of the self as an unstable aggregate of *skandhas*),
give his body, at any rate, a seemingly transcendent perspective.

As Margolis reminds us, this produces only analogies of
the indescribable for the intellect. Don Juan as *philosopher*
leaves his academic apprentice about where Wittgenstein
ended his *Tractatus*: with the idea that manifestations of
"what is mystical" can only be witnessed. Nevertheless,
Wittgenstein continued to write after the *Tractatus,* and
whatever *basis* don Juan's analogies might have continues
to provoke explanations from the mind of the reader. For,
as Joseph Margolis also admits, "what is ineffable is ineffable, though that appears to have discouraged no one."

Thus, the concluding reaction to the don Juan writings
accurately reflects the tremendous intellectual strains both
the *Tractatus* and *Tales of Power* produce as they lead us
with their authors up a mountain to a precipice beyond
which propositions and concepts cannot support us in the
least. If we are able to make it that far, we foresee, perhaps, a leap into our real lives, a challenge to self-knowledge grounded in the thin air of symbols and stories.

JOSEPH CHILTON PEARCE
Don Juan and Jesus

All logical systems, East-West, scientific-religious, cyclic
or linear, originate in an analysis of the way reality is structured. Then, by various techniques, the system develops as
an attempt to use the analysis to obtain some particular
product from the process analyzed.

The idea of eschewing products, and seizing the very
process by which reality *organizes* is the radical departure

found in don Juan's Way of Knowledge, and in Jesus' Way of Truth. Don Juan and Jesus consider the world to be an arbitrary construct, not an illusion as in the East or a fated absolute as in the West. Since the world is an arbitrary construct, the means of construction, not a particular construct, or the products of a construct, are the focal point of attention.

Don Juan and Jesus believe the materials of the world to be subject to dramatic alteration and reorganization by an activity of the mind. Both systems work to lower the threshold between reality-adjusted thinking and autistic thinking, and without loss of identity. Both systems have analyzed the way by which reality events shape, and have then dared to dissolve the structure of a common domain, the selective world agreed upon in ordinary social thinking. Such a dissolution would ordinarily threaten the ego-personality which has been centered and formed *by* the common domain, and this is a risk assumed.

Both don Juan and Jesus have as a goal the seizure of the ontological function itself and both attempts hinge on a complete surrender to the function. Through a sacrifice of self and absolute obedience to the *way* of the system, union with the process of reality is achieved. There is a single underlying way by which all reality forms and "union" with this procedure is possible. However, the system or means of achieving such union determines the *kind* of reality then shaping as experience for the person involved. There is a single unitary core of reality-functioning, but it is not available in a "pure form." It is, in actuality, according to the method of *actualizing* it. The subject's approach to the function determines his realization of it.

Don Juan recognizes the ordinary world to be but one of an endless number of possible constructs. The man of courage and daring in his culture will explore as many possibilities of this as he can, simply because the possibilities are there and that is what life is about. Man can re-structure reality in freely-synthesized ways. Though death is the final victor, to live a strong, hard life, in which reality opens its endless possibility, is the mark of a warrior, a man of knowledge, and the only conceivable way to live.

Jesus aims to restructure particular events *within* the world. He aims toward a special consensus concerning the ordinary reality. Non-ordinary reality is used only for the sake of the ordinary world. Achieving a new and different "editorial hierarchy of mind," the follower of the *Way* serves as catalyst for new syntheses when our fated and autonomous blindnesses, split from our whole mind as they are, lead us into inescapable dilemmas.

Don Juan seizes the ontological process to construct paths of "breathless wonder." Jesus seizes the process to bridge the modes of mind. Don Juan is in love with eternity. He is a kind of hedonist of the psyche. Jesus is in love with time. He is a pragmatic Hebrew, concerned over his fellow man. The esthetic differences of goals, of techniques and disciplines, give dramatically different results. But the process of attainment is similar.

Eastern thought viewed the world as a fated illusion and yearned for the *real* world. This is a proposition denied by both don Juan and Jesus, who know the world to be perfectly real. Greek-Stoic thought viewed the world as a fixed mechanical unit, distinct from the mind of man. This, too, is denied by don Juan and Jesus, who see the world as a matrix for continual resynthesis. Both recognize the world as an agreed upon and practiced construct in a continuum of possible worlds.

Don Juan created private but equally-real worlds for personal adventure, and accepted as a natural part of his path the isolation within his created point of view. Carlos experienced this as "the aloneness of a single person on a journey." Jesus recognized that no communicable shared reality is possible except by agreement between the participants of that world. So his system was to carry don Juan's open synthesis *into* the ordinary world. Jesus will break with the world of common agreement, but only under special circumstances and for special goals.

The crack in the egg is sought by Jesus to restructure

some specific problem area in ordinary reality. His system works only in relationships between people. His non-ordinary states are created as *shared* states by the constant focus on the needs of the other. No isolation is engendered. Two or three can gather together and reach a non-ordinary consensus, a point of agreement different from that of the ordinary world. Group agreement gives a mutual feedback of verification, sustaining the non-ordinary even in the ordinary. Carlos might call feeding the five thousand a special consensus of non-ordinary reality, or healing the man with a withered arm a special consensus about ordinary reality. In all cases, filling some need is Jesus' motivation and this proves to be the only way his particular crack is sustained.

Don Juan spoke of learning by doing as the only way to knowledge. There was no act of grace suddenly bestowing the goal. And yet there was the ally, a helper available once the subject had proved himself and learned to open to and control the technique of bringing about states of special reality.

Jesus' knowing, too, could only be obtained by doing, a course of action and thinking as rigorous as don Juan's. In conjunction with reality-adjusted thinking went an unambiguous single-minded organization similar to Bruner's "thinking for the left hand." Once this kind of thinking was practiced the world no longer split against itself, and there was freedom to "intervene in the ontological constitution of the universe," as Eliade put it, since conscious thought then had ready access to that point in the continuum where there was no judgment, no distinction between kinds of organization.

Neither don Juan nor Jesus could offer intellectual procedures or explanations of their way, since logic and reason are only the surface part of mind, the part splitting a total awareness. Both deny absoluteness or "sanctity" to any particular system, and, eschewing the products of systems, they are equally offensive to all systems. The only thing sacred to don Juan and Jesus is the way in which systems are built. Allegiance can only be given the *process* if balance of mind is to be achieved and sustained. Unbending intent is don Juan's requirement, a passionate concern. Idolatry, Jesus would say, is considering as absolute or true any *product* of the reality process. The *process* is the only truth, the only absolute, and the way to freedom.

Don Juan would have but one apprentice in his life, as his own benefactor had had but one. Many might be called to Jesus, but few would be chosen. Few would ever find the Narrow Gate. Both systems were esoteric, difficult to attain, and harder to sustain. Both demanded a risk of life— the world turns and rends its heroes—and, more seriously, a risk of soul or mind.

Growth within the way was not automatic or assured. The continuing response of the person gave the context for growth. Peter could be either the Keys to the Kingdom, or Satan, depending on his use of all his faculties and openness to the guide.

In his evaluation procedures, don Juan had set the expectancies shaping Carlos' future experiences. He did this by strong negative and positive reactions to the contents of Carlos' preliminary ventures. Jesus, too, reacted with quick negatives and positives to his follower's responses, questioning and probing their reactions, attempting to determine their expectancies associated with the Way.

Both systems required "frugality" or conservation of energy. Every aspect of life had to be reserved for the path. This implies no nonsense of a limited or fixed quantity of "libido" in a Freudian sense, but ultimacy of commitment and unambiguous intent. Extraordinary effort was needed to break with the broad stream that makes up the self-mirroring world of the ordinary. The activity of restructuring in the face of the strength of statistical reality called for extremes of energy and determination in Jesus' Way. And restructuring in the wake of psychedelic dissolution called for the same commitment and strength in don Juan's Way.

Shelter, nourishment, companionship, and so on, are the needs ruling the split man. They are the products by which short-circuited demonic power is wielded by one man over another. All these products of the broad way must be ruthlessly cut out, boldly denied. Fasting played a role in both systems. One became a "eunuch" for the sake of the Kingdom. Don Juan kept telling Carlos that he thought about himself too much. Self had to be forgotten. Only the path was important.

Both don Juan and Jesus were figures for transference, and both provided the clues for the initiating of the way. Both promised a helper or ally who would come and open one to ever-greater levels of growth and power. Power, an automatic result in both systems, was a crucial point of danger. The Temptations in the Wilderness graphically typified the main categories of misuse of power and loss of the Way. In don Juan's system any power once attained was never lost. Unless voluntarily surrendered, however, and given over only for the furtherance of more knowledge, the power became immediately demonic and blocked all further possibility of growth. Double the talents, Jesus promised, and you would be given twice that many more—for more doubling, if *invested*. Otherwise all were taken away.

Any attempt to use power for personal ends destroyed the Way in Jesus' system as well as don Juan's, and a practical, functional reason, not a "spiritually moral" one, was the cause. Desire for freedom from the tensions of reality as found in mystical systems or desire to use the potentials of the whole mind for ego-interests are out-of-balance maneuvers; the point of rapport with the whole mind is simply lost. In mystical experience the self is dissolved, if only temporarily, into the continuum. In desires of the ego, the imbalance is toward self, breaking the rapport with the whole mind, and further trapping the person in the fixed products of the ordinary world.

In Jesus' system concern *for* others on the one hand, and total allegiance to the autistic "spirit" on the other, achieved the otherwise impossible balance. Clarity of

mind, a clear understanding of one's own motivations, was
necessary in both systems. Single-vision, or non-ambiguity,
was the prime criterion. The path had to be chosen freely,
as ultimately desirable, having counted the costs of following it.

There was no free directing of the path itself, however.
Personal responsibility was a surrender to the peculiar
qualities of the path. A cultural hierarchy of values helped
give the guidelines for action. A continually-renewed commitment was necessary, though, for the only known goal
was the process of movement along the path itself. The
path was an open structure forming only as one moved
along it. The "obligatory acts" in Jesus' system were much
more dependent on the context of the moment than were
don Juan's.

Death was a contingency in both systems. In Jesus' system death was the ultimate demonic, accepted and assumed as an unavoidable property of the split mind but
not of the integrated one. The demonic was controlled by
denying absoluteness to those aspects of life over which
the demonic has power. The soul never "sinning," never
granting allegiance to the products of a system, and allying
only with the function of systems building itself, would
never die. Only when concern for the path was greater
than concern for self could the self achieve security.

In don Juan the capacity for exertion of extraordinary
energy had to be effective, quite literally, for survival.
Non-survival had to be accepted, however, as the mark of
profound belief. No goal could be entertained by mind except the goal of the path itself. And this path was its own
end. Don Juan had no prospect of survival. Death was the
final victor.

With Jesus, agreement, if only among two or three,
could establish a non-ordinary reality by consensus within
the group. This kind of autistic bridge between people is
found in don Juan, who brought about non-ordinary
events shared, unhappily, by Carlos in non-hallucinogenic

ways. It was, in fact, this conscious restructuring by don
Juan of ordinary events, right out in the light of day, that
finally defeated Carlos by their sheer horror.

Fear had to be accepted, faced, admitted, and then gone
beyond. Until one recognized the reason for fear he was
not fully aware of the qualitative distinction between his
new Way and the world's Way. The follower was then still
double-minded and divided in intent. The real onslaught
of fear arose at recognition that the events of ordinary reality were arbitrary. Langer's fear of "collapse into chaos
should our ideation fail" is strong. We are a built-in function of delineation, defining, delimiting, constructing by
ordinary consensus a tight little island in a sea of apparent
randomness. This is genetically, psychologically, and inherently, the strongest motivation we have, the skeleton of
our minds, egos, ways of being. To threaten it is worse
than death. The crack in the egg is no small threat.

Don Juan exerted all his dramatic abilities and knowledge to maneuver Carlos into just the position where his
certainty that the reality of everyday life is implicitly "real"
would be undermined. Only the complete collapse of that
certainty could remove the last barrier to accepting the existence of separate but equal realities, those realities of
"special consensus." The component elements of ordinary
reality could be denied and thus open to restructuring.
Carlos sensed in this that there was no guarantee that he
could "provide himself indefinitely with consensus," and
this abyss of apparent chaos drove him back into the broad
stream.

The break with ordinary consensus is thus profoundly
serious. This is what Jesus meant when he said that we
must give up our life to find greater life, and that while the
animals had a definite place, the Son of Man had none.
Such cures for psychic ills are strong medicine, no matter
how sick the patient.

Jesus could exert great sway in an event of the moment,
but was frustrated that the import of his maneuvers faded
from his followers' awareness. His followers centered their

faith in his personality, while *his* constant aim was to center their faith in the function of faith itself. His problem was similar to that of transference in psychoanalysis. As a transference-agent he could catch his followers up in the restructuring of an event, but they could not see the transference function as itself the crack in the egg. They made the common error of idolatry—making Jesus into the source of magic. And it was the function of reality formation toward which Jesus pointed, toward which he tried to be "transparent."

No line can be drawn between what don Juan was, what he taught, and what his Way of Knowledge was. But *he* was not the end product; he considered himself impersonally in respect to his path. Similarly, only by making himself the focus of attention could Jesus reorganize the concept-percept structure of his followers and open them to the crack. Function and man appear synonymous because the function can only be pointed toward by *being* the function. There is no being except in a mode of being.

In Chapter VI, I mentioned the psychology professor walking the fire by holding the fakir's hand. Without the fakir as trigger, without seeing him actually walk, it is difficult to see how the professor could have been so seized. But the fakir was neither the reason for the phenomenon nor the bearer of magic. The restructuring ability was innately within the professor all along, a part of the very mechanism of his being.

Leonard Feinberg came away from Ceylon convinced that somehow the god Kataragama was an operative and real force within the accepted fourteen-mile radius of his temple. The dramatic events of the ceremonies were capped by peculiarly synchronous after-effects that disturbed Feinberg's western point of view as much as the fire-walking. The tough-minded scholar and the classical Christian react to this sort of thing with equal scorn, appropriate to their belief's esthetics. The scholar's contempt will be that a fortuitous congruence of events should be interpreted superstitiously, which means outside the accept-

ances of the scholar's own path. The Christian's scorn will
be that an efficacious god could be a viable fact within a
twenty-eight mile circle. Both scholar and Christian are
functioning in identical ways, just under different metaphor, and both are evading the mechanics of being.

Carlos never resolved his half-suspicion, half-conviction,
that the god Mescalito was somehow synonymous with the
peyote plant itself; that the unique quality of Mescalito was
within the properties of the hallucinogen in some independent way. He knew the hallucinogen of itself led nowhere. Aldous Huxley's experiences with mescalin, the
synthetic of peyote, bore not the faintest resemblance to
Carlos' experience. Carlos recognized the handiwork of
don Juan; but Mescalito's person and total experience
were not dismissible as just hallucination.

Those with ears to hear would understand. Jesus spoke
of his "Kingdom" as like a leavening, the kind the
housewife puts in her flour to give life to the inert ingredients. Only a tiny bit of leavening is needed to work and
raise large quantities of flour. Beware, though, Jesus
warned, of the leavening of the Pharisee, the world of legalistic split-thinking and rationale; and beware the leavening of Herod, the world of power battening on the
brother's blood, the final demonic, the forces of death. Beware because *all* leavenings work, all raise the flour, and
equally well. Leavening is ontological, neutral, impersonal,
natural. Jesus said that his "Father" judges not. God is the
function of leavening, not the capacity for choosing types
of leavening. Judgment is given to the "Son." Man
chooses, God responds automatically. That is the way the
process works. Don Juan said there was an infinite number
of paths, and that we should choose our paths with care.

It is not just fortuitous that the metaphors Jesus used to
describe both the way to and the resulting state of his
"Kingdom" show remarkable similarity to Hilgard's outline for hypnotic transfer. Reality-adjusted thinking was
Jesus' point of departure. He did not break with logic or
"law," the reasoning functions of mind. He spoke of per-

fecting logic in order to go beyond it. His child-metaphors have meaning only against an adult background. The first demand he makes is that the ego-centered, reality-thinking personality must be surrendered. Unless you hate your life you cannot follow where he goes—not just because ambiguity would result from trying to hold two orientations at once; more, unless you are willing to give up your world view structured from infancy, those concepts directing your percepts cannot be restructured.

An indeterminately-wide capacity for resynthesis is incorporated in the structure of our minds. This capacity is blocked, though, by the very system of logic which *must* be developed to structure the mind to the point where resynthesis is then possible. Paralleling Piaget and Hilgard makes this clear. No resynthesis is possible to us until an initial synthesis gives a ground on which to stand.

It is not just fortuitous that somewhere around age twelve logical development begins to firm up, and that this is the age of the archaic transformation rites. Neither is it fortuitous that this is the age when our educational system breaks down most seriously (try teaching in a junior high school), or that mythological overlay gave this as the setting for Jesus' first manifestations of seizure, and so on.

The material of the common domain, the clearing in the forest cons in process, must be the materials for synthesis, for there are no other materials. If a kingdom of heaven is desired, it must be synthesized from the available stuff. The world is no trivial illusion blocking a pure soul's vision of heavenly vistas. The world is the matrix from which all things must operate. To be realized, made real, is to be born into the world. In order to be in the world, one's world view must shape according to the shape of that world. The logical process of structuring the mind into a modified relation with the world of man may be arbitrary, but it brings about the only reality available. Any restructuring is then equally arbitrary, a matter of choice and commitment, but it is a restructuring.

There are many forms of trance-thinking, and every

system or discipline incorporates some aspect of it. Sometimes this state is only a temporary lowering of the threshold of the logical mind to incorporate a new experience not available to logic. Recall Hans Selye's observation that every great scientific postulate-illumination had *happened* to the scientist in a hypnogogic state. With don Juan, the new states created were entered into for adventure, becoming as valid as the ordinary reality, little by little firming up into tangible structures, each building on the other. Don Juan's process imitated the way by which The Creation itself is brought about. The flaw in his system, and the probable reason for its obsolescence, was the ego-isolation within the construct. It gave only a private world.

With Jesus the same function is used, but only as a shared venture. Creating only *interventions* in the common domain, one remained *in* the world, the "larger body of man" was kept intact. His "interventions in the ontological constitution of the universe" were on two levels. The first was when the logical process broke down, as in conflicting personal relations or when logical choice had created insoluble problems, and the crack was opened as a way down and out. This was "forgiveness." No problem was "solved" as such, in some brilliant logical analysis. Rather, the situation was simply retructured, giving a clean slate, a new possibility for synthesis. The procedure could be repeated infinitely, there was no heavenly hierarchy of value judgment determining its granting. The only criterion was that the materials had to be surrendered *for* the resynthesis. Since no logical prestructuring was possible, it was an unknown venture each time, a kind of "little death" as Blake called it.

The second category of intervention was the ordinary cause-effect mechanisms of reality. Without fire burning, charcoal-broiled steaks are not possible, nor the joy of the hearth. There are times of ultimate concern, though, when a way down and out from this universal mechanism is needed. When the ordinary mechanics break down or lead to destructive results, disease, disaster, and so on, the crack is needed to restructure events. Since the ordinary mechanics are infinitely contingent, accident is inevitable. But the crack opens to that mode of thinking itself infinitely contingent, and capable of infinite synthesis. The way down and out is an instantaneous restructuring of some isolated, specific point of relation, a carrying of the non-ordinary to the ordinary, and an equally instantaneous establishment of the ordinary mechanics. Hypnotic anaesthesia is a minor case in point. Blood circulation and nerve response are vital mechanisms—else the whole house of cards tumbles down—but in certain instances can be suspended as needed.

The end goal of don Juan's way was adventure. The end goal of Jesus' way was solving problems of individual and society in the shared adventure of group life. Interventions are made only to correct, alleviate, fill out the inevitable shortcomings of a system limiting an infinitely openness to specific actualities. The crack in the egg was utilized only for the good of the egg, never for self. But since the self is also the egg at some point, the self was taken care of peripherally and automatically by caring for the egg. "Man, if you know what you are doing" (when you use the crack), "you are blest."

It would have been a neat system. It could have achieved the unity of man in the only practical way—attainment of desire for every man. It would have been rather a universal mutual-back scratch, through which all our itches, beyond personal reach, could be tended. It would have been a massive *power for,* rather than our current demonic and fragmenting *power against.*

Cracks in the egg cannot be built into a cosmic egg. They can only come about when the embryonic form expands and needs room beyond its genesis. The crack is found by the time-tested technique found in all systems, of necessity, the only one that works: a repeating of the initial process of world view formation. A surrender is made as a "child" to a father-figure who gives sureness and confidence that one *can* give over his life, his conceptual framework, to the image and receive it back enlarged.

In all education, *metanoia,* or change of concept, there is some form of duplication of this world view structuring. Those whose initial experiences, of entry into fantasy and return to reality with their parents, were rewarding may have an edge here. Perhaps we can see why education fails so sadly; why there are at best mostly technicians and too few physicists; why "hardness of heart" may be built in from infancy.

It is not fortuitous that Jesus used the father-figure as his symbol for transference, neither is it just an echo of Old Testament archaisms—which it very soundly is, in spite of Harvey Cox, and for good reason. Nor is it at all just coincidence that Jesus used the child-metaphor for the subject making the transference.

The symbol of transference determines the nature of the resulting hierarchy of mind. Sadly, I will never know don Juan and so can never experience his Path of breathless wonder. When Jesus said "no man comes to the Father but through me" he was simply stating this very case. His "father" is a very specialized and carefully-delineated symbol of transference designed to give that "loosing on earth" that we want "loosed in heaven."

Both the systems of don Juan and Jesus were end products of ancient cultural drifts. Don Juan's was so completely developed that no innovations were possible within it. Don Juan was the remnant of an ancient though disappearing culture. Jesus was the culmination of a long-building synthesis, incorporating his own culture and even beyond. "Before Abraham was, I am," indicates an "inflation of the psyche" seized by an archetypal imagery long in building. He was the *Eureka!* illumination of a long process of synthesis brought to fruition through extremes of cultural crisis. He was the focal point of a passionate quest centuries in building, and the translator of the answer into the common domain.

In our day we tend to dismiss suggestions of "unconscious" cultural forces, since we deny properties of mind other than those of an electrochemical, biological nature. This notion makes it difficult for us to understand culture in general. Only recently have anthropologists broken from this narrow and pedantic error. An unconscious exchange is apparent between Carlos and don Juan, and the suggestive force of that exchange went far *beyond* the person of don Juan. This contributed to Carlos' perplexity about the reality of Mescalito. Recall Cohen's observation that under LSD the Freudian patient immediately reflected and thus verified the analyst's assumptions. An indeterminably ancient set of archetypal assumptions and "sets of expectancy" underlay don Juan's Way of Knowledge. As with Jesus, Carlos sowed a wind—and reaped a whirlwind.

A cultural hierarchy, represented as the Two Brothers, directed the contents of the aboriginal Dream-Time. No syntheses outside the cultural set of expectancies ever resulted; there was no antisocial behaviour. A cultural hierarchy directed the Balinese in their seizures. The material for the restructurings had been automatically absorbed as part of the overall cultural conditioning. A strict protocol controlled the content of the seizures. The trance state never led to antisocial behaviour.

A cultural synthesis was the "hierarchy" in Jesus' *metanoia*. His "father-symbol" was the sum total of the human venture. As Bruner said, life creates myth and finally imitates it. Jesus, seized by the catalytic synthesis of the long quest, translated the answer in flesh and blood, giving a concrete symbol of the new cultural synthesis. He set up the expectancies for new possibility and gave the pattern for the best representation we could make of life for the best mirroring response. He used dramatic restructurings of ordinary reality as examples of the possibilities— whenever he could find a person willing to suspend an ordinary world view and enter into a subset with him. He used these restructurings as don Juan did with Carlos, to try to show the arbitrary character of ordinary reality, and the equality of other possibilities. He emphasized a decorum and respect for the world, while yet giving a criterion for deciding when you should "hate" this world and break with its statistics and employ the non-statistical openness.

Don Juan was contemptuous of those who would try halucinogens without the proper disciplines. In the same way, the logical processes of mind, the disciplines, "law or judgment" in terms of his day, were never evaded by Jesus. Unless your "righteousness exceeded that of the Pharisees and lawyers," you would never get through to the crack in the egg. Dissolution of ordinary consciousness, or isolation in non-ordinary states, plays no part in Jesus' system since the entire concentration of "obligatory acts" is on one's fellow man. This kept the follower *in* the world, while hopefully not of the world.

A new hierarchy of concept, such as don Juan's or Jesus', organizes the new kind of reality event, but only on the spot, so to speak, out of the materials given from the ordinary context of reality. There is small probability of finding out what the new reality is like *first* and then deciding to try a switch of allegiance. The forest shapes according to the light of the clearing. In scheming out the possibility of an "after life," Jesus realized there could be no such thing *a priori* to his actions. He would have to go and "prepare a place" in that "house of many mansions," the open possibility of synthesis.

The systems of don Juan, Jesus, and other cracks in the egg produce unique events not available to the non-committed person. Fire-walking can be observed by others, but the walking itself is another matter. With don Juan, becoming the process was the only way to discover what it was about. The same holds for Jesus. The rewards of the system could not be displayed to a non-believer to convince him that the plunge was worth the risk. A person had to *enter into* creation of the state in order to share in it. That is why healing stood a good chance of being a bridge over the gap in Jesus' time. There were simply not many rivals. And this is why healing stands far less chance of bridging the gap today. *Agreement* between two or three on what is being done is the key. Agreement is freedom from ambiguity. Double-mindedness fragments.

Ignored to this day by Christian orthodoxy is that Jesus was *helpless* to create non-ordinary events unless his hearers surrendered their hierarchy of mind to him, at least for the moment and at least in regard to the problem at hand. Jesus could trigger a "special consensus" about reality, and so change events, among those who had *nothing to lose,* those country dwellers and city poor, those crippled and diseased without hope, those whose world was terrible enough to make the risk of suspension of ordinary criteria, with its overtones of a "collapse into chaos," the lesser of evils. Things were different indeed with the clever intellectuals, the people in power, the "doctors of law." "Hardness of heart" is as much indicative of success within an established system as it is some sort of moral failure. No one abandons a game which he is winning. Jesus pities the rich young ruler unable to grasp the new reality because he could not let go of the old. Can you imagine Richard Nixon becoming an apprentice to don Juan?

The empty category can be filled, but it must first be created. Long centuries of sacrifice by hook-swinging took place in India before broken by that believer seized by the notion that he really *was* the temporary incarnation of the god, as the priests had represented for centuries. Once that notion had been realized, dramatically concretized and made real, no bodily harm ever came again to the "victim." The mythos leads the logos.

Don Juan had entered a firmly-established path through a long and hard apprenticeship to his own benefactor. No such system was handed Jesus. His illumination was probably symbolic, of necessity, as was Kekule's hypnagogic imagery giving rise to the benzene ring hypothesis, for instance. The genius of the man was called into play to translate the experience into reality. A high degree of improvisation and innovation is found in Jesus' sayings and actions. Hugh Schonfield brilliantly portrayed this venture in his *Passover Plot,* though in another work I have contended with him on several points.

The common materials of common reality had to be Jesus' materials for translation since the common world was his focus of concern and since there *was* no other material. The Greek-Stoic perversion of Jesus' imagery has projected his magnificent display of courage and genius onto an "out there" Olympus. To translate the imagery of his *Eureka!* into a communicable form, however, Jesus had to *be* that imagery, act it out, give it flesh-and-blood reality, fill the empty category with the only material available, himself, knowing that the average man can grasp concepts only as a concrete, workable image is given him.

Recognizing that "what we loose on earth is loosed in heaven," Jesus tried to give the *kind* of loosing we should do, the kind of representation we *should* make of God, or life, if we want the non-judging mirroring process of reality to work to our best advantage. It was a purely practical, pragmatic venture. He set up a pattern of representation, an image of transference, a pivot for restructuring, by which we can, "becoming as little children," achieve a new hierarchy of mind, a way down and out to freedom from fate.

On the other hand, he recognized and warned that *any* representation of God or life was *true* insofar as believed in. Any leavening fills the flour. Kataragama is as true and real as his Hindu followers. He works. Science works. Carlos found Mescalito a functional fact.

The unknown continuum of potential, the dark forest with its circles *ad infinitum,* the large category of the unknown, rains on just and unjust alike. This function "judges not." Any question asked with ultimate seriousness merges into this unjudging ultimacy and tends to express itself. Any sowing enters this contingency and tends to set up its own reaping. Any world view organizes a world-to-view. Any representation of God produces accordingly. Understanding and accepting responsibility for this function can make us free.

The whole character of don Juan's or Jesus' system was interlocking. The only way by which the ally could be brought about in the mind was by surrender and commitment to the initial transference figure, who was also the content of imagery by which the synthesis could organize. Recall how P. W. Martin's *Experiment in Depth* carried its own materials for synthesis. The same self-verifying procedure takes place in physics.

Fasting entered into Jesus' Way as it does in all non-ordinary systems. His forty-day fast in the wilderness, duplicated in our day from necessity by marooned travelers, was the way of breaking with the world of necessities and statistics. Fasting bypasses the logical blocks. Jesus refused food, saying he had nourishment his followers knew nothing about. Don Juan commented casually that food would not be needed for their several days' trip to the mountains where they would be guests of the god Mescalito. The ways of the world would not be essentials when one had opened to the ways of the god. Don Juan never made an issue of the two- and three-day fasts that preceded new steps along his path, such was simply a natural part of the tradition.

To move against the certainties and energies of "the world" calls for an equally sure conviction and a concentration on balance of mind. To center all the forces on the restructuring of an ordinary event in a non-ordinary way called for exceptional organization of self.

Jesus *sighs heavily* as he goes to raise Lazarus. In his growing and reckless confidence, he delayed two days, not only to make sure Lazarus would be dead but to gather the forces of mind necessary to illustrate this extreme example of the "glory of God," the open-ended potential of being. Jesus *sighs heavily* as he moved to heal the deaf man. The fire-walker *sighs heavily* as he walks to the pit of fire. There is a childlike quality in bringing the dream state through the crack to fruition. Such an inner state is balanced by a tough and resilient clarity of mind in the outer self. One is like a lamb to the inner spirit but like a fox to the outer world. This is the balance of mind.

As with don Juan's "ally," Jesus' "Holy Spirit" would instruct in the "right way to live." This "instruction" was only a synthesis of the instant moment itself, however, not any sort of foreknowing. The "ally" is only a catalyst acting on all parts of the immediate context. In Jesus' move-for-the-world this means all those other persons who are also the autistic, also the "father son"; they also contain the kingdom of heaven within them. To prestructure, or "take thought of the morrow," would set up logical blocks of expectancy preventing free synthesis. The synthesis would of necessity have to include the instant moment of, and move for, all parts of the context equally, since all parts are equally the context to the non-judging autistic.

Eternity is still in love with time. The desires arising out of time are the organizing nucleus for whatever "eternity" might be. In every case of Carlos' meeting with Mescalito, the god could only ask: "What do you want?" Jesus promised his followers: "Whatever you ask in my name will be given you."

"What do you want?" is the only question eternity can ask of time, and it is our divine gift to answer by asking our own question. Desire, passion, curiosity, longing, novelty, daring, creativity, productivity, lust for life, ecstasy, joy, adventure, all these are the highest thrusts of life, the most divine of attributes, the most sacred of possessions. And all these have been the attributes *mistrusted* and *condemned* by that dark priesthood probing for control, domination, and battening on the brother's blood. Without these seeds from time, however, without these vital gametes from the larger body of man, the womb of eternity is barren.

In another study I have attempted a defense of Jesus as a genius with radically new ideas, an evolutionary *Eureka!* development by which life tried to develop a new aspect of potential. I have tried to outline how completely the massive "failure of nerve" of that period, epitomized in Stoicism, and seen by Singer to have destroyed early science, was the victor in the struggle for man's mind. This same failure of nerve is the very psychological contradiction dominant today, the perennial cause of the split mind. This frozen logic of Stoicism not only triumphed but then incorporated the imagery of Jesus, inverting and negating his entire thrust. Thus was the "rushing torrent of the river of God" turned into a "broad but feeble stream" called Christendom, to use Edwin Hatch's metaphor.

One or two comments by Augustine, that final death-knell of Jesus' Way, indicate how the symbols of the Way had been absorbed into Greek logic until indistinguishable. Writing of the Stoic Seneca for instance, Augustine exclaimed: "What more could a Christian say than this Pagan has said?" Concerning the Platonists, Augustine stated that "the sole fundamental truth they lacked was the doctrine of the Incarnation." Since this "doctrine" was itself purely Greek, foreign to a Hebraic background and undetectable in the ideas, sayings, or actions of Jesus, we see how the new wine had long since been put in old skins.

Considering the world an immovable fated cycle, and man a tragic incidental on its surface, with God an abstract "pure essence" off in his ninth circle or wherever, the Greeks were unable to ask or hear a Job-like ultimate question. To the Greeks nothing could ever happen to the cosmic egg, only to incidental man. And to the Greeks, boxed in by their own logic, no answer came.

Stoicism rewrote Jesus' crack in the egg as a mythological once-for-all happening. Their projection placed the Way out of bounds for man. Thus man was really no longer responsible for his world, but only responsible to the priesthood organizing the dogma. The open-potential catalyst is completely unpredictable, and the forces of social control, feeding on predictability, quickly shut it out.

The "Will of God" shaped as the new metaphor for the old Greek Fate. The "Son of God" was no longer rational man; the "father" no longer the logos-shaping mythos, the symbol of transference; the "Spirit" no longer the threshold of mind; "God" no longer that divine-demonic, non-judging, amoral, raining on just and unjust alike, the hard taskmaster reaping where he sows not, doubling the talents, any talents, mirroring any desire, and crying "More! More! Less than all will never satisfy." By the Greek perversion these became Olympian figures rather than psychological symbols of ontology. They were abstracted from all reality. Jesus' Way, the greatest of human *Eureka!* ventures, became a fairy tale, a maudlin, ridiculous, pious fraud.

Actually, none of the accounts of Jesus' "non-ordinary" reality maneuvers need be discounted. A miracle is a nonordinary state in the don Juan, fire-walker sense, rather than in the Greek mythological fire-from-Olympus sense. Christendom has largely ignored Jesus' insistence that acts greater than his would be a product of his system. Based on Greek logic as it is, rather than on the non-structured and open Way, theology never understood or really believed in those happenings. Since miracles represented cracks in the egg beyond all probability, the self-styled guardians of the egg, determined to protect man *from* himself, projected those cracks into the nethermost regions of inaccessibility.

The "interventions in the ontological construct" attributed to Jesus and promised for his followers are as logical within *his* premise and system as are different reality states in don Juan's, fire-walking in the Hindu's, or atom bombs in the scientist's.

And surely, from the evidence I have tried to bring together in this book, it should be obvious why Hugh Schonfield's thesis of Jesus' taking a drug to simulate death so seriously misses the point, and places Schonfield, in spite of his remarkable work, squarely in the camp of those theologians he challenges. Such a notion of trickery on Jesus' part, double-mindedness of the first rank, would have automatically fragmented the very state of mind that was the *only* weapon Jesus had.

The technique, improbable as it sounds, by which one might open to this way even today has been outlined in this book. The Laski-Wallace-Bruner outline of creative thought (Chapter IV) is easily traced in Jesus' own seizure and translation, and was clearly established as the pattern for his followers. The reason for the similarity is simple—there is no other way for newness to come about. We are dealing with the ontological way of all things, not heavenly mysteries or occult secrets.

Surely the obstacles to any crack are many and formidable. The scientific allegiances are no more powerful checks than theologians—those standing at the gate preventing others from going through.

Greatest of the several tragedies of the Stoic inversion of Jesus, culminating in Christendom and still operative under various guises, was *representing God as reason,* considering God to be *rational*. Again, it is a case of projection. Reason and logic are the qualities of limitation and definition produced by man's conscious thinking. We are, to use religious imagery, "made in the likeness of God" in that non-logical, autistic mode of mind, the mode we cannot get at directly and manipulate, but which is closer than our very consciousness, the breath of life making all things real. God became only an extension of *man* through this classical view. This inverted view trusts only its own logic and mistrusts God's unruly and unpredictable characteristics which then are considered Satanic. The Classical view, as Blake and Northrop Frye point out, inverts the true situation and mistakes reality-thinking for the *autistic*, which is, ironically enough, claiming man to be god, the *very error* theologicans have been most strident in condemning. Down through the centuries they have been yapping at their own image in the mirror.

Man is the imaginative tool or technique by which life "thinks" in a rational, value-giving and limited way, selecting that which might be real. We have received only a mirroring of our own limitations, and have thus seen ourselves fated, by the Classical view. Calling God "Nature" has not changed the resulting fate. A change of metaphor will not make a bad idea good. To attribute human qualities to God is to have mirrored back *just this quality* of limitation, trapping us in our own logic.

The man who challenges: "If there *is* a God, why doesn't he do something about things?" must grasp that the part of mind thinking in this "why" kind of way is the rational mode of life, reasoning man. The closest thing there will ever be to a God responsible for the question is the *asker* of that question. The capacity to fill empty categories is not selective, or the breeder of categories. "God's mode" for thinking selectively is *man*.

There is no magician up there pulling strings if his whim and fancy can just be tickled by the right words. There is no Moral Governor of the Universe, no oriental tyrant able to grant amnesty if we can but find flattering enough incantation. There is no divine mind with beautiful blueprints. There is no super-computer behind the scenes able to out-figure the statistics if we could but hit on the right combination to trigger the mechanism.

The formative process of life is non-ambiguous since it is equally all possibilities. Any non-ambiguous idea becomes an organizing point for realization in this process. Ordinary logical thinking is ambiguous and enters only indirectly as one of an infinite number of random contingencies which may or may not be decisive. Non-ambiguous impressions and notions are generally "below the limen of feeling," and so appear to happen as fate when becoming points for formative realization. Fear, for instance, takes on an ultimate, non-ambiguous nature and tends to create that which is feared. Hatred is the same, trapping the hater in his own hell. A conscious, passionate, singleminded intensity tends to dampen out ambiguity and achieve a realization. Ultimate ideas in that "secret place of mind," the rock-bottom of real belief, shape one's ground of being.

We *must* become aware of the force of mind and develop a balance between the modes of thinking. The materials for achieving this wholeness have been in the common domain for two millenia now, though continuously evaded by our failure of nerve. The current dilemma allows no further evasion. Langer's "boldness of hypothesis" is not just desirable but crucial for survival.

Surely we see each nation groping for protection in this present nightmare, and each further developing the capacity to obliterate all life. But this is merely making outward and evident an inner condition previously projected "out there" as fate. We are finally confronting the mirror of our true selves—we are that fate. We are in our own hands.

Our leaders, placed in positions of power, immediately succumb *to* that power and speak of "dealing from positions of strength," which translates into power *over* and *against*—a desire to be God. The great hopefulness exhibited by that long-gone America of the Marshall Plan and the young United Nations, moving for others as the best protection for ourselves, has been eclipsed in a mirroring of our adversary's paranoia. Now we find that it is we ourselves, not that perpetual enemy, who are considered the "nightmare of the world," as Toynbee plainly called us.

We could have risked our lives to serve and been saved. Inflated with power we have succumbed to don Juan's first stumbling block. We have undergone a temptation in the wilderness, hideously failed, and ironically claimed divine sanction for our folly. What will we do about total power, for soon we will all have it   not just the "most powerful and richest nation on earth," but even these tiny and backward nations whose faces we have ground in the dust of our concupiscence and lust. Soon they, too, will hold the trigger to our mutual demise. What then? Having cast our bread on the waters it will surely be returned. Sowing, we must surely reap. Nothing can mitigate the mirroring we subject ourselves to—nothing but turning from this path that has no heart, this path that can only kill.

Invested in a furtherance of life's thrust toward awareness and expansion of potential, our power could lead to stars and all the "joys and pleasures" in them if we so desired. Used against ourselves to prove our "leadership," to prove that we cannot be pushed around, all development will cease. Power will become ultimately demonic, and this little venture into awareness, in this little corner of infinity, will simply cease to be. Don Juan and Jesus understood this—stood under and responsibly accepted—within their own framework of imagery and representation. And we need their understanding.

We face new situations—but new techniques are arising. Through these current ventures, briefly mentioned in this book, we are creating pieces for this new puzzle, and we will yet fit them together into an even larger image of man. The picture must encompass those pieces already created, however, for it is only by placing one foot firmly in the past that .we have firm ground for a step into the future. Our emerging picture will find its true dimension, in that frame of continuity encompassing our total heritage. Our next step will hinge on opening to the total process of mind and that means that shadowy area encompassing the whole development of psyche. In Jesus, and even don Juan, we find such symbols for the larger body of man. Triggered through such imagery of the total man, the *autistic* process can synthesize from that enormously rich trial and error understanding reaching through the whole thinking phylum of our living earth.

Do you not see why balance of mind and the non-ambiguous process can only be utilized by passionately holding to some symbol of *wholeness,* a symbol that stands equally for *all* parts of the process itself—which means the absolutely other to us, the neighbor? Do you not see why anything *less* fragments us and isolates us in our surface limitations? Do you not see how logical thinking, in order to even function, must limit to a specific, and that this specific is then the only apparent reality—and how this fragmented form of thinking then orients' quite naturally around the notion of *scarcity,* the idea that in order to *have* we must take from and deprive others, since only a limited amount can be seen? Do you not see that fragmented thinking turns all others into potential enemies, until we live, as Northrop Frye said, as armed crustaceans, damned to a perpetual alarm and crisis, where life itself is a threat to life? Can you not see that opening to the whole mind must open to a constant yield always sufficient, always ample? The cause of the need is the cause of the fulfillment of the need. The empty category is an ontological function. Stepping out into nothingness is impossible—though nothing can be seen, something always forms underfoot. Our universe is not a fixed and frozen machine grinding out in entropy. It can always be what we have need of it to be. The eternal mental life of God and Man has enough to go around—eternally round and round—by moving for and not against.

The new directions outlined here in my book can be seen as harbingers of a new and larger season in our own cycle, and we will manage, I do believe, to hold through this winter of confused discontent. Leonard Hall, Carlos Castaneda, Lévi-Strauss, Polanyi, Hilgard, Bruner, Langer, and all the rest—these tend toward recognition of the arbitrary character of reality. There is a growing acceptance of Carl Jung's understanding of mind, though his insights are adopted under different imagery, and his genius not credited as the source. The impressive impact of Teilhard de Chardin may well resist attempts by cyclic thinkers to warp his illumination into their deadly circles. Parapsychology suggested a direction, but a more tangible and "scientific" approach will probably be the key, since this is the path already taken. The scientific tool may well prove the bridge, but even so there will come a time when such intermediary devices and projection techniques are obsolete. Such a transition will be gradual and natural; one stage will fuse easily into the other. We may always be simply "discovering Nature's Laws."

In Berkeley, California, for instance, the Carnegie Institute has pioneered a program for developing a kind of free intuitive creativity in young children. The young child is presented with problem-filled adventure readings, situations *without* formal, logical conclusions, where no prestructured logical "answer" exists, even in the minds of the creators of the system. The child has to create a "solution" freely in order to continue the adventure, and the self-motivated technique avoids those arbitrary absolutes which act as constricting, goal-oriented motivations in ordinary education. With no *a priori* answer, and no outside criteria, the child develops a trust and confidence in an inner, open logic too often stifled by formal schooling. Developing this free-synthesis capacity has led, in turn, to impressive leaps of the intelligence quotient itself—that questionable gauge of reality-thinking.

The whole experiment is a gesture toward bridging the modes of mind, and the results could reach beyond science fiction. We may yet see the day when the tragedy of school is overcome.

Prophetic, in a Teilhardian way, was Arthur C. Clarke's little mythos-fantasy, *Childhood's End.* Here science and all intermediate mechanisms of projection had finally given way to a direct "intervention in the ontological constitution of the universe." There was an absorption and loss of individuality implied in Clarke's little dream, reminiscent of a problem never solved by Teilhard. But there was also an odd, if strained, similarity between Clarke's extrapolation and that "coming again in glory" of Jesus' misplaced and misunderstood Apocalypse.

For now the kind of non-ambiguous thinking demanded by a don Juan or a Jesus seems highly improbable. Too many priesthoods have too tight a control and domination over our fragmented minds. That *Childhood's End* wherein we might "level this lift to rise and go beyond" will have to encompass, perfect, and make obsolete a vast number of brilliant but restricting disciplines. We will have to become more righteous than a host of Pharisees, but we will get around these stumbling blocks by the only creative method—which is "agreeing quickly with your adversary," the way to use stumbling blocks as stepping stones.

As for myself, however, today is the day, and I dare not wait for some slow cultural drift finally to pave the way that I might easily float into some nebulous social salvation. I cannot depend on "them" "out there" to order into coherency this small sphere of my only present now. And I find, fortunately, that the process of reality remains unchanged. Ultimate allegiance to a symbol of openness really does open things. The search for the proper materials, the passionate intensity, the decorum and respect, the willingness to be dominated by that desired, leads now as always to the needed synthesis. The fusion still arcs across the gap—the crack surely follows.

If some single, lonely reader is desperate enough, and "hates" an obscenely mad world sufficiently to give it up and open his mind to a restructuring for love *of* that world, things can be different for him, even now. And if he could find two or three to gather with him and agree on what was mutually needed, in this highly-specialized form of agreement even more things could be different. That—strangely—is the way, and the only way by which the broad social drift itself will ever be changed for the better.

So I would urge you to remember, when the forces of despair and destruction hedge you round about, that you need not succumb to their dark statistics. The non-statistical is even here—closer than your very self, and it is yours, and it works. The relation of mind and reality has been but dimly grasped—surely only hinted at in these pages of mine—but even these brief glimpses are blinding. As Whitman said "I am ever shutting sunrise out of me, lest sunrise should kill me." And surely we must channel with care, and take our waking slow, for even in these tentative gestures of ours, outlined here, even in this our infancy of awareness—people *do* walk fire. We *are* an open possibility.

JAMES W. BOYD
The Teachings of Don Juan from a Buddhist Perspective

Whether they are "fiction" of the Hermann Hesse type or scholarly studies of Mexican Indian shamanism, the fact that Carlos Castaneda's three volumes have found thousands and hundreds of thousands of buyers in the U.S.A. is evidence of today's increasing interest in mysticism. Cas-

taneda, readers will recall, spent years—or so he says—
under the tutelage of an old Yaqui sorcerer whom he calls
Don Juan. His account of that experience—in *The Teachings of Don Juan: A Yaqui Way of Knowledge* (T), *A Separate
Reality: Further Conversations with Don Juan* (S), and *Journey
to Ixtlan: The Lessons of Don Juan* (J)—won him an M.A.,
and eventually a Ph.D. in anthropology from the University of California at Los Angeles.

My concern is not to dispute the factualness of Castaneda's reports but rather to define the fundamental motifs of the teachings he presents as Don Juan's. Though
these teachings are by no means identical with those of the
Buddhist tradition, there are remarkable parallels between them. And since of the two systems Buddhism is the
more familiar, a comparison of its tenets with Don Juan's
may clarify the latter.

A STATE OF DIS-EASE

The fundamental Buddhist assertion is that human existence is out of joint (Sanskrit *duhkha*). Where Judeo-Chris-
tianity asserts that life is fundamentally good (cf. the doctrine of creation), Buddhism declares that, ordinarily, to
live is to be ill at ease and that this state of dis-ease is inherent in the very structure of existence. Therefore it seeks to
provide a means of radically changing this undesirable experiential state for the better. Through the realization of
"insight wisdom" (*prajñā*), the individual who follows the
Buddhist path of discipline can attain true knowledge
(*dharma*). If he is fortunate, he will have a teacher to guide
him step by step, but basically he must depend on his own
efforts: he must "come and see" (*ehi paśyika*) for himself
what the Truth is. No one can give another the final
benefit of his experience of knowledge, or describe that
experience to another who has not yet broken through the
structures of existence to Truth.

Although Don Juan's teachings are less metaphysical in
their import, his path of discipline, apparently based on an

evaluation of life similar to Buddhism's, prescribes techniques for altering this state of being quite radically. He points out that the only thing his apprentice Carlos knows is how to seek [negative feelings] (J, p. 221). Because most men take everything in the ordinary world as real and "for sure," they end up bored to death with themselves and with the world (J, p. 35). But men should deliberately seek well-being (J, p. 221)—should seek to live as happily as possible (J, p. 110; T, p. 158). He can attain well-being by becoming a *man of knowledge* and learning how to *see* (J, p. 233). Yet the only way one can "stop the world" of ordinary existence and break through to knowledge is by one's own efforts. Don Juan can be a guide, a teacher—he himself had a teacher; but Carlos will learn only as he follows the path himself.

BALANCING TERROR AND WONDER

Neither Don Juan nor the Buddhist offers a paradise on earth. Both admit that to live is to be condemned to a world of men (samsaric existence and T, p. 158). Even if a man succeeds in "stopping the world" in which he feels disoriented, he still remains subject to the common human lot—joy, pain, sadness, struggle (J, p. 138; S, p. 33) What the Path of the Buddha and the Yaqui Way of Knowledge offer is the artistry of a significant life style which brings the realization of Nirvana into ordinary life and balances ["the terror . . . with the wonder . . ."].

Both Don Juan and the Buddhist castigate man's dishonesty about life's limitations. The only thing that is real, the Yaqui says, "is the being in you that is going to die" (J, p. 239), for no man's life will continue indefinitely (J, p. 110). The fact of life's impermanence should not only be acknowledged; it should also be a constant corrective to misperceptions and misaligned values. Don Juan urges Carlos to focus his attention on the link between his own life and his own death (J, p. 112), to use his death as an adviser (J, p. 55) in establishing each moment's life. Don

Juan's meaning is vividly illustrated when he recommends
to Carlos that one way to help a friend of his who is having
trouble raising a nine-year-old boy is to advise the friend
to have his boy touch the corpse of a dead child. [The boy
has to see a totally different world after such a confrontation.]

The Buddhist says that because of his impermanence,
man anxiously tries to construct a mental world (*mithyā
dṛṣṭi*) in which he feels more comfortable even though that
world is based on ignorance (*avidyā*). Thus he devises religious systems which posit an eternal God who has the power to bestow eternal life upon man; or else he conceives of
himself as already possessing an eternal soul. Or again, if
he is more secular-minded, he eschews the notion of soul
in favor of a common-sense metaphysic and develops an
understanding of himself as a personality that is real, as a
self who experiences a certain continuity through space
and time.

But the Buddhist questions the reality of a limited, temporary self and, even more, of an eternal soul-essence. He
asks: Does one have a direct experience of a body, sensations, perceptions and conscious mental activity (*skandhas*)?
All these "parts" make up the "self," but there is no experience of a "self" as such, just of parts. Or the Buddhist asks:
What is a room? Answer: A room is an ordered combination of a floor, walls, ceiling and, probably, a door. But
again these are "parts." What is "roomness" itself? One can
only define "room" in terms of its component parts. Hence
the realization that the word "room" is simply that, a word
or concept, an intellectual tool for designating a certain aggregation of parts. Likewise with the word "self": it is a
mental construct used to designate a certain aggregation
of parts—body, sensations, perceptions, etc. And these
"parts," in turn, are abstractions referring to other com-
binations of other aggregates. "Body" is merely a broad re-

ference to a combination of bone, blood, flesh, etc. But to suppose that because there is a mental referent "self" or "body" there is in fact a self or body is to commit a basic error, the fallacy of misplaced concreteness. In this nominalistic manner the Buddhist teaches that the world the ordinary man considers real is only a mental tapestry into which he has woven himself and, in consequence, has lost sight of the true world of experience.

Don Juan, similarly, views man as recoiling from the fact of his own death by constructing mental schemes which "establish" important, permanent "realities." In his attempts to undermine Carlos's deeply imbedded sense of self-importance and reality, Don Juan often mentions Carlos's own death and says he is puzzled how anyone can feel so important when he knows death is stalking him (J, p. 55)—not only to get rid of his self-importance but to "drop" his personal history. Don Juan says of his own life [that he has no past; deciding he did not need it, he moved methodically "to chop it off . . ."] (J, p. 29).

Our strong attachment to our own personal history, to our "selves," is simply one facet of our attachment to the world which we and our teachers from childhood have constructed. In fact, Don Juan asserts, the [common reality of our perception is only perceived as it has been described for us (J, pp. 8, 302), so that, interpreting it moment by moment on that basis, we mold it into an unnatural form (J, pp. 9, 95)]. Imposing conventional interpretations on "raw experience," thinking in categories (cf. Kant) in order to arrange sense data, is what Don Juan calls *doing*. We continually, consciously, intentionally *do* this, and then (committing the fallacy of misplaced concreteness) suppose it to be the real world marked by ill-being and confusion. It is *doing* that makes the world what it is for us (J, p. 227), Don Juan says; and to make his point he tells Carlos as they sit in a restaurant [that the two of them were constantly participating in the actual creation of their immediate surroundings, including "the *doing* in this room . . ."] (J, p. 252). Continuing to use a metaphor similar to the Buddhist metaphor "chain of being," Don Juan asserts that from birth [we possess "rings of power" which are "hooked to the *doing* of the world"] (J, p. 252). In other words, we think we perceive the world as happening to us, we think it is outside man and he experiences it, when in fact it is the projection of categories, a something we *do,* not a something happening to us.

REVERSING THE WHEEL OF LIFE

Like Don Juan, the Buddhist considers man's mental world of description a stubborn barrier to the attainment of real experience, of insight knowledge. And like Don Juan, he has a technique for breaking through conceptual categories; namely, by exposing the disciple to a new description of the world—a radically different experiential world in which the perceptual interpretations of ordinary phenomena are inapplicable. The result is a gradual undoing of the rigid and binding limitations of normal perception—a process the Buddhist calls "turning back the wheel of life" (*bhavacakra*)

A characteristic Indian Buddhist technique for reversing the wheel of life is called "dharmic analysis." Basically, this is an extension of the type of analysis noted above, which analyzes "self" and "body" into component parts. Critically examining each of the so-called parts of the phenomenal world, the Buddhist discovers that all phenomena initially supposed to be real are in fact a combination of still smaller "parts," which in turn are simply abstractions for other units. As the analysis continues beyond the empirical realm, a theory of the "atomic" structure of all phenomena results. All phenomena are made up of *dharmas* ("atomic units"). Even the dharmas, however, are not substantial self-existents; rather, they too are designations for a composite of smaller, conditioned and interdependent parts (*pratītya samutpāda*). All phenomena appear to be empty (*śūnya*) of any identifiable permanent essence.

Dharmic analysis is not merely an academic exercise; it is

meant to be a deliberate, attentive mode of behavior. Through it the Buddhist seeks to empty himself of emotional-mental perceptual patterns, of all those "realities" we call rooms, selves, bodies, trees, etc. Then, continually practicing not-seeing "trees," he begins to alter and remold his basic patterns of response and enters a radically different experiential world. No longer is he viewing "persons," "trees" or whatever; he has *undone* that world of description which is no longer applicable to his new world.

ACTION IN NONACTION

Taoist and East Asian Buddhists (Chinese Ch'an and Japanese Zen) follow a different technique for acquiring a new description of the world. Rather than undertaking a detailed analysis of all phenomena into separate parts, they undo the world by attempting to tune into the natural, spontaneous flow of events. This type of not-doing, called *wei-wu-wei* (action in nonaction), is often effected by dwelling on aspects of phenomenal existence which one normally does not consider. Rather than seeing a bowl as a container, one is referred to the "emptiness" of the bowl which allows it to serve its purpose. The "hole" in the middle of the wheel rather than the spokes, the "shadows" of the valley rather than the high mountains, are the mental referents which allow the Taoist to undo his normal mental preoccupations and gradually enter into another descriptive dimension. The seeming paradox here, as in the Indian Buddhist technique, is that abandoning oneself to another mode of perception requires deliberate effort.

Don Juan's techniques for stopping the world are shamanistic variations on those of the Buddhists and Taoists. While his use of psychotropic plants finds no parallel in Buddhist tradition, drugs are not the only avenue for communicating his teachings (J, pp. 7-8). Seeking to lead his apprentice to the experiential realization of a new description of the world, he tells Carlos on one occasion to perceive attentively a porous rock. Focus on details, he says, in order to reduce the world and eventually enlarge it in a new perspective. Carlos examines the rock and reports that, in the small area where his eyes were focused, the detail [became so clear and well-delineated to him that he began to see a "vast world," until Don Juan deliberately cut off his focus and the rock once again assumed the blurred features of an inconsequential aspect of ordinary reality] (J, p. 237). Don Juan calls this technique a form of *not-doing.* Focusing on the details of a rock is similar to dharmic analysis in that it begins with a deliberate mental effort to discriminate details which make up the rock. When Carlos begins to construct a perception of a more significant whole, Don Juan interrupts. He blocks the light to prevent his apprentice from getting lost in a new vision which itself would need to be dissipated by further analysis. For through mental habit Carlos ahd begun to turn *not-doing* into doing (J, p. 236), into making another world.

On another occasion Don Juan tells Carlos to focus on the shadows of the leaves on one single branch of a tree, and then, eventually, without letting his eyes go back to the leaves, on the whole tree, thus allowing his body to *not-do* (J, p. 217). Carlos reports [the striking impact of being able to arrange the shadows into a whole in the same way that he "normally grouped the foliage . . ."] (J, pp. 217-218). Note here that Carlos's attempt to "group" the dark masses of shadows underscores once again how routine and habitual our patterns of perceptual response are and how difficult it is to uproot them. The technique used to overcome that response is similar to the Taoist-Buddhist technique for accomplishing *wei-wu-wei.* Carlos observed shadows—i.e., the recessive, dark, passive and shadowy aspects of ordinary phenomena—in the effort to realize the mood of action-in-nonaction.

DISCARDING THE RAFT

Thus far, we have been considering methods, not final aims. In both Don Juan's view and Buddhism, a disciple or

apprentice who experientially enters into a radically different perceptual world in order to turn back the wheel of life
or stop the world has not necessarily attained "insight wisdom" or "seeing"; he is only on the brink of attaining it.
This stage in the path of the learner is the most difficult,
for he has to take the next step alone; the teachings can do
no more than lead him up to the point of breakthrough.
That is why the Buddhist stresses the importance of a
seeker's *vow* to attain Enlightenment; he must have utter
conviction to pursue the Path to the end. Don Juan calls
this conviction "spirit" and says it is indispensable if the apprentice is to go through all the hardships of learning to
become a "warrior" determined to gain real power (J, p.
26).

The Buddhist speaks of "killing the Buddha" at this
stage in the Path; that is, of discarding the raft of teachings
once it has helped the disciple to cross the river of ordinary life. The danger is that he will want to hold on to the
raft. But he must not. He must cast it aside, must empty
himself not only of the nominalistic, relativized description
of the world, but also of the teachings of the emptiness of
all things. Buddhist teachings are only techniques, *means*
to the attainment of wisdom, not definitions of the Real.
The Buddhist does not attempt to define the Real. He de-
nies the possibility of a definition by asserting that Nirvana
is samsara, that the state of Enlightenment *is* the state of
ordinary existence. Obviously, such an assertion puzzles
those of us who are grounded in the world of ordinary
perception.

Don Juan's teachings also are techniques. Once Carlos
has attained access to the world of sorcerers he is at the
end of his apprenticeship, and his teacher can offer him no
directive which would enable him to *see*. Don Juan even
warns Carlos not to get "pinned down" in this new, exciting and bizarre world (J, p. 300); rather, Carlos is to aim at
the "crack between the two worlds, the world of the diableros and the world of living men" (T, p. 195). In any case,
he says, "it really doesn't matter whether or not all this is

true" (J, p. 230). Carlos asks in amazement, "Do you mean that neither the world of ordinary men nor the world of sorcerers is real?" (J, p. 300). Don Juan answers, "They are real worlds." Yet it really does not matter if his answer is true or not, because *seeing* the final accomplishment—(J, p. 233), which is contrary even to sorcery (S, p. 204)—is not confined or defined by the terms of either of these two perceptual worlds. When one *sees* "there is no difference between things because there is no one there to ask about the difference" (T, p. 18). "*Seeing* makes one realize the unimportance of it all" (S, p. 24). Don Juan might just as well have said, "Nirvana *is* samsara."

The way of mysticism, then, is meant to lead to the same goal, whatever the techniques its travelers use. He who ventures into that way must "leave behind" an entire world, including the teachers whom he loved and who loved him. At the conclusion of Carlos Castaneda's latest book Don Juan, having said farewell, walks off without looking back at Carlos. The teacher's task has come to an end. From this point on, the true "warrior" or the bodhisattva must seek the goal unaided.

JOSEPH MARGOLIS
Don Juan as Philosopher

Carlos Castaneda's four books appeared serially but, once read, they cannot be viewed separately. In fact, with the appearance of each new book the remembered volumes come to acquire a tone anticipating their successors and the successor volumes display the unsuspected structure of their antecedents. There is no mystery in this. The point is pretty explicit in *The Strategy of a Sorcerer,* in the last book, *Tales of Power.* Don Juan says quite plainly that it is a recapitulation. He means it in an extraordinarily detailed way. But what this suggests is that the books were prepared or planned at the same time and in their own way form the basis for *our* apprenticeship to the magic presence of Don Juan through the sorcery of Carlos himself. The evidence of this each may find for himself simply by noting how, by the time he reaches the fourth volume, the sympathetic reader is prepared for whatever mystery or marvel Carlos recounts in spite of the fact that he cannot possibly understand the details of the sorcerer's exercises or explanations. Of course, to put matters this way is to be deliberately paradoxical—but not, I trust, perversely so. In effect it signals the unusual position of the reader, compellingly drawn and even enchanted by what Don Juan progressively discloses of an unfamiliar but apparently surrounding world.

It is essential to concede that the reader cannot understand the details and that he has actually been told so again and again—just as Don Juan tells Carlos that he cannot make him understand. He can only lead him to the Unknown. Before the disclosure of the "warrior's" final discovery, perhaps the work of the last two chapters of *Tales of Power*, no mere description could possibly be adequate since what is experienced is obviously so utterly alien; and within that experience (if it may even be called an experience) description proves to be utterly inadequate in principle. We are therefore reduced to being witnesses at a second remove· witnesses to the *tales* not the *acts* of a sorcerer (as Don Juan himself acknowledges: *Tales of Power*, p. 62).

Conceivably, some readers may have already sampled experiences rather like those that Carlos undergoes. Chances are, these are linked to the hallucinogens of his early training, which seem more designed to break the grip of his habitual conceptions than to dignify a drug culture as a self-sufficient mode of life. Obviously, as Carlos approaches the warrior state, the use of drugs recedes in importance and the direct discoveries of the later exercises are not available at all, in the sense that as readers we could hardly be a party to what obviously depends on the most rigorous, sustained, and arcane discipline. The usual association will be made with the great religious systems of the East, with Taoism perhaps or with Zen or Yoga, and one may well suppose that, both as a reader and as something of an initiate in those systems, one can readily understand the lessons that Don Juan has prepared for Carlos. But this view depends on two serious limitations: for one thing, one needs to know firsthand what Don Juan is teaching in order to confirm the resemblance (and we simply lack the evidence); for another, what Don Juan is teaching, where we can follow his instruction, must be the same as is offered in certain Oriental systems that are said to have discovered a hidden world behind the world (and that seems to be false—for reasons that go to the heart of Don Juan's distinctive teaching).

But this emphatically is not to detract from the compelling power of the books: they are in fact a "place of power" themselves, a setting for the contemplative exercises of a reader at a remove from the necessary site of full discovery. Why is this?

The answer is simply Don Juan. From the very moment that Carlos encounters him in a border town in Arizona, he becomes a formidable presence in the reader's life. Not as a fictional creation but as a compelling teacher who obliges one to review step by step with Carlos in his own transformation the details of whatever analogue of the warrior's apprenticeship to knowledge each of us can sustain. We are at a second remove but not from ourselves. There is a genuine longing to be worthy in Don Juan's eyes. In fact—I trust this is not just a personal confession—there is a palpable and very sweet sadness in coming to the close of each book in turn (spaced as their publication was) as if taking final leave again and again of a teacher who has strangely illuminated and dignified our own familiar lives by reference to an entirely original and ultimately unfathomable alternative—the "way of knowledge" of the Indian *brujo*.

Carlos seeks him out by chance, out of his preoccupation with medicinal plants. A year later he finds that he himself has been selected to be Don Juan's apprentice, and in retrospect we see that he had signaled his own readiness and aptitude from the first moment that he avoided Don Juan's eyes. There is surely a counterpart experience in the reader who returns, like Carlos himself, after a year or so's separation, from one set of conversations to another. The proof is in the structure of the books themselves. For example, the episode about the eyes is repeated in different ways in the first three books. In *The Teachings of Don Juan* we barely learn of Carlos's initial uneasiness and are plunged at once into the sort of superficially organized explorations that a focused student or a modern Western man might pursue: Everything is skewed by Carlos' preconceptions and interests; and indeed the closing "structural analysis" is as much a joke as evidence, in retrospect, of the impossibility of Carlos's continuing within the boundaries of ordinary reason. In *A Separate Reality* we return to the episode in the bus depot where the power of Don Juan's gaze is hinted at a little more explicitly now that the baffling evidence of the first conversations has been collected. In *Journey to Ixtlan* we return to the first full force of "that stupendous look" and its implications for Carlos' apprenticeship. Thus, in the same good-humored and patient way with which Don Juan tricks Carlos into reviewing his experiences, we ourselves are very gently led to understand the developing import of what we are just told. In *Tales of Power*, on the other hand, there is no Introduction at all. The account begins at once, with fresh details. Obviously, we ourselves have been waiting to pick up the thread of the conversation. So that when Carlos is finally introduced to the distinction of the *tonal* and the *nagual* so are we. But it is the author who has prepared us. And if we had been told the doctrine at the first encounter, we should, like Carlos himself, not have understood at all.

In this sense, it makes no difference whether the books are a record of an actual encounter or whether Castaneda is the author of a clever fiction. In either case Don Juan is an utterly unforgettable presence—not merely a character and more than a man. Whatever affinities there may be between the teachings and the gifts of Don Juan and the

standard philosophies and mystery cults of the world, we
ourselves are confronted by the teacher himself, face to
face without intervening allusions, references, research,
theories. Nothing but the transcript retold in a graduated
way. Either Castaneda is recording an encounter with a
master of the most remarkable sort or else he is himself
that master. There is really no other possibility. All the sly
doubts about the authenticity and seriousness of Don
Juan's teachings—for that's what the books are and that's
what they're said to be—is simply the reverse side of an uneasy, dawning realization of the gathering presence of
Don Juan himself.

The books are a kind of temporally spaced training
manual—for witnesses of tales, not warriors, that is, for
those who may one day, but not merely as readers, confront the actual lessons. They are after all not verbal lessons—or at least they are not fully intelligible apart from
the experiences the apprentice undergoes. And Don
Juan's presence is simply the source of an entirely spontaneous, effortless, and unending stream of distinctions,
perceptions, instructions, interpretations of everything
that comes within our notice. What holds us is the incredible detail: at once almost totally unfamiliar, unified
in a conceptual order marked by its own specialized
vocabulary, linked to experience by way of a vast set of instructions and exercises that collect a distinct tradition, im-
penetrable to our own familiar categories and therefore
seriously threatening and upsetting, gradually recogniz-
able as we adopt the apprentice's own discoveries, oddly
plausible and convincing in spite of merely reading about
it, affectionate and humane and informed over all with the
excitement of a new meaning and dignity in our mortal
passage. The first book is obviously dedicated to Pablito
and Don Genaro or (perhaps more doubtfully) to Nestor,
who do not yet appear. Every important detail resonates
through all the books though the ordering changes as we
ourselves become better oriented and more receptive. In
fact, the pace between our own discoveries and those of

Carlos is increasingly synchronized as we advance from book to book; and in the last one we are learning side by side though unequally.

Tales of Power is the most explicit of course, and it is there that one might hope to gain more than an inkling of Don Juan's system. But it is utterly useless to disengage the apparent theory from the lessons spaced through all the books, of quite particular exercises concerned with *dreaming, not-doing, acquiring an ally, the gait of power, splitting, stopping the internal dialogue, seeing, controlled folly, erasing personal history, shrinking the tonal, grabbing with the will, dreaming the double, opening the bubble, closing the mortal gap.* These obviously involve very specific forms of discipline— all utterly alien. They're alien, it must be emphasized, not merely because they are unfamiliar. After all, a precise description of an unfamiliar portion of the world—the Arctic, say—would make it more familiar. They're alien because no extended description of *this* world, the ordinary world that we know, would make *that* world more familiar *and* because there is apparently no other way to be in touch with that other world (where—and only where—Don Juan's descriptions make clear and specific sense) except through the exercises he himself has provided. Furthermore, the theory of the *tonal* and the *nagual*, which is at once Don Juan's metaphysics and the clue to the sorcerer's accomplishment ultimately organizes what is disclosed through the exercises themselves. We are obliged therefore to understand the account only in analogical terms.

There *are* affinities to be noted of course, but they are not altogether satisfactory. This is due jointly to the fact that whatever distinctions Don Juan teaches us are intended to illuminate the range of exercises and experiences that all four books collect *to which we ourselves are not a party* and to the fact that the ultimate conceptual lesson to be learned is *the inherent inadequacy of conceptual distinctions themselves.* The problem is to understand the orderliness and attraction of the teachings in spite of these two extraordinary constraints. For in a sense we ourselves are led to imitate—in a much paler mode of experience to be sure—the stumbling and developing enlightenment of Carlos. "The *nagual* has no limit," says Don Juan (p. 141); it is the "unspeakable" (p. 265); it cannot be compared with experience or consciousness (p. 141); it is only the counterpart in us of the "indescribable void that contains everything" (p. 271). Such remarks are bound to encourage comparisons with Taoism and the like, and perhaps they are justified. But they will be made at a purely verbal level, without the grounding of the apprentice's discoveries.

More suggestively, Don Juan identifies the *tonal* with whatever we know (pp. 124, 125); the *nagual* lies beyond that (p. 127); we are said to be *nagual* at birth and for a short time after (p. 128); and when we become *tonal* we distinguish "pairs" (p. 128); birth and death define the *tonal*, but the *nagual* has no end (p. 141). To the question what may be found where the *nagual* is located, no answer can be given. If he were to say, Nothing, Don Juan explains, he would merely reduce the *nagual* to the *tonal* (p. 128 *f.*).

Perhaps an experimental association can be made to one of the surviving fragments of the pre-Socratic philosopher Anaximander of Miletus (*c.* 560 B.C.). I select it because of its apparent aptness and because it is unlikely to be considered by those with cultish interests. It's worth a try in any case. Anaximander says: "The Non-Limited is the original material of existing things; further, the source from which existing things derive their existence is also that to which they return at their destruction, according to necessity; for they give justice and make reparation to one another for their injustice, according to the arrangement of Time."[1] But it is unsatisfactory after all, for we have neither a reliable account of what Anaximander means by "material" or "necessity" or "justice" or "time" nor any inkling of any program of discipline that Anaximander may have associated with his teaching. Still, there is in both a contrast between an indeterminable source and determinate and therefore limited things that exist for an interval, as well as a suggestion that the generation or the intelligibility of things accords with opposing pairs of distinctions: Anaximander speaks of justice and injustice; Don Juan of the negative and the positive (p. 128). Anaximander is also thought to have believed that there were an unlimited number of universes. But then, we know nothing for certain of Anaximander's intention in so speaking and Don Juan is, however serious he may ultimately be, clowning in the manner of the lecturer.

There are also two very brief attempts on Carlos' part to associate Don Juan's distinctions to others that he's familiar with. For one, just when these distinctions are being explored, Carlos mentions the Kantian contrast between the Transcendental Ego and the Empirical Ego—Carlos actually says that he had insisted European philosophers had analyzed what Don Juan called the *nagual* (p. 140). But Don Juan sees through this at once; since it is the only thing capable of judgment, of disclosing reality within consciousness, the so-called Transcendental Ego must be the *tonal*. The refutation of course is absolutely valid: Whatever is conceptually ordered and conceptually discriminated is the *tonal*; the *nagual* erases *that*; hence Carlos must be mistaken. The other episode occurs in *A Separate Reality* (in section 13). Carlos had been reading the *Tibetan Book of the Dead* and was trying to compare Don Juan's remarks on death and on one's own death with the Tibetan account. But Don Juan had put his remarks in terms of the phenomenon of *seeing*; hence he observes very sensibly that if the Tibetans could *see* in his sense, then they wrote what they did because they knew it made no difference, otherwise what they wrote is simply nonsense. We are, in short, forever drawn back to the connection between the exercises and the apparent theory.

Here, a critical difficulty arises. Because if the *nagual* is inexpressible, what is the status of our attempt to identify it and to contrast it with the *tonal*? The answer is utterly baffling and yet dialectically sound. Don Juan has no hesitation about it: We must talk about the *nagual* in terms of the distinctions of the *tonal*; hence we do not seek to explain it but only to identify its effects (p. 131). Of course this means that even the specification of the *nagual* as other than the *tonal* and as having some distinctive effect on us is the work of the *tonal*. Otherwise, what Don Juan is teaching (and what Anaximander appears to claim) would be straightforwardly self-contradictory. What is ineffable is ineffable, though that appears to have discouraged no one.

In a famous passage Wittgenstein says: "My propositions serve as elucidations in the following way: anyone who understands me eventually recognizes them as nonsense, when he has used them—as steps—to climb up beyond them. (He must, so to speak, throw away the ladder after he has climbed up it.) He must transcend these propositions and then he will see the world aright. What one cannot speak about we must pass over in silence."[2] But of course Wittgenstein's entire book of propositions precedes the remark.

Wittgenstein may very easily be the single most influential philosopher of the twentieth century, and the *Tractatus* from which the excerpt comes is thought by many to be the single most important philosophical book of our time. It is admittedly a cryptic book, a book of the greatest difficulty. But it has the extraordinary property of having been pondered by nearly every Western intellect concerned with the ultimate intelligibility of all possible things at the same time that it reconciles that question with a closing emphasis—usually termed mysticism—on the ultimate ineffability of reality. Hence it is not altogether tactless perhaps to attempt a comparison of the strenuous views of these two masterly teachers. Ironically, it may even render a service to Wittgenstein's memory as well as to Don Juan's, since most of those affected by the *Tractatus* seem to have discounted (or to have been embarrassed by) the mystical passages.

Wittgenstein's essential puzzle concerns the profound difficulty of the remark, "A proposition is a picture of reality. A proposition is a model of reality as we imagine it" (4.01). The one-to-one correspondence between the picture and reality depends on their having something in common—a logical form in virtue of which "the possibility of all situations" is captured (2.014; 2.022); but "a picture cannot depict its pictorial form: it displays it" (2.172). Pictures cannot *say* what they have in common with what they picture. Here is a strenuous thesis that cries out for explanation. Still, though the combination of these two points appears to depart from Don Juan's contrast between the *tonal* and the *nagual*, the final comment of the book (6.54; 7) makes one wonder. On Wittgenstein's view, the very purpose of our deepest conceptual efforts, the formulation of propositions that depict the structure of reality—in fact the structure of all possible states of affairs—itself generates its own inherent failure We advance beyond it by a mystical absorption in an ineffable reality. For if we should presume to *state* or *say* what we *picture,* we should merely then have stated something that, on the correspondence view, might actually picture what we claim it does: to know *that* we should have to be poised between language and reality and, commanding the one and belonging to the other, grasp (inexpressibly) that the mute structure of the world was the very structure that, using language, we claimed it had. Hence, the very success of language entails its ultimate failure even at the point of success; though at that point, failure itself opens on to a new and inexpressible success.

Wittgenstein also says, "*The limits of my language* mean the limits of my world. Logic pervades the world: the limits of the world are also its limits. So we cannot say in logic, 'The world has this in it, and this, but not that.' For that would appear to presuppose that we were excluding certain possibilities, and this cannot be the case, since it would require that logic should go beyond the limits of the world; for only in that way could it view those limits from the other side as well" (5.6; 6.61). And this seems tantalizingly similar to the (informal) remarks made by Don Juan, in which he notes that, though it cannot really create or change anything, the *tonal* does in a strange sense create the world since we judge, perceive, appraise the things of the world. That is, the *tonal* provides the conceptual rules by which we apprehend the world, and that is a sort of creation (p. 125).

The genius of the *Tractatus* lies in the attempt to provide us with a *sense* of the logical form every possible notational system or form of representation must share if pictures or propositions are to be able to picture reality at all (2.18). That this itself is an impossible task is at least part of the point of the final remarks of the *Tractatus;* though even within the enterprise attempted inherent difficulties shatter the prospect. However, Wittgenstein also says that "there are indeed things that cannot be put into words. They *make themselves manifest.* They are what is mystical" (6.522). So the convergence between Wittgenstein and Don Juan—an outrageous suggestion in many ways—is even more tempting to consider. There are at least two themes of agreement that are instructive. First of all, the inexpressible *shows* itself: Don Juan says that nothing said about the *nagual* makes sense, though there is a sense in which the body witnesses to the *nagual* (p. 158). Secondly, whatever conceptual scheme is mine is the limit of my world but another might represent it in an utterly different way (always supposing Wittgenstein's constraint of logical form to obtain, that is, that he has discovered the structure of all possible ways of representing reality—an astonishing claim). For his part, Don Juan says that the *tonal* must be made to understand that there are different worlds that can be visually seen (p. 173); also, more profoundly, that what we learn is not *the* nature of the world but merely one descriptive scheme in accord with which we habitually recognize the world (p. 123)—which, however informally expressed, is really quite sympathetic to the point of Wittgenstein's claim.

In a sense, then, Castaneda's books provide us with a demonstration—or as close to a demonstration as we can come, being witnesses only of *tales* of power—of these two truths (that is, that the inexpressible shows itself and that the limits of one's conceptual scheme are the limits of one's world). For there is no question that the sorcerer's view of the world is utterly unlike our own (unless, *per impossibile*, at least Wittgenstein's ultimate constraint regarding logical form obtains). Even here, more recently in philosophical circles, under the spreading influence of Thomas Kuhn's theory of scientific revolution,[3] it has been held that perceptual discourse and actual perceptual discrimination are controlled by one's commitment to an antecedent theory and that in principle it would be possible for two scientists to share no perceptual distinctions in common because their theories shared no relevant concepts in common. In short, approximately, what Don Juan and Wittgenstein both claim (and what Kuhn is quite explicit about) is that what we see is what the system of our beliefs and concepts permit us to see, in visual contact with the world. Ultimately, there may be nothing that we share with another. Hence we move between the undemonstrability, perhaps the meaninglessness, of Wittgenstein's constraint to the radical tolerance, perhaps the incoherence, of Kuhn's concession. But more than this, we see the sense in which the apprentice's experience is utterly unfamiliar.

The truth about mysticism is more difficult to specify. It is, as we have seen, merely announced in Wittgenstein. Apparently Wittgenstein had in mind rather special problems like that of values. "All propositions are of equal value," he said; "the sense of the world must lie outside the world"; "if there is any value that does have value, it must lie outside the whole sphere of what happens and is the case" (6.4; 6.41). Don Juan's concern is, rather, with one's "totality." The point seems to be that the very theory of the *tonal* and the *nagual* which finally collects all of the instructions and experiences that have gone before is required by the warrior's effort to live and die with that totality (p. 133). The final lessons hinge on this and seem therefore to be deeper than merely theoretical. For, after all, if what

has already been said is seriously intended then it can be
no more than an expression of the *tonal*. Don Juan trans-
forms these theories into "personal knowledge." Power, he
tells Carlos, teaches that the awareness of death is essential
to the phenomenon of *having* to believe, of commitment in
the world. Without that, life is trivial and undistinguished.
The imminence of death makes the world a mystery (p.
116). Paradoxically, then, the warrior believes without believing; doesn't believe but *has* to believe (p. 110); or else
having to believe the world to be unfathomable is simply
"the expression of a warrior's innermost predilection" (p.
117). The world *is* the *tonal* for those who must believe so;
it is the *nagual* or both the *tonal* and the *nagual* for those of
another predilection. What ultimately matters is to be an
"impeccable" warrior: In that sense alone one enters both
the *tonal* and the *nagual*; in fact the *tonal* is finally as mysterious and as unfathomable as the *nagual* (p. 270). For
very much in the spirit of Wittgenstein's remarks, we can
construct an appropriate *tonal* (appropriate to whatever
way of life we pursue) only by contact with the *nagual*. Perhaps, here, there is a hint of an important convergence between Don Juan and Wittgenstein. For in attempting to
clarify the paradox of the luminous beings, Don Juan
straightforwardly says that the *tonal* merely reflects the inherent order of the unknown; and the *nagual* merely
reflects the encompassing void itself (p. 270 *f.*). Now, what
he appears to mean is that there is in each of us two centers
of awareness, the *reason* and the *will,* that the *tonal* is
reflected through the one and the *nagual* through the other (since both are ultimately indescribable), that *there is* an
inherent order in reality that reason reflects in its own distinctive way, and that sorcerers have learned to witness
(but not to describe) through the *will* the effects of the
nagual (pp. 269–270).
    The lesson is obviously extremely difficult. What we are
offered seems to be a remarkable development from an
anthropologically familiar doctrine. Carlos himself summarizes the standard account. Apparently the *tonal* was (in

certain Mexican cultures) an animal spirit or a guardian spirit acquired at birth and linked to that life; and the *nagual* was either an animal that a sorcerer could transform himself into or such a sorcerer himself. (The *Popol Vuh* of the Quiche Maya seems to confirm this.[4]) Obviously Don Juan has transformed these two notions into cosmic categories. But the deep import of the distinction construed in terms of the personal discipline of the sorcerer is given in the inexplicable summary addressed to Carlos: Each of us is a "cluster" (p. 265). Out of the void, some ordering power binds the necessary elements together and we emerge into the *tonal* (p. 266). We must of course remember that all of this is analogical. And yet Carlos himself attests to an experience that is beyond experience in any ordinary sense, for he has an awareness of breaking into a colony of separate awarenesses which have a certain affinity for one another (p. 262). This apparently clarifies the thesis that we may see other worlds, alternative conceptualizations of some ulterior order—a view not unrelated to the sense of Wittgenstein's thesis. But it also is designed to clarify another point, namely, that the witnessing of the *nagual* is quite concrete if inexpressible. Admittedly this runs the risk of contradiction (as do Wittgenstein's propositions). But what Don Juan seems to intend is that there is some center of sensitivity or awareness (the *will*) that uses a second center of awareness (the *reason*) in order to provide even the paradoxical descriptions of one's encounter with the *nagual* in accord with which at least the orderly process of apprenticeship may proceed and the warrior may accomplish the task of gaining command of his totality (p. 248).

Here, no more can be said. The details of the two chapters The Strategy of a Sorcerer and The Bubble of Perception are simply extraordinary. To understand them one has plainly to undergo the exercises. Still, apart from the special discipline of the warrior and his privileged experiences (which is nearly all but not quite all that we are told) the dignity of the account affects us at our second remove.

For we are left with the inexhaustible mystery of reality, the contingency of every conceptual scheme, and—grasping the final sublime clowning of Don Genaro—the love of the earth and one's personal encounter with the void. Yet even here the parallel with Wittgenstein is instructive. For Wittgenstein says, "The contemplation of the world sub specie aeterni is its contemplation as a limited whole. The feeling of the world as a limited whole is the mystical feeling" (6.45). It is hard to deny that Don Juan's notion of the warrior's witnessing to the *nagual* lends itself to this conception and that in different ways their accounts of the intelligible order of things positively presuppose a mystical form of cognition. In fact, both regard that as a mode of feeling—some sensitivity on the side of personal identity, more profound than rational distinctions can capture, of an unfathomable source with respect to which identity itself is perhaps no more than a transient but marvelous precipitate.

Notes

[1] Kathleen Freeman, *Ancilla to the Pre-Socratic Philosophers* (Oxford: Basil Blackwell, 1948), p. 19.

[2] Ludwig Wittgenstein, *Tractatus Logico-Philosophicus,* translated by D. F. Pears and B. F. McGuiness (London: Routledge and Kegan Paul, 1972, corrected), 6.54; 7.

[3] *The Structure of Scientific Revolutions* (Chicago: The University of Chicago Press, 1962).

[4] *Popol Vuh: The Sacred Book of the Ancient Quiche Maya,* English version by Delia Goetz and Sylvanus G. Morky, from the translation of Adrian Recinos (Norman: University of Oklahoma Press, 1950), pp. 84 *n*, 198 *n*.

SUGGESTIONS FOR FURTHER READING

The following titles were chosen from references made in the various selections above and also include other works which seem to relate especially well to the themes of Castaneda's tetralogy. Unless indicated by a (c), the books suggested are available in a paperback edition.

BARFIELD, OWEN, *Poetic Diction: A Study in Meaning*. Third edition. Middletown, Conn.: Wesleyan University Press, 1973.
————, *Romanticism Comes of Age*. Enlarged edition. Middletown, Conn.: Wesleyan University Press, 1967. (c)
————, *Saving the Appearances: A Study in Idolatry*. New York: Harcourt Brace Jovanovich, 1965.
BARTHELME, DONALD, *Guilty Pleasures*. New York: Farrar, Straus & Giroux, 1974. (c)
BEARDSLEE, WILLIAM A., *Literary Criticism of the New Testament*. Philadelphia: Fortress Press, 1970.
BECKER, ERNEST, *The Denial of Death*. New York: Free Press/Macmillan Co., 1973. (c)
BELLAH, ROBERT N., *Beyond Belief: Essays on Religion in a Post-Traditional World*. New York: Harper & Row, 1970. (c)
BERGER, PETER L. and THOMAS LUCKMANN, *The Social Construction of Reality: A Treatise in the Sociology of Knowledge*. Garden City, N.Y.: Doubleday, 1966.
BORGES, JORGE LUIS, *In Praise of Darkness*. Translated by N.T. di Giovanni. New York: Dutton, 1974.
BOYD, DOUG, *Rolling Thunder: A Personal Exploration Into the Se-*

cret Healing Powers of an American Medicine Man. New York: Random House, 1975. (c)

BROCKMAN, JOHN, Afterwords: Explorations of the Mystical Limits of Contemporary Reality. Garden City, N.Y.: Doubleday, 1973.

BROWN, NORMAN O., Love's Body. New York: Random House, 1966.

BURNSHAW, STANLEY, The Seamless Web. New York: George Braziller, 1970.

CAMPBELL, JOSEPH, The Flight of the Wild Gander. Chicago: Henry Regnery Co., 1972.

———, The Masks of God. Four volumes. New York: Viking Press, 1959–70.

———, editor, Myths, Dreams, and Religion. New York: Dutton, 1970.

CAPPS, WALTER H., editor, Ways of Understanding Religion. New York: Macmillan Co., 1972.

DOTY, WILLIAM G., Contemporary New Testament Interpretation. Englewood Cliffs, N.J.: Prentice-Hall, Inc., 1972.

DOUGLAS, MARY, Natural Symbols: Explorations in Cosmology. New York: Vintage Books, 1973.

DUNNE, JOHN S., The Way of All the Earth: Experiments in Truth and Religion. New York: Macmillan Co., 1972.

DURKHEIM, EMILE, The Elementary Forms of Religious Life. Translated by J. Swain. New York: Free Press/Macmillan Co., 1963.

ELIADE, MIRCEA, The Sacred and the Profane: The Nature of Religion. Translated by Willard R. Trask. New York: Harper & Row, 1961.

———, Shamanism: Archaic Techniques of Ecstasy. Translated by Willard R. Trask. Princeton, N.J.: Princeton University Press, 1964.

ELLWOOD, ROBERT S., Religious and Spiritual Groups in Modern America. Englewood Cliffs, N.J.: Prentice-Hall, Inc., 1973.

FARADAY, ANN, The Dream Game. New York: Harper & Row, 1974. (c)

FINGARETTE, HERBERT, The Self in Transformation. New York: Harper & Row, 1965.

FRYE, NORTHROP, Fables of Identity: Studies in Poetic Mythology. New York: Harcourt, Brace & World, 1963.

FURST, PETER, editor. *Flesh of the Gods: The Ritual Use of Hallucinogens.* New York: Praeger, 1972.

GARFINKEL, HAROLD, *Studies in Ethnomethodology.* Englewood Cliffs, N.J.: Prentice-Hall, 1967.

GENDLIN, EUGENE T., *Experiencing and the Creation of Meaning: A Philosophical and Psychological Approach to the Subjective.* New York: Free Press/Macmillan Co., 1962. (c)

GREGORY, R. L. and E. H. GOMBRICH, editors, *Illusion in Nature and Art.* New York: Charles Scribner's Sons, 1974.

GUENTHER, HERBERT V., *The Tantric View of Life.* Berkeley, Calif.: Shambhala Books, 1972. (c)

HALL, EDWARD T., *The Hidden Dimension.* Garden City, N.Y.: Doubleday, 1966. (c)

———, *The Silent Language.* Garden City, N.Y.: Doubleday, 1959. (c)

HALLOWELL, A. I., *Culture and Experience.* New York: Schocken Books, 1967.

HARNER, MICHAEL J., editor, *Hallucinogens and Shamanism.* New York: Oxford University Press, 1973.

HESSE, HERMANN, *Siddhartha.* Translated by Hilda Rosner. New York: New Directions, 1951.

HOPPER, STANLEY R. and DAVID L. MILLER, editors, *Interpretation: The Poetry of Meaning.* New York: Harcourt, Brace & World, 1967.

HUSSERL, EDMUND, *Ideas.* New York: Macmillan Co., 1962.

HUXLEY, ALDOUS, *The Doors of Perception.* New York: Harper & Row, 1954.

———, *The Perennial Philosophy.* New York: Harper & Row, 1970.

JAMES, WILLIAM, *The Varieties of Religious Experience.* Garden City, N.Y.: Doubleday Dolphin books, n.d.

JONES, W. T., *The Sciences and the Humanities: Conflict and Reconciliation.* Berkeley, Calif.: University of California Press, 1965.

JUNG, C. G., *Memories, Dreams, Reflections.* Edited by Aniela Jaffé. Translated by Richard and Clara Winston. New York: Vintage Books, 1961.

KAFKA, FRANZ, *Parables and Paradoxes.* New York: Schocken Books, 1961.

KEEN, SAM, *Apology for Wonder*. New York: Harper & Row, 1969.
————, *To A Dancing God*. New York: Harper & Row, 1970.
KELEMAN, STANLEY, *Living Your Dying*. New York: Bookworks/ Random House, 1974. (c)
KERMODE, FRANK, *The Sense of an Ending: Studies in the Theory of Fiction*. New York: Oxford University Press, 1967.
KLINKOWITZ, JEROME and JOHN SOMER, editors, *Innovative Fiction: Stories for the Seventies*. New York: Dell Laurel Originals, 1972.
KUHN, THOMAS S., *The Structure of Scientific Revolutions*. Second edition, enlarged. Chicago: University of Chicago Press, 1970.
LEARY, TIMOTHY, RALPH METZNER, and RICHARD ALPERT, *The Psychedelic Experience: A Manual Based on The Tibetan Book of the Dead*. New Hyde Park, N.Y.: University Books, 1964. (c)
LA BARRE, WESTON, *The Ghost Dance: The Origins of Religion*. New York: Dell Delta Books, 1972.
————, *The Peyote Cult*. Revised edition. New York: Schocken Books, 1969.
LAING, R. D., *The Politics of Experience*. New York: Pantheon Books, 1967.
LAMB, F. BRUCE, *Wizard of the Upper Amazon: The Story of Manuel Córdova-Rios*. Boston: Houghton Mifflin Co., 1975. (c)
LAME DEER and RICHARD ERODES, *Lame Deer: Seeker of Visions*. New York: Simon and Schuster, 1973.
LEACH, EDMUND R., *Rethinking Anthropology*. Atlantic Highlands, N.J.: Humanities Press, 1971. (c)
————, editor, *The Structural Study of Myth and Totemism*. New York: Barnes and Noble, 1968.
LEE, DOROTHY, *Freedom and Culture*. Englewood Cliffs, N.J.: Prentice-Hall, 1959.
LÉVI-STRAUSS, CLAUDE, *The Savage Mind*. Chicago: University of Chicago Press, 1966.
————, *Structural Anthropology*. Translated by C. Jacobson and B. G. Schoepf. Garden City, N.Y.: Doubleday, 1967.
————, *Tristes Tropiques*. Translated by John Russell. New York: Atheneum, 1968.
LILLY, JOHN C., *Center of the Cyclone: An Autobiography of Inner Space*. New York: Bantam Books, 1973.

MARWICK, MAX, editor, *Witchcraft and Sorcery.* Baltimore: Penguin Books, 1970.

MASTERS, R. E. L. and JEAN HOUSTON, *Varieties of Psychedelic Experience.* New York: Dell Delta Books, 1967.

MERLEAU-PONTY, MAURICE, *The Phenomenology of Perception.* Translated by Colin Smith. Atlantic Highlands, N.J.: Humanities Press, 1962. (c)

————, *The Primacy of Perception.* Edited by James M. Edie. Translated by William Cobb, *et al.* Evanston, Ill.: Northwestern University Press, 1964.

MOISÉS, ROSALIO, JANE HOLDEN KELLY, and WILLIAM CURRY HOLDEN, *The Tall Candle: The Personal Chronicle of a Yaqui Indian.* Lincoln, Neb.: University of Nebraska Press, 1971. (c)

MYERHOFF, BARBARA, *Peyote Hunt: The Sacred Journey of the Huichol Indians.* Ithaca, N.Y.: Cornell University Press, 1974. (c)

NATANSON, MAURICE, *Literature, Philosophy and the Social Sciences.* The Hague: Martinus Nijhoff, 1962.

NEEDLEMAN, JACOB, *The New Religions.* Revised edition. New York: Pocket Books, 1972.

NIN, ANAÏS, *The Novel of the Future.* New York: Collier Books, 1970.

NOEL, DANIEL C., editor. *Echoes of the Wordless "Word": Colloquy in Honor of Stanley Romaine Hopper.* Introduction by Joseph Campbell. Missoula, Mont.: Scholars Press, 1973.

NOVAK, MICHAEL, *The Experience of Nothingness.* New York: Harper & Row, 1970.

OATES, JOYCE CAROL, *New Heaven, New Earth: The Visionary Experience in Literature.* New York: Vanguard, 1974. (c)

ORNSTEIN, ROBERT E., *The Psychology of Consciousness.* San Francisco: W. H. Freeman, 1972.

PEARCE, JOSEPH CHILTON, *The Crack in the Cosmic Egg: Challenging Constructs of Mind and Reality.* New York: Pocket Books, 1973.

————, *Exploring the Crack in the Cosmic Egg: Split Minds and Meta-Realities.* New York: Julian Press, 1974. (c)

POLANYI, MICHAEL, *Personal Knowledge: Towards a Post-Critical Philosophy.* New York: Harper & Row, 1964.

POPE, HARRISON, JR., *The Road East: America's New Discovery of Eastern Wisdom.* Boston: Beacon Press, 1974.

RADIN, PAUL, *The Trickster.* New York: Philosophical Library, 1956. (c)

REICH, WILHELM, *Character Analysis.* New York: Simon and Schuster, 1974.

―――, *The Function of the Orgasm.* New York: Simon and Schuster, 1974.

ROSZAK, THEODORE, *The Making of a Counter-Culture: Reflections on the Technocratic Society and Its Youthful Opposition.* Garden City, N.Y.: Doubleday, 1969.

―――, *Where the Wasteland Ends: Politics and Transcendence in Postindustrial Society.* Garden City, N.Y.: Doubleday, 1973.

ROTHENBERG, JEROME, editor, *Shaking the Pumpkin.* Garden City, N.Y : Doubleday, 1972.

―――, editor. *Technicians of the Sacred.* Garden City N.Y.: Doubleday, 1969.

―――, and George Quasha, editors. *America a Prophecy.* New York: Vintage Books, 1974.

SHUTZ, ALFRED, *Phenomenology of the Social World.* Translated by George Walsh and Frederick Lehnert. Evanston, Ill.: Northwestern University Press, 1967.

SEGALL, MARSHALL H., DONALD CAMPBELL, and MELVILLE J. HERSKOVITZ, *The Influence of Culture on Visual Perception: An Advanced Study in Psychology and Anthropology.* Indianapolis, Ind.: Bobbs-Merrill, 1966. (c)

SNOW, C. P., *Two Cultures: And a Second Look.* New York: Cambridge University Press, 1969.

SNYDER, GARY, *Earth House Hold.* New York: New Directions, 1969.

SOLTIS, JONAS, *Seeing, Knowing and Believing: A Study of the Language of Visual Perception.* Reading, Mass.: Addison-Wesley, 1966. (c)

SPICER, EDWARD H., editor, *Perspectives in American Indian Culture Change.* Chicago: The University of Chicago Press, 1961. (c)

STEIN, CHARLES, *Poems and Glyphs.* Preface by Richard Grossinger. Plainfield, Vt.: Io Books, 1973.

STEVENS, WALLACE, *The Collected Poems.* New York: Alfred A. Knopf, 1968. (c).

———, *The Necessary Angel: Essays on Reality and the Imagination.* New York: Vintage Books, 1951.

———, *Opus Posthumous.* Edited by S. F. Morse. New York: Alfred A. Knopf, 1966. (c)

STONEBURNER, TONY, editor, *Parable, Myth, and Language.* Cambridge, Mass.: Church Society for College Work, 1968.

STRENG, FREDERICK J., *Emptiness: A Study in Religious Meaning.* Nashville, Tenn.: Abingdon Press, 1967. (c)

SUKENICK, RONALD, *The Death of the Novel and Other Stories.* San Diego, Calif.: Serendipity Press, 1969. (c)

———, *98.6.* New York: Fiction Collective/George Braziller, 1975.

———, *Out: A Novel.* Chicago: Swallow press, 1974.

———, *Up.* San Diego, Calif.: Serendipity Press, 1970.

———, *Wallace Stevens: Musing the Obscure.* New York: New York University Press, 1967.

SUZUKI, D. T., *Zen Buddhism: Selected Writings of D. T. Suzuki.* Edited by William Barrett. Garden City, N.Y.: Doubleday, 1956.

TART, CHARLES, editor, *Altered States of Consciousness.* Garden City, N.Y.: Doubleday, 1972.

THOMPSON, WILLIAM I., *At the Edge of History: Speculations on the Transformation of Culture.* New York: Harper & Row, 1972.

The Tibetan Book of the Dead. Translated by Lama Kazi Dawa-Sandup. New York: Oxford University Press, 1960.

TRUNGPA, CHOGYAM, *Cutting Through Spiritual Materialism.* Edited by John Baker. Berkeley, Calif.: Shambhala, n.d.

———, *Meditation in Action.* Berkeley, Calif.: Shambhala Books, 1969.

VAN DEN BERG, JAN H., *Things: Four Metabletic Reflections.* Pittsburgh: Duquesne University Press, 1970. (c)

√VAN DER WETERING, JANWILLEM, *The Empty Mirror: Experiences in a Japanese Zen Monastery.* Boston: Houghton Mifflin Co., 1974. (c)

WASSON, R. GORDON, *Soma: Divine Mushroom of Immortality.* New York: Harcourt Brace Jovanovich, 1972.

WATTS, ALAN, *In My Own Way: An Autobiography.* New York: Vintage Books, 1972.

————, *The Joyous Cosmology.* New York: Vintage Books, 1962.

————, *This Is It and Other Essays.* New York: Collier Books, 1967.

WEIL, ANDREW, *The Natural Mind: A New Way of Looking at Drugs and the Higher Consciousness.* Boston: Houghton Mifflin Co., 1972.

WHEELIS, ALLEN, *The End of the Modern Age.* New York: Harper & Row, 1972

————, *The Illusionless Man: Some Fantasies and Meditations on Disillusionment.* New York: Harper & Row, 1971.

WHEELWRIGHT, PHILIP, *Metaphor and Reality.* Bloomington, Ind.: Indiana University Press, 1968.

WITTGENSTEIN, LUDWIG, *Philosophical Investigations.* Third edition. Edited by Kenneth Scott. New York: Macmillan Co., 1973.

————, *Tractatus Logico-Philosophicus.* New edition. Translated by D. F. Pears and B. F. McGuiness. Atlantic Highlands, N.J.: Humanities Press, 1974.

WOLFE, TOM, *The Electric Kool-Aid Acid Test.* New York: Bantam Books, 1969.